Plans des forts faicts par le Regiment
Carignan Salieres sur la Riviere de
Richelieu dicte autrement des Iroquois en
la Nouuelle france—

Fort Ste Therese
fait par Mr de Salieres
sur la Riviere des Iroquois

Ce fort est haut de 15 pieds auec
Double palissade qui a vne Banquette
en dedans esleuée d'vn pied et demy
dessus le sol

Lac Ontario ou des Iroquois

Les Cinq Nations Iroquoises

The Good Regiment

The Good Regiment

The Carignan-Salières Regiment in Canada 1665–1668

JACK VERNEY

McGill-Queen's University Press
Montreal & Kingston · London · Buffalo

©McGill-Queen's University Press 1991
ISBN 0-7735-0813-9

Legal deposit first quarter 1991
Bibliothèque nationale du Québec

Printed in Canada on acid-free paper

This book has been published with the help of a grant
from the Social Science Federation of Canada, using
funds provided by the Social Sciences and Humanities
Research Council of Canada.

Canadian Cataloguing in Publication Data

Verney, Jack, 1919–
    The good regiment
    Includes bibliographical references.
    ISBN 0-7735-0813-9
    1. France. Armée. Régiment de Carignan-Salières.
    2. Canada—History—1663–1713 (New France).
    I. Title.
    FC369.C37V47 1991 971.01´63 C90-090519-0
    F1030.V471991   70478

The typeface used in the text is ITC Garamond® Light
with old style figures from the Adobe Garamond Expert
Collection® set by the Instructional Communication
Centre at McGill University.

Endpapers:
The Iroquois country and plans of forts on the Richelieu River.
From Reuben Gold Thwaites, ed. and trans., *The Jesuit Relations
and Allied Documents,* 73 vols. (Cleveland: Burrows Brothers
Company, 1896–1901), 49: facing p. 266. Photograph courtesy of
the National Library of Canada.

Contents

Illustrations vi

Preface vii

1 Canada Bound 3

2 Forts in the Wilderness 18

3 Courcelle's Ill-fated March into Mohawk
  Country 37

4 Questions of Peace and War 54

5 Tracy's Splendid Victory Denied 71

6 The Colony at Peace 85

7 Misdeeds, Marriages, and a Miracle 92

8 The End of the Mission 108

9 Conclusion 122

  Appendix A: Equipment 129

  Appendix B: Nominal Roll 145

  Notes 187

  Index 217

Illustrations

1 The probable route of Tracy's march to the Mohawk villages, 1666   77

2 Seigneurial grants near the Richelieu Valley made to former officers of the regiment, 1672   120

Preface

The story of the Carignan-Salières Regiment, which Louis XIV sent to Canada in 1665 to secure the colony from Mohawk attacks, has been distorted by what historian Mason Wade described as "a golden haze of glorious legend."[1]

The impetus for that distortion came from the Abbé Lionel Groulx and is found in his lectures delivered on the Montreal campus of Laval University, later the University of Montreal, in the years between the two world wars, and in his copious writings, especially those essays published by the right-wing nationalist group, Action française. The models for it were his too and are contained in his *Chez nos ancêtres* and *Notre maître le passé,* both highly subjective idealizations of everyday life in pre-Conquest Canada.

The goal of his crusade was to turn the province of Quebec into a spiritual and national homeland for Franco-Americans, a refuge wherein Catholicism, the French language, and the inspiration of a utopian past would combine to provide a bulwark against the advancing tide of Protestant, English-speaking materialism. The trouble was that although Catholicism and the French language were well entrenched in the province, historiography, far from concerning itself with the virtues of habitant life, was becoming increasingly preoccupied with the ideal of one nation, united from coast to coast. If Franco-Americans were to aspire to a national identity of their own, that emphasis had to be changed. The story of the simple lives led by their forebears, shaped by the dictates of the land, the seasons, the church, and the community, had to be elevated to a place of primacy to serve as an example of what they should all strive to become. The result was that the history of pre-Conquest French Canada began to be lifted from the mould of pan-Canadianism and reshaped so as to conform with the Abbé's teachings.

Following his lead, French-Canadian historians, stirred by his nationalistic credo, produced works in keeping with it, and similarly motivated teachers made full use of them in the province's classrooms and lecture halls. So great, in fact, did the demand for such material become that some publishers, unable to find enough new manuscripts to meet it, turned to earlier works in a similar vein and republished them. One such work was *Le Régiment de Carignan* by Benjamin Sulte.

Sulte's monograph, published in 1922, was essentially the same as a paper he had presented to the Royal Society of Canada twenty years earlier, and it wends an erratic way through a regimental history that is often factually flawed and generally sparsely documented. Despite the shortcomings of the book, its acceptance was assured, not because of its significance as an objective piece of scholarship, but because of its appropriateness to the needs of the time. Its emphasis on those soldiers who remained in Canada after 1668, reputedly to follow that simple way of life extolled by the Abbé Groulx as the ideal, commended it to his disciples and made it a part of the growing body of literature available to them to help advance his ideas. As Gérard Malchelosse observed in the preface to the book, "Its [the regiment's] organization and history are of particular interest to us at this time when there is such a great desire to show our roots in the best possible light."[2]

Three years later, in 1925, Malchelosse cooperated with Régis Roy to produce what they described as "a corrective supplement and complement" to Sulte's study.[3] It was also entitled *Le Régiment de Carignan,* but the identical titles should not be construed as an attempt to confuse, for the two works are so interlinked that they have to be considered parts of a single larger one. It is, however, Roy and Malchelosse's that bestowed the legendary status on the regiment. After rejecting any suggestions that it was not a handpicked body of men, the authors proceeded to attribute the soldiers' deeds to spiritual motivation and to expound a somewhat mystical account of the part they, and their descendants, had played over the years in furthering the cause of the Abbé Groulx's particular form of Franco-American nationalism. As they stated:

These are those who made up the bands that the Comte de Frontenac sent out to the south and to the west. These are those who hastened to the aid of Quebec in 1690. These are their sons, brave men like them, who stand in a place of honour beside Montcalm, and their grandsons at the side of Salaberry at Châteauguay in 1812–14. It is their blood, vigorous, generous and ardent blood, which flowed in the veins of more than one of our patriotes of 1837–38, and of our crusaders who sped to the aid of the Holy

Father in 1870. In the same way, this valiant Carignan blood pulsed more strongly yet in the breasts of our dear Canadians in 1914, when they set foot on the sacred soil and could say, "France, we are here! We are the descendants of those soldiers you sent us in 1665 to suppress the barbarous hordes which threatened our land, and we have come to you in your hour of peril."[4]

In other words, if pre-Conquest Canada was the Abbé Groulx's Camelot, then its spirit of knight-errantry survived in the descendants of those Carignan-Salières veterans who settled in the country and who stood ever ready to hurry to the defence of its French and Catholic heritage.

Since 1925 historians, English or French, have added to the reputation of those books by using them as sole sources for accounts of the regiment in works of their own. By that means they have been instrumental in perpetuating the story as Sulte and Roy and Malchelosse told it, even though their readers may no longer be concerned with the advancement of Groulx's teachings. The best-known and probably the most widely read such work in English is T.B. Costain's *White and Gold,* a popular history of New France published in 1954, but it is by no means the only one.

The intent of this present work, however, is not to demean or diminish the regiment's reputation, but simply to disperse enough of the "golden haze" to reveal it for what it really was, a workaday seventeenth-century infantry unit sent to fight overseas. To that end, the contents of surviving documents that shed light on the story will form the basis of the narrative. They will be supplemented by material from authoritative secondary sources only to the extent necessary to permit the writing of a connected and logical account. As for the men who served in the ranks, it is hoped that they too will benefit from the process and emerge from the haze, not as knights in shining armour perhaps, but as real infantrymen – a few of them saints, a few of them sinners, but most of them ordinary foot soldiers, who coped with peril, privation, and incompetence as stoically as their kind has been doing since time immemorial.

Before turning to their story, though, I must first acknowledge some assistance I have received in getting the manuscript ready for publication. A few years ago, Robert-Lionel Séguin helped me decipher the document that became the basis of appendix A; then, some time later, Michel Wyczynski, of the Manuscripts Division in the National Archives of Canada, steered me towards unsuspected documentary sources; and, most recently, Audrey Hlady helped me get the manuscript into a form that was fit to be printed. Their help has been invaluable.

The Good Regiment

CHAPTER ONE

Canada Bound

On 18 March 1664 Jean-Baptiste Colbert, Louis XIV's minister of finance, advised François de Laval, bishop *in partibus* of Petraea and vicar apostolic in New France, that "His Majesty has resolved to send a good regiment of infantry to Canada at the end of this year, or in the month of February next, in order to destroy these barbarians [the Iroquois] completely."[1] The minister was almost as good as his word: a little over a year later, on 19 April 1665, the first four companies of the Carignan-Salières Regiment sailed from La Rochelle bound for Quebec.[2] Despite all appearances to the contrary, that event marked not so much the beginning of a bold enterprise as it did the culmination of years of pleas and petitions from Canada for troops to subdue the Iroquois. As well, it represented the successful completion of a logistical operation that had extended France's supply and shipping capabilities to their utmost, and even beyond.

It all stemmed back to the early years of French settlements in Canada, to the time of Champlain when the fur trade had become the dominant feature of their economy and had increasingly forced them into trading partnerships with their Indian neighbours to secure the flow of beaver pelts into their warehouses. That dependency quickly entangled the French in the intertribal warfare existing between their trading partners, the Montagnais, the Algonkins, and the Hurons, and the sworn enemies of those groups, the Senecas, the Cayugas, the Onondagas, the Oneidas, and the Mohawks, the Five Nations of the Iroquois Confederacy. The French might not have been aware of it at the outset, but they very soon discovered that to be the cost of doing business. If they wanted to preserve the arrangement, they had to be prepared to resort to force of arms. It was a price they seemed willing to pay, and the result was that from 1608 to 1665 their tiny enclaves along the north shore of the

St Lawrence were seldom free from attacks by war parties from one or another of the Five Nations with whom the French had few other contacts, since those Indians traded with the Dutch at Fort Orange on the Hudson River.[3]

What made the French settlements particularly vulnerable throughout those years was their chronic underpopulation. This fact was never more evident than during the years after the Huron dispersal, in 1648, when the French just did not have the manpower to counter effectively the almost unremitting attacks upon them, and upon their Indian allies as they brought their cargoes of furs to the St Lawrence. An idea of the degree of that underpopulation can be gained by examining the demographic statistics for 1663: in that year there were 3,035 people living in Canada, 1,928 persons who might be classified as adults, and, of them, around 63 per cent, or about 1,200, were males, perhaps 800 or 900 living in Quebec and no more than 200 in both Trois-Rivières and Montreal.[4]

Blame for that perilously small population is often attributed to the fur trade monopolists for neglecting to fulfil their undertaking to bring in settlers, but that was not entirely the case.[5] By and large the Compagnie des Cent-Associés, or the Compagnie de la Nouvelle-France, did meet its obligations and regularly brought indentured workers into the country.[6] The problem lay in the large number who returned to France at the end of their three-to-five-year period of indentured service. Rather than stay on as settlers in a country that had little to offer by way of creature comforts and security, with its forbidding winters, the difficulty of clearing land for agricultural use, the shortage of marriageable women, and the constant threat of Iroquois attack, they went back to France where conditions were far more hospitable.[7]

The situation was desperate, and if outside help was not forthcoming quickly, there was every likelihood that, before too long, the Canadian settlements would be overwhelmed and their residents slaughtered. A number of appeals for help had been made to France by both secular and religious leaders, including Paul de Chomedey de Maisonneuve, Bishop Laval, Marie de l'Incarnation, and Governor Davaugour, but to no avail.[8] Even as late as 1661, when Pierre Boucher, the governor of Trois-Rivières, went to Paris to plead for military help, he met with not much more than polite, but noncommittal, sympathy.[9] The king's concerns at that time were all European ones, and until someone could convince him that benefits could be gained from his American colonies, Canada would have to face the Iroquois alone.

The French settlements had to wait for Jean-Baptiste Colbert, with his talk of mercantilism, to bring about that change of mind. In Colbertian terms, mercantilism was a state enterprise rather than one oriented towards private gain, but otherwise it was very little different from that practised elsewhere in Europe. It was based on the precept that a finite amount of wealth existed in the world and that any increase in one country's portion of it could be achieved only at the expense of another's. The shining example of the system in operation, the one that aroused the most envy in the hearts of kings, was that practised by Spain, who, while protecting her domestic commerce from foreign competition, exploited the wealth of her Latin American colonies to finance the Hapsburgs' dynastic ambitions in Europe. If French wealth were to be similarly enhanced, Colbert preached, the king would do well to develop and exploit his overseas empire, to encourage settlement in it, to build up a merchant fleet to monopolize the carrying trade to and from its shores thereby eliminating the Dutch and the British from any share of the traffic, and to erect a protectionist barrier around France to keep out foreign goods.[10]

The prospect of the increased wealth flowing into the royal coffers, which mercantilism promised, appealed to Louis, whose plan to give his realm a more readily defensible frontier along the natural boundary of the Rhine was already well formed in his mind. He knew that it would be a costly undertaking. Providing himself with suitably splendid surroundings, in keeping with the grandeur he saw himself attaining as monarch, would also be expensive. If mercantilism could provide the resources for all he envisaged, it certainly warranted his attention.

Seen from that standpoint, the settlements along the St Lawrence suddenly took on a new aspect for the king. If he brought them under this personal control, he, and his treasury, rather than a consortium of speculators seeking personal gain, would be the beneficiaries of their bounty.

It is not known exactly when the decision to set up the structure that came to be known as royal government was made, but it was most likely towards the end of 1662, and Louis accomplished it in four well-defined steps. First, in February 1663 he requested the Compagnie de la Nouvelle-France to relinquish its monopoly. The company acceded to the demand, and by mid-March he was able to announce that New France had formally been brought under his personal rule.[11] Second, in April 1663 he established the Conseil Souverain in Quebec to administer the colony in his name with the proviso that, at all times, its acts were subject to his veto, should he disapprove of them.[12] Third, in November 1663 he appointed

Alexandre de Prouville, Marquis de Tracy, his lieutenant-general, with vice-regal authority to oversee the putting in place of the infrastructure of royal government in the whole of New France, a move to ensure that it was all done in strict accordance with the royal wishes. The importance of the appointment can be judged by Tracy's rank of lieutenant-general. There was only one higher in the French army, that of marshal of France.[13] Fourth, in May 1664, acting on Colbert's recommendation, he granted letters patent to a new monopolist, the Compagnie des Indes occidentales, which, despite its name, was actually a Crown agency through which he could exercise strict control over his colonies. The company was to enjoy a monopoly of all the commerce in New France and along the west coast of Africa from Cape Verde to the Cape of Good Hope. Also, as Grand Seigneur in Canada, it would enjoy wide powers pertaining to government, justice, commerce, defence, the appointment of officials, and the signing of treaties.[14]

The measures were all very good in theory, but it was unlikely that they would have the desired effect unless one important prerequisite existed in Canada, that of peace. If the Iroquois continued to harass the colonies along the St Lawrence, as they had been doing, the king's plans were doomed to failure, and nobody knew that better than Colbert. For that reason, he hastened to reassure Mgr de Laval in March 1664 that military help was forthcoming. Even so, there was a delay of eight more months before he was able to advise Tracy, who was already in the Antilles, that the chosen regiment would be setting out in the new year.[15] Thus it finally transpired that on 23 January 1665 Michel Le Tellier, the minister of war, ordered the intendant of Rochefort to make all the necessary arrangements for the dispatch of the Carignan-Salières Regiment to Canada.[16]

Colbert de Terron, a cousin of the better-known Jean-Baptiste Colbert, was the intendant, and his importance in the events surrounding the regiment's departure for Canada, as well as in its maintenance there afterwards, cannot be overemphasized. He was of the new generation of bureaucrats who had the responsibility of implementing royal policies, and it fell to him to arrange for the mustering and accommodation of an entire regiment, a thousand men or more, in the embarkation area near the port of La Rochelle. Once it was ensconced in transit camps there, he had to ensure that its twenty companies were up to strength, properly clad, and fully equipped. In addition he had the job of finding enough ships to transport the regiment across the Atlantic, no easy task since the French merchant fleet was pathetically small at that time.[17]

The job would have been difficult enough had there been a precedent to draw upon, but never before had an enterprise of such magnitude been undertaken in France. The only experience Colbert de Terron had to guide him was what he had learned the previous year when the Marquis de Tracy had sailed for the Antilles with four companies of soldiers. Compared with his latest task, however, that had been a relatively small operation.

While the intendant of Rochefort set about the considerable job of preparing for the Canadian venture, the Carignan-Salières Regiment, already detailed for overseas duty, was foot-slogging across France towards La Rochelle.

The unit had been formed only in 1658 when the Carignan and the Salières regiments had been amalgamated as part of a military reorganization following the restoration of peace between France and Spain. So far as can be determined, its brief history was unmarked by battle honours, although its two component regiments had both seen active service in the Thirty Years' War, in the factional strife of the Fronde, and in the late war with Spain.[18]

It was organized like most French infantry regiments of the day. It had twenty companies, each with an established strength of a captain, a lieutenant, an ensign, and fifty enlisted men included among whom were two sergeants, three corporals, five anspessades – a rank approximately equivalent to lance-corporal or private first class – two drummers, a fife player, and a surgeon.[19] The enlisted men were all volunteers and were recruited by the captains into their own particular companies, rather than into the regiment. Thereafter the captains paid them, clothed them, and fed them out of money provided for those purposes by the king, acting through his minister of war.[20]

In the second half of the seventeenth century, little difficulty was encountered in recruiting all the men needed, not because of any great yearning for glory among young Frenchmen, but mainly because of recurrent economic distress in the country. French agriculture, the backbone of the economy, was in a state of disarray resulting from an almost nonexistent interprovincial distribution system, which, across the country as a whole, was responsible for a chronic state of imbalance between supply and demand. It was really no more than a reflection of the disjointed nature of a state wherein such central authority as did exist resided in the king's person, and the few central agencies that had been set up, for example, the War and the Finance departments, served the king's needs rather than those of his subjects. One outcome was that, in farming areas, wildly fluctuating prices for agricultural produce contributed to wildly fluctuating demands for labour. At the same time, in towns and other nonproducing areas, food prices could soar beyond the reach of the poorer classes so that near famine prevailed among them. Thus, in town and country alike, the net result was the same. In both there was a growing number of men looking for some form of employment that could provide them with a livelihood, and for those who were young and able-bodied, the beat of the recruiter's drum offered an alternative to crime by beckoning them to the king's service.[21]

As for the officers, with few exceptions at the regimental level, notably that of the colonel, they belonged to an emerging caste of career soldiers, a burgeoning officer corps made up of impoverished members of the *petite noblesse,* sons of bureaucrats, and other young men of bourgeois origins. They filled all but the ranks of colonel and above, which the king continued to reserve for members of the old *noblesse de l'épée.* All officers, however, regardless of their antecedents, served the king neither as mercenaries nor out of any feudal obligation, but as his servants. In return he paid them a wage according to a prescribed scale, which, in most cases, was their main source of income. The only way it could be increased was by promotion, which could result only from some form of distinguished conduct that had been brought to the notice of the king by his minister of war. What worried a number of the officers in the Carignan-Salières Regiment in January 1665 was that any such conduct that took place somewhere in a Canadian wilderness could well go unnoticed by a king who was five thousand kilometres away in Paris, and consequently no advancement would result.[22]

The outcome was that some of those officers, mainly lieutenants and ensigns, hurriedly absented themselves from duty on a variety of pretexts, which, almost without exception, were inspired by an overwhelming desire to avoid overseas service. Their absence, contributed to an erosion of discipline among the enlisted men, who were already somewhat disgruntled at being uprooted from the relative comfort they had been enjoying in garrison towns such as Marsal in Lorraine and Arras, near the border with the Spanish Netherlands.[23] Apprehensive about the prospect of going to Canada, they were further unsettled by the officers' conduct.[24] It was not that they resented the officers' shirking of duties so much as that their esprit de corps was diminished by the fact that their leaders were, very likely, just as unsettled as they were. The result was that the regiment's progress across France was marked by outbreaks of disorder and violence.

The first documented incidents occurred in the villages of Marchenoir and Peronaille, near Orléans, and it is possible only to hazard a guess as to what caused them.[25] Such events, however, were not uncommon in seventeenth-century France, many of which were the outcome of problems with billeting and victualling.[26]

The question of providing for troops on the march had been a concern for over a hundred years, ever since the mid-sixteenth century when Henry II had first established military supply depots at regular intervals along the major roads travelled by troops on the march. The move had been designed to avoid the often violent confrontations that had occurred with civilians over the provision of rations and quarters. It is not unlikely, therefore, that the trouble at Marchenoir and Peronaille had its cause rooted in the circumstance that, during the latter part of its march to La Rochelle, the Carignan-Salières Regiment did not follow any of those particular roads, most of which radiated from Paris towards towns on, or near, France's land frontiers.[27] If that were the case, then it would have devolved upon the regimental billeting officer to requisition, or commandeer, whatever food and shelter were needed for the troops along the way.[28] If, in this instance, the villagers had been unwilling, or unable, to meet his demands, it is not difficult to imagine how the disorders might have begun.

Whatever it was that touched them off, the subsequent events were serious enough for the intendant of the province to conduct an inquiry. The intendant, whose duty it was to oversee the passage of troops through his province and to investigate and report on any extraordinary occurrences, forwarded his findings to the minister of war, along with a request that in future he be notified in advance of any troop movements planned through the area under his jurisdiction.[29]

Le Tellier had no intention of doing anything of the sort, and although his reply was polite, it was unyielding. The king, he wrote, while agreeing that the incidents were most unfortunate, wanted to be lenient because the regiment was bound for Canada. Beyond urging the Marquis de Salières to tighten up his discipline, he proposed taking no other action. The request that advance notice be given of troop movements got even shorter shrift. The minister left no doubt when he stated that, in all such instances, the king's wishes had to be paramount, and local concerns, such as those expressed in the intendant's letter, could not be permitted to interfere with his wishes being carried out.[30]

Not so lenient was the king's attitude in the case of an ordinary soldier who, shortly after the Marchenoir and Peronaille incident, was brought before a regimental court martial charged with having stolen several lengths of cloth and some items of tableware. The court found the man guilty as charged and summarily sentenced him to six years in the galleys, a punishment in which a convict served as an oarsman on one of the royal naval vessels, usually in the Mediterranean. The king quickly confirmed the verdict and ordered that the prisoner be placed in chains until he could be transferred to Marseille to begin his punishment.[31]

The apparent inconsistency in the king's reaction to the two cases seems to suggest that he used a double standard when sitting in judgment, but that was not really so. His conclusion in both instances has to be considered against the background that he constantly sought ways to strengthen his monarchy to a point where his authority would be respected and unquestioned from one end of France to the other. At the same time, it must be taken into account that, first, those close to him suspected that sometimes provincial intendants lent an unduly sympathetic ear to the complaints of the common people, and, second, he needed the army to suppress any open opposition to his royal authority.[32]

Besides serving as his bulwark against outbreaks of civil unrest, which were not uncommon at that time, a major uprising having occurred in the Boulogne area in 1662 and another in the southwest of the country in 1664, the army was the very embodiment of that authority.[33] The troops had the additional quality of being able to enhance his glory by means of victories on the battlefield. It is not surprising, therefore, that it occupied a position of some prestige and privilege in his kingdom, for, without it, Louis XIV would have been vulnerable to every faction that looked for opportunities to curb the consolidation and further growth of his power.[34]

Under those circumstances, condemning the regiment merely at the urging of an intendant, whose motives might have been open to question, could have been seen by some as a sign of weakness and of a proneness to bow to provincial pressures. At the same time upholding the court martial's decision was clear evidence to all of his continuing concern to see discipline maintained in the only body upon which he could rely to enforce his authority and to suppress any rebellious subjects who might try to usurp it.[35]

A further expression of that concern was contained in a letter form the minister of war to the Marquis de Salières, which confirmed the sentence that consigned the soldier to the galleys. The letter went on to urge the colonel to look again at the bothersome matter of the absentee officers. Salières was instructed to submit forthwith all their names to the minister, along with those of any junior officers he could recommend for immediate promotion. With that information in hand, the king was prepared to cashier the absentees without any further warning and, at the same time, to confirm the promotion and appointment of their replacements.[36] The solution may have sounded draconian, but, nonetheless, it was the sort called for if the regiment was to be up to its established strength when it embarked for Quebec, and if the related questions of an uncertain discipline and a wavering morale were to be remedied too.

Those two problems, however, were not entirely attributable to that one cause. A contributing factor was the continual influx of recruits, who, until they adjusted to the regimen of military routine, had an unsettling effect on the regiment. In addition, the method of securing their enlistment very often proved to be a source of trouble in itself when townsfolk, already unhappy about having troops billeted on them, became further displeased at the sight of young, able-bodied men being encouraged to join the army.

The technique of recruiting was simple enough. A drummer, accompanied by an NCO or an anspessade, would be positioned at a busy street corner or in the marketplace to attract attention. The NCO would direct any likely looking candidates to an officer, generally located in a nearby tavern. Using all the blandishments at his disposal, the officer would try to secure their commitment to join up for a three-year engagement.[37]

It was in a small town named La Mothe-Saint-Héray, about fifty kilometres south of Poitiers, that those very activities provoked what turned into another unfortunate incident along the way to La Rochelle.

As the La Fouille Company was well below strength, its captain, Jean-Maurice-Philippe de Vernon, Sieur de La Fouille, decided to try to enlist a few recruits in the town. Accordingly, one of the company drummers, a man known as La Noiray, was ordered to commence beating his drum at a street corner. He had not been at it long when he was accosted by a local magistrate, the Sieur Bonneau-Chabot, who began to berate him in a loud and insulting manner. Then knocking La Noiray down, the magistrate forcibly confiscated his drum. That evening, still smarting from the verbal and physical abuse he had suffered, La Noiray gathered up six or seven of his comrades and, intent upon revenge, they lay in wait for Bonneau-Chabot. The magistrate must have been expecting some sort of trouble because, when he did appear, he too had several well-armed friends with him. A battle royal ensued. In the melee the soldiers had the advantage, and when they left the scene, they had not only killed the magistrate but had also mortally wounded one of his companions. Soon afterwards the company moved on, but that did not prevent the case from being brought before a civilian court at Saint-Maixent where the soldiers were tried in absentia and convicted.

Five of them, including La Noiray and the company commander's nephew, were sentenced to death, but by that time they had passed beyond the jurisdiction of the district court.[38]

What seems the most astounding aspect of the whole affair is that at no time did the military authorities make any attempt to cooperate with their civilian counterparts. It was almost as if the two belonged to different worlds which viewed each other as adversaries. Given the king's own attitude towards his subjects, this outlook becomes at least partly understandable.

A very similar incident took place near Saint-Jean-d'Angély, not far from Rochefort, where another fight broke out between civilians and soldiers when the regiment passed through. During the fracas the brothers of one of the local notables, the Sieur de Paille, killed Sergeant Hivars of the Rougemont Company. Outraged by the killing, another NCO, Sergeant Yvon, and several enlisted men returned to town later, revenge uppermost in their minds. On that occasion, however, the civil authorities intervened before any more blood could be shed. They arrested the sergeant and his henchmen and brought them before the magistrates, thereby forestalling a possible repetition of what had happened at La Mothe-Saint-Héray. The incident, however, had an interesting outcome, one that again emphasized the inferior position occupied by the general population vis-à-vis the army in Louis xiv's France, where the system served to maintain that inferiority. After that incident, the minister of war authorized the regiment to post guards in any towns through which it passed in order, he said, to protect the soldiers from civilian attacks. While they might have been the cause of the trouble at Saint-Jean-d'Angély, Le Tellier's action, despite his caution that the guards should not be used to intimidate civilians, effectively imposed martial law on any town through which the regiment, or any part of it, happened to pass.[39]

Bearing in mind that these documented cases possibly represent only the most serious of a larger number that actually took place, they suggest that, during the latter stages of its march across France, the regiment's conduct was less than exemplary. If that was indeed the way it was, all that can be said in extenuation is that in the seventeenth century violence was not uncommon. The soldiers of the day, by virtue of their calling and the role they played in the state, were expected to be violent men, and the conduct of the Carignan-Salières Regiment was neither much better, nor much worse, than that of any contemporary unit, French or otherwise, under similar circumstances.

By the beginning of April, however, the cross-country march was over and the whole regiment had reached the assembly area near La Rochelle. There, on the king's orders, it was dispersed in camps on the offshore islands of Oléron and Ré, an expedient that had three very obvious advantages.[40] First, it enabled the entire regiment to be concentrated in two relatively small areas, which facilitated the final preparations for embarkation; second, it effectively isolated the troops from the civilians in La Rochelle on the mainland, and thereby minimized the chances of clashes between the two; and third, it deterred would-be deserters, since it required the collusion of a boatman for them to get away. The surrounding sea, therefore, formed a most effective barricade around the men, many of whom, including the officers, must have by then been viewing the future with increasing apprehension as they found themselves caught up in the final preparations for crossing the Atlantic, an undertaking that in 1665 was still fraught with peril both from disease and from disaster.

What made an already anxious period worse was the continuing absence of a number of officers. The king's threat to cashier them had certainly persuaded the few truant captains to return to duty, but the same could not be said for the twenty-eight lieutenants and ensigns who persisted in absenting themselves. If the regiment's fortitude was to be bolstered sufficiently for it to face up to what lay ahead with some equanimity, something had to be done without delay to eliminate that nagging problem before spirits sank any further. Fortunately for that situation, the king's patience ran out and on 13 April the minister of war sent twenty-eight blank commissions, twelve for lieutenants and sixteen for ensigns, to the Marquis de Salières. The accompanying instructions ordered him to fill the vacant lieutenancies from the ranks of his most promising ensigns, and then to elevate as many cadets, or other capable persons, as were needed to make up his complement of officers.[41] Nothing is known of the fate of the absentees except that they were posted as deserters and left to be dealt with according to the king's pleasure. So it was that, after weeks of indecision, the regiment's body of officers was finally brought up to strength. The only remaining concerns were to complete the outfitting of the regiment and to get it aboard ship, both duties which fell very much to the intendant of Rochefort.

Bureaucratic procedures, by reputation, are not conducive to expeditiousness. As a result, military officers, the nature of whose duties calls for a certain decisiveness and impatience in their dispositions, soon develop an intolerance for them and their practitioners. That temperament, without a doubt, was one reason the routine followed by Colbert de Terron in preparing the regiment for embarkation proved so irksome to the Marquis de Salières and caused him such wrath. It made enough of an impression on the intendant for him to complain to his cousin, months afterwards, that "his [Salières's] bad temper is part of his nature, it is nothing to do with anything else; I remember him well at La Rochelle."[42]

Another reason for the anger was that as an old soldier, whose career extended back many years, the colonel had grown more than a little jealous of his authority, particularly so when he felt that others were encroaching on areas of responsibility he considered to be rightfully his, such as looking into the regiment's preparedness for service in Canada, which Colbert de Terron was doing. He took offence even though the intendant's concerns were most likely identical with what his own would have been had he been the inspecting officer.

Among those concerns would certainly have been whether the twenty companies were up to strength. Although most had more than their entitlement of fifty enlisted men, inspection showed that one, the Froment Company, was seriously undermanned. It is impossible to determine the cause, but it was not deemed to be the captain's fault. It was corrected by simply transferring two men from the overstrength companies and reimbursing their commanding officers fifteen *livres* a man – the sum estimated by the minister of war to be the amount expended on recruiting and outfitting them.[43]

Not all the reasons for subjecting the regiment to inspections, however, were concerned with determining its readiness for war. Of no less importance to the minister was the need to ensure that the money he had provided the captains with to pay and outfit their companies had been used for its intended purpose. Opportunities for abuse abounded in this system, and it was not uncommon for officers to try and augment their incomes by misappropriating some of the funds for their own use. Falsifying the number of men on the companies' rosters and other similarly fraudulent practices were commonplace, and Le Tellier was ever anxious to detect and bring to account those engaging in them.[44] One frequently used trick was designed to take advantage of the situation that, save for the regimental cockades worn on the right shoulder, there was no prescribed uniform for the French army before 1670. It was up to each captain to decide just how he would clothe his men and, as one might expect, some were more honest about it than others.[45] The result was that, within a regiment, the cut, the cloth, and the overall quality of the garments issued to the enlisted men varied considerably from company to company. Any money the less scrupulous captains managed to save by buying inferior goods they pocketed, and, were it not for the inspection process, their dishonesty was not likely to have been detected.

Inspection to ensure conformity with the required quality of clothing and accoutrements and to ensure honesty among those entrusted with the spending of royal funds were two of the more important outcomes of the army reforms introduced by Michel Le Tellier. If the case of the Carignan-Salières Regiment is any indication, it effectively achieved those ends. When Colbert de Terron found that four companies, which had boarded ship and were about to sail, were wearing what he considered inferior clothing, he had no hesitation in ordering their captains to replace it forthwith. Until they did, sailing was held up.[46]

By 1665, on paper at least, inspection had developed into a well-defined procedure with several layers of responsibility. Overall supervision of infantry regiments was in the hands of the inspector general of infantry, the famous Lieutenant-Colonel Jean Martinet. Since the Carignan-Salières Regiment was bound for New France, however, its readiness to sail had to be assessed by the controller of the navy, while its weaponry and other military matériel came under the surveillance of a commissioner of supplies. In practice, though, it appears that Colbert de Terron carried out most of the on-the-spot inspections and reported his findings to the officials on whose behalf he had conducted them.[47]

The newly appointed intendant of New France, Jean Talon, also kept a close watch over the final preparations for the Canadian venture. Since he would be responsible for replacing any worn or unserviceable items once the regiment landed in Canada, he was concerned that excessive demands for replacement items would place an unacceptable burden on the limited amount of cargo space available in the small number of ships that sailed to the St Lawrence each year. Therefore it was important for him to be satisfied that every man who sailed to Quebec was as well and as durably outfitted as possible.[48]

Gradually all the prescribed equipment and supplies reached the embarkation area, including the latest development in small arms, flintlocks, to replace the old matchlocks, the standard personal weapon for many years.[49] The issue of the new gun meant that the men had to be familiarized with its operation, a procedure that, in a way, was a godsend, for it helped relieve the tedium of days spent waiting for suitable ships to be found and readied for the Atlantic crossing.

The Marquis de Tracy's departure for the Antilles the previous year had denied Colbert de Terron the use of two of the largest ships in the French merchant fleet, the eight-hundred-ton *Brèse* and the only slightly smaller *Terron*. But for their size, which made them difficult to manoeuvre in the narrow, shallow channels of the St Lawrence, they would have been able to carry a large part of the Carignan-Salières Regiment all the way to Quebec.[50] The navigation of that waterway, however, was best accomplished by vessels having a much shallower draft, ones that, as the records show, displaced no more than three hundred tons. Ships of that size could carry up to four companies of soldiers in addition to their crews, although, with that many people aboard, conditions would have been extremely cramped and uncomfortable during the voyage that could last up to four months.[51] In that situation, the danger was that soon after the last of the fresh food had been consumed, scurvy was likely to break out and rampage unchecked through the overcrowded holds.

Six ships in all were required to transport the Carignan-Salières Regiment to Canada, together with its equipment and provisions. The assembling of a fleet of that size was, perhaps, the biggest single problem that Colbert de Terron had to overcome because of the limited resources of France's merchant marine. The fact that it was not equal to so large a task became apparent the minute the first contingent of men boarded the *Joyeux Siméon,* a two-hundred-ton Dutch ship chartered by Pierre Gaigneur, a La Rochelle merchant and an old hand in the trans-Atlantic trade between his home port and Quebec.[52] It was a recourse that had a certain irony to it, since one of the avowed aims of Colbert's mercantilist policies was to put France in a position to exclude the Dutch and the English from the carrying trade to and from its colonies.

Nevertheless, it was the only way that a suitable ship could be on hand at La Rochelle on 12 April to take on board the first four companies of troops. Seven days later she was towed clear of the harbour to hoist her sails and to head west into the Atlantic.[53]

Another month passed before any other vessels were ready for the voyage, a delay brought about by the dilapidated state of one of the two that Colbert de Terron had earmarked for the trip. Both were royal ships, the *Paix,* a good Atlantic vessel, and the *Aigle d'Or,* a teredo-riddled old tub that was kept afloat only by the numerous patches on her worm-eaten hull.[54] Nor was that the end of the delays. It was discovered that neither ship had any bedding aboard so that five hundred palliasses had to be found and filled with straw.[55] At last, by the end of the first week in May, all was finally ready and a further eight companies went aboard, four to each ship, and both sailed for Quebec on the thirteenth.[56]

By the third week of the month two more ships, the *Saint-Sébastien* and the *Justice*, were ready for loading. They too were royal vessels and had also been delayed while hull repairs had been carried out. They took on board the remaining eight companies, as well as the newly appointed governor of New France, Daniel de Rémy de Courcelle, and the new intendant, Jean Talon, both en route to their posts in Quebec.[57] Thus it was that on 24 May 1665 the last of the Carignan-Salières Regiment sailed for Canada. All that remained for Colbert de Terron was to see that the supply ship, the *Jardin de Hollande*, was loaded and sent on her way, an event that took place on 22 June.[58]

By that time the *Joyeux Siméon* had already reached Quebec and had disembarked the vanguard of the regiment, an event that inspired Marie de l'Incarnation to write: "It [the regiment] is resolved to make its faith and courage conspicuous. The soldiers are being made to understand that this is a holy war, in which is involved only the glory of God and the salvation of souls."[59]

Her words may not have been entirely appropriate for the men whose recent march across France had been marred by what can only be called a series of sordid incidents, but it is unlikely that she would have known that. What is more to the point is that, like most of the clergy and the religious in the colony, she failed to recognize that their mission was a secular rather than a sacred one, and that God was involved in it only to the extent that Louis XIV considered himself to be king by divine right.

CHAPTER TWO

Forts in the Wilderness

On 19 June 1665, sixty-one days' sailing from La Rochelle, the *Joyeux Siméon* docked at Quebec to disembark the advance party of the first regiment of French regular troops to serve in Canada.[1] Of the five contingents from the Carignan-Salières Regiment that crossed the Atlantic that spring, it was the one most blessed with favourable winds to speed it to its destination. As a result, the men were in fine fettle, both physically and mentally, when they stepped ashore, apart from a little ungainliness as legs grown accustomed to nego-tiating heaving decks encountered solid ground again. With a lightness to their step and an air of well-being about their bearing, which spoke of happiness at being back on dry land, they set off up the road that wound steeply from the waterfront to the Upper Town. Neither was the joy restricted to the troops; it also pervaded the whole settlement, for King Louis XIV had finally responded to its pleas for help and, to show its gratitude, the townsfolk flocked into the streets to give the soldiers a welcome such as they had probably never seen before. It was the very antithesis of the sort of reception they had come to expect in France, which, generally, lay somewhere between sullen resentment and open hostility.[2]

That reception, enthusiastic as it was, however, paled beside the one given to the Marquis de Tracy eleven days later when he came ashore after an unforeseen delay in the Gulf of St Lawrence. His ship, the *Brèse,* was too large to risk in the treacherous waters of the estuary ahead where adverse winds added to the already con-siderable perils to navigation posed by shoals and narrow channels. It had waited at anchor off Percé, at the easternmost tip of the Gaspé Peninsula, for the better part of a month waiting to trans-ship the general, his entourage, and the four companies of soldiers that accompanied him to two smaller vessels for the voyage upstream to Quebec. He finally reached that destination on the last day of June to face a tremendous outpouring of public acclaim.[3]

The sixty-two-year-old Tracy, weary from weeks at sea and debilitated by a persistent fever, declined all formal welcomes and, attended by his considerable retinue, immediately set about lumbering up the hill to the church.[4] There, at the main door, stood Mgr de Laval, resplendent in his pontifical vestments and supported by numerous clergy and acolytes, all waiting to greet him and to conduct him to the choir where a prie-dieu stood ready for his use. Despite his poor health, though, Tracy ignored it, preferring to suffer the discomfort of kneeling on the flagstones all through the ritual of the Te Deum. The gesture was, perhaps, as much an expression of his relief at being back on land as it was of his piety, for in 1665 French soldiers were landsmen all and were not used to having to travel to their duties by sea.[5]

Needless to say, Tracy's arrival with two hundred soldiers, following hard upon that of the first four companies of the Carignan-Salières Regiment, was not without its problems. Overcrowding became an immediate and urgent cause for concern in Quebec where, in a matter of eleven days, the population had undergone a sudden and dramatic increase of about 25 per cent. Even though it was the largest settlement in Canada, its available accommodations were few, consisting of several institutional and governmental buildings and a mere seventy houses.[6] What made the matter even more pressing was that a further eight hundred soldiers were expected daily so that if the problem was left unresolved for long the warmth of any afterglow of the recent joyous welcomes could quickly cool to the chill of resentment. It was, therefore, a question of some urgency for Tracy.

Equally urgent was the question of the best way to set about tackling the Iroquois. It took him less than three weeks to decide on the direction to take. The course became clear when he recognized that it was not the Iroquois Confederacy as a whole that was the immediate enemy, but only the Mohawks. The other four nations, for one reason or another, were preoccupied elsewhere and were not involved in the most recent attacks on the French enclaves, or in impeding the flow of beaver pelts to them by blockading the Ottawa and St Lawrence rivers.[7]

Following the dispersal of the Hurons and their allies, Iroquois leaders had looked forward to enjoying the fruits of their victory, which, besides giving them access to extended hunting grounds, were calculated to put them in a position to control the flow of furs to the St Lawrence via the Lake Ontario artery. That advantage, however, did not last long. It lost much of its effectiveness the moment the Ottawas, an Algonkian tribe, moved into the vacuum left by the Hurons and, assuming the role of intermediaries in the fur trade, diverted its traffic from the west to more northerly waterways that they controlled, thereby circumventing the Iroquois blockade.[8]

Had the entire Confederacy acted in concert, it is likely that the blockade would have succeeded, and the French would almost certainly have been compelled to submit to Iroquois terms if they wished to continue in the fur trade. Perplexing as it might appear at first sight, it was primarily the Mohawks alone, not the Confederacy as a whole, who sustained pressure on the fur-trading settlements.[9]

In reality the Confederacy never did constitute a tightly knit alliance in the European sense. Its five component nations acted in concert only if expediency dictated it, as was the case on occasion during the systematic destruction of the Hurons and their allies between 1642 and 1657. At other times they went their separate ways, and open warfare between some of them was not unknown. Add the fact that the Senecas, Cayugas, and Onondagas were far too preoccupied with running a blockade imposed on their own trade by the Susquehannocks, as well as a disinclination on the part of the Oneidas to trust the Mohawks, who they suspected of pursuing their own exclusive interests, and the Confederacy is at once revealed as having less than a united front.[10]

Vital to Mohawk interests was the Lake Champlain – Richelieu River corridor, darkly referred to by some as the Iroquois Lake and the Iroquois River, although, perhaps, the name Mohawk would have been more apt under the circumstances, since it was the one nation that made extensive use of the route. Certainly it was not a commercial lifeline for anyone, Indian or European, but it was the main approach route for Mohawk war parties en route to the settlements along the St Lawrence and to the all-important Ottawa Valley.[11] Any interruption of the traffic passing through the valley could seriously affect the conduct of the fur trade and add to the discomfiture of the French.

Therein lay the key to Tracy's plan of action, which was most likely based on information gathered in conversations with well-informed persons in the colony, particularly men like Paul Ragueneau, the Jesuit father superior. Ragueneau, who regularly briefed Colbert on conditions in Canada, was well acquainted with the ways and workings of the Confederacy, a knowledge acquired during many years of missionary experience among the Iroquois and the Hurons. It did not, therefore, take Tracy long to conclude that as a first move towards making the colony and its trade secure, he had to deny the Mohawks access to the St Lawrence, an operation that could best be accomplished by closing off the Richelieu Valley to them.[12]

As a means to that end, he decided to fortify the waterway by dispatching detachments of troops, more or less as they arrived from France, to build forts at strategic locations along its length, from Lake Champlain in the south to its confluence with the St Lawrence in the north. It was a plan that would also solve the overcrowding problem in Quebec. It could be argued that Tracy's Richelieu Valley forts served little military purpose because any Mohawk war party, intent upon attacking the settlements along the St Lawrence, would simply portage around them. The forts, however, were never intended as purely defensive installations, which that argument implies. From the outset they were meant to serve three main purposes, all of them offensive. First, they allowed troops to be deployed closer to the enemy than would otherwise have been possible. Second, they provided bases from which to patrol the surrounding country, thereby denying the Mohawks freedom of movement in it. Third, when the need arose, they would serve as forward bases and supply depots for any expeditions into the Mohawk lands.[13]

The first of the planned forts was to be built between the Richelieu Rapids, about sixty kilometres up the Richelieu, at its nearest point of approach to the Ottawa River. Construction was entrusted to Captain Jacques de Chambly, who set out from Quebec on 23 July, with the four companies of soldiers recently arrived from La Rochelle. Also in the party were about one hundred local men and a number of friendly Indians under the general supervision of fur trader Jean-Baptiste Legardeur de Repentigny, who had frequent contact with most of the Indian nations engaged in that trade, as well as the Jesuit Fathers Charles Albanel and Pierre-Joseph-Marie Chaumonot, both of whom had travelled extensively in areas associated with the missions and the fur trade and were no doubt knowledgeable about those Indians who dealt with the French.[14]

Leaving the comparative safety of Quebec for an area in which the Mohawks were known to range at will, as well as having to travel in nothing more substantial than native canoes and shallops built especially to negotiate the shallow, turbulent waters of the Richelieu River, was cause for some qualms among the soldiers in that first detachment.[15] At least we can assume so if the reaction of two of the company commanders was indicative of a more wide-spread uneasiness. The first, the elderly Captain de La Tour, had taken a profound interest in the career of one of his company

drummers, a nineteen year old named François Moussart. Not wishing
the young man, who was an accomplished musician, to have to
face the perils and the rigours of the wilderness, the captain arranged
for him to enter the Jesuit college to further his education. The
second, Captain Pierre de Froment, also an elderly officer, handed
a considerable sum of money, one hundred *louis d'or* (about thirty
thousand dollars) to the Jesuits for safekeeping, together with instructions for the money's disposal should he not return from the expedition.[16]

As if to confirm everybody's worst fears, the journey to the
Richelieu was not without its alarms. The convoy had gone barely
sixty kilometres from Quebec before word reached it that Trois-
Rivières was under attack by the Mohawks. Uncertain as to the
reliability of the news, Chambly ordered a halt while he dispatched
a small party to try to discover if the report was true. Happily it
turned out to be unfounded, but by then the wind had veered into
the northwest and the flotilla had to put into Trois-Rivières to wait
until it shifted to a more favourable quarter. There the troops
remained, weatherbound, for two weeks, much to the joy and relief
of a population still recovering from the shock of a recent Mohawk
raid.[17]

The enforced halt proved eventful for the soldiers as well. A day
or so after the start of their unscheduled stopover, four to five
hundred members of the Ottawa nation paddled in from the west,
bound for Quebec, with a huge cargo of beaver skins worth many
thousands of *livres*.[18] Although the significance of the event was
probably lost on most of the troops, it was, in fact, a glimpse of
the reason for their dispatch to Canada, for it was the king's wish
that the regiment should free the fur traffic from harassment so that
it could make its way to the French settlements along the St Lawrence
unmolested and with its cargoes intact.

Shortly after that, the general air of well-being that had pervaded
Trois-Rivières ever since the soldiers had arrived was suddenly dis-
pelled to be replaced by one of grief. It happened on 6 August
when a soldier from the Froment Company – one Sépulture de
Coue, known in the regiment by his nom de guerre of La Fleur –
was killed by the inadvertent firing of a cannon.[19] The pall of gloom
brought down on the soldiers did not even begin to lift until after
the funeral, and only then when a shift in the wind permitted M.
de Chambly to order them back to the canoes.[20]

In the meantime, two of the regiment's ships were approaching
Quebec, after having been considerably delayed at the mouth of
the Saguenay River while the one, the leaky *Aigle d'Or,* had more

patches added to its rotten hull. The other, the *Paix,* had stood by until her worm-eaten escort had been rendered seaworthy enough to complete the voyage upstream. They ultimately reached Quebec during the third week of August, fourteen weeks after leaving La Rochelle, and disembarked eight more companies from the regiment.[21]

Among those who came ashore from the *Aigle d'Or* was the Marquis de Salières, who, of all the newly arrived officers, alone found cause to complain of his treatment while at sea.[22] Like the Marquis de Tracy, he was a landsman through and through, and what little is known of him leaves the impression that he found travel on water completely odious and to be avoided if at all possible. If that was in fact so, and if it is considered along with his bad humour, which had been so evident at La Rochelle and which was unlikely to have abated much during the voyage, it is not difficult to imagine that a rather cantankerous old man stumped ashore at Quebec, anxious to commit his complaints to paper and to send them to France on the first possible ship.

Neither was that to be the last of his outbursts of bad temper in Canada. Most of them, however, were brought on because he was not consulted about decisions affecting him or his regiment, not just because of the sourness of his disposition. To eliminate the lengthy delays that would have resulted if every question of military import had to be referred to Paris, the normal command structure was modified by adding a Canadian decision-making body made up of the Marquis de Tracy and Governor Courcelle, who were empowered to decide on the deployment and use of troops in the colony.[23] In Europe the king would have made such decisions, with the advice of his minister of war, who would have been well briefed by the colonel of the regiment involved. After all, the colonel was the king's man, appointed by the king, and answerable to the king for the regiment.[24] It is understandable, therefore, that the Marquis de Salières disliked the new arrangement, for it seemed to deprive him of any part in the decision-making process. Nevertheless, there is nothing to suggest that he allowed his obvious displeasure to impair his performance as an officer. He continued to carry out his duties in an exemplary manner and showed himself to be both a model and an inspiration to those under his command.

Two days after their arrival, the eight companies were drawn up in review order for inspection by Tracy. The glorious display of military might served not only to impress the townsfolk and the Indians but also to provide an opportunity for the general to make an assessment of their readiness for service in the Richelieu Valley.[25] In the absence of any evidence to the contrary, it can only be assumed that, militarily, the companies passed muster. It was a different matter, however, when the church came to look at their spiritual fitness. Then they were found to be wanting by Canadian standards.

In France, whether a man was a practising Catholic was of little interest to army recruiters; for them it was sufficient that he was willing and able to take up arms on the king's behalf. In Canada, though, that was not good enough. There the king had given the church considerable political power, so much, in fact, that it was literally a partner in government, with the vicar apostolic, Mgr de Laval, holding the second most important position on the Conseil Souverain.[26] Moreover, for much of his life, Laval had been very closely associated with the Jesuits so that although he was not of the Society of Jesus, he was very sympathetic towards its aims and objectives.[27] It follows, therefore, that he did not subscribe to even the minimal degree of religious tolerance provided for by the Edict of Nantes, and neither was he likely to be sympathetic towards the moderate view on the subject expressed by the king in 1665: "Those who profess it [the Huguenots] are not less faithful than my other subjects; they should not be treated with less regard and kindness."[28] The vicar apostolic saw the mission of the Carignan-Salières Regiment as essentially one of waging holy war on behalf of Catholicism; it was thus necessary for its soldiery to be within the fold of the church. Having taken that position, he must have been dismayed to learn of the presence of a sizeable number of relapsed and unconfirmed Catholics in the ranks of those eight companies and, what was even worse, more than a few Huguenots. The situation called for immediate and drastic measures.[29]

The Huguenots were weeded out and catechized until they saw the error of their ways and recanted their heresy, although some circumspection was observed when it came to dealing with the abjuration of an officer, Captain Alexandre Berthier, who had accompanied Tracy from the Antilles. It was not deemed politic to let it be widely known that His Most Catholic Majesty, Louis XIV, by God appointed, had actually commissioned a Huguenot to lead his troops into a crusade. The outcome was that the captain recanted his Calvinism in camera with only clergy and a few government dignitaries present to witness the event.[30]

Relapsed and unconfirmed Catholics were also dealt with expeditiously. An emergency program of rehabilitation and instruction was initiated by the Jesuit Father Claude Dablon. By means of two powerful sermons delivered on consecutive mornings, he succeeded in having them all ready for confirmation, or for readmission to the sacraments of the church, a mere five days after they had landed in Canada.[31]

Such a triumph over heresy and indifference had to be celebrated in a fitting manner, and the very same evening, with soldiers and clergy looking on, Mgr de Laval and the Marquis de Tracy sanctioned the day's doings by jointly putting the torch to a gigantic bonfire. There was perhaps a touch of irony to the form of the celebration, for only a few hours earlier Tracy had issued an order requiring the civilian population of Quebec to provide eight hundred cords of firewood for the troops who would be wintering there. Good churchman that he undoubtedly was, and no matter whether his personal inclination was towards the Gallican or the Ultramontane view of Catholicism, he was, first and foremost, a king's man and was careful to ensure that his royal master's interests took second place to none, including those of the Canadian clergy. For political direction he looked steadfastly to Paris where Louis xiv enjoyed virtual dominion over all but the liturgical and doctrinal affairs of the church in France, and not to Rome as the Jesuits did.[32]

What might seem a little perplexing about the incident is that Tracy, who had been thoroughly briefed by Colbert, not only about the Jesuits' zeal and fervour in the missionary field, but also about their part, in collusion with Laval, in trying to discredit two former governors, Davaugour and Mézy, seemed quite unconcerned about activities that were contrary to any policy of religious toleration that the king might have expressed.[33] There are a number of possible explanations, but the most plausible by far is that what passed for religious toleration in France was more a matter of political expediency than of conviction. Although the king paid lip service to it, many close to him felt that the country would be better off without it, for as one writer of the day expressed it, "Diversity of belief, of cult, of ceremony divides subjects and creates reciprocal hate and scorn between them from which conflict and war are born."[34] By taking the position he did, therefore, Tracy was probably reflecting a sentiment shared by many others of his standing; at the same time he was allowing a possible source of discord to be eliminated from the ranks of his troops.

Another cause for some perplexity is the reportedly exemplary conduct of the soldiers during their first weeks in Canada, a phenomenon that gave Marie de l'Incarnation cause to rejoice: "Fully five hundred soldiers have taken the scapular of the Blessed Virgin ... Every day the soldiers say the rosary of the Holy Family with so much faith and devotion that God has shown by a miracle that their fervour is pleasing to him."[35] It is difficult to equate those words with the men who had marked their progress along the road to La Rochelle with outbreaks of disorder and indiscipline. More appropriate to them is the account of their impact on Montreal by the Sulpician François Dollier de Casson in which he implies that they were not the paragons of virtue Mère Marie made them out to be. He struck a far more credible note when he wrote darkly of "vices which have, in fact, risen and grown here since that time [when the troops arrived], along with many other troubles and misfortunes which had not up to that time made their appearance here."[36]

A glimpse of those vices, troubles, and misfortunes might be gleaned from an entry in the *Journal of the Jesuits,* dated 21 October 1665. It tells of an incident involving a member of the regiment in which "the two des meres – who, while under the influence of wine, had killed a soldier, were flogged; and the guiltier of the two was branded with the fleur-de-lys by the Executioner."[37] The revealing thing about that report is the comparative leniency shown towards the two culprits in a jurisdiction in which the criminal justice system was both swift and severe. It seems to indicate that some mitigating circumstances had been taken into account, which saved them from the hangman's noose – circumstances such as that soldier was not necessarily the victim of an unprovoked attack, but had incited it in the first place.

Even if we put the worst possible interpretation on any surviving reports or hints of lawlessness, there remains a lingering impression that although the troops' conduct might not have been beyond all reproof, it was generally better than it had been in France. If that impression is correct, then it immediately raises the question why?

Possible causes include the following: (1) the troops had been so well received by the civilian population that they did not feel like social outcasts in Canada; (2) the influence of the church had a salutary effect on the men's conduct by turning their minds towards more contemplative activities than would otherwise have been the case; (3) the men's relief at having survived the Atlantic crossing and at being safely back on dry land tended to moderate their conduct; (4) the fact that the troops formed such a large proportion of the population led to a feeling that there was no need for further intimidation; (5) the loss of desertion as a practical option for those finding army life intolerable compelled them to make the best of their lot by avoiding trouble; and, finally, (6) the movement of most of the men into the Richelieu Valley to help build forts, soon after they disembarked, reduced the likelihood of outbreaks of disorder in the towns.

Alternatively, the impression of better behaviour might have been nothing more than that, just an impression given by contemporary accounts written by priests and religious, among whose concerns were those of portraying Canada as a land where people walked in virtue and breathed sanctified air. Their interests could conceivably have led them to avoid detailing any incidents that might detract from that overall picture for fear of discouraging support for their particular order.

Whatever the truth, Tracy had no intention of keeping hundreds of men pent up in a town the size of Quebec, which had neither the facilities nor the resources to cope with them. Accordingly, on 25 August, the day after the festive bonfire, he took a step towards relieving the pressure by ordering Captain Pierre de Saurel to proceed with his company to the mouth of the Richelieu River, there to start rebuilding the derelict fort, Fort Richelieu, which had been destroyed by the Mohawks in 1646.[38]

Saurel had been in Canada less than a week when the order came for him to move out. It provoked the Marquis de Salières to protest most vehemently, not apparently because of the order itself, but because he, the colonel of the regiment, had not been consulted about the matter before the decision was made, as, he insisted, custom demanded.[39] Tracy, seemingly, was not concerned with custom, and neither was he prepared to have his authority questioned. He responded to the complaint in terms that could have left no doubt in the colonel's mind. He intended, he said, to proceed in such a manner whenever troop movements were made. He would send whomever he chose to wherever the need existed and whenever he felt the situation called for it. What struck an even more radical note, so far as a man like the colonel was concerned, was the additional remark that he, Tracy, would not hesitate to put the man best suited for the job in charge of any operations he planned, even if it necessitated putting a lieutenant in charge over a captain.[40]

The colonel's protest, of course, was doomed from the outset, for there was no question where authority really lay in Canada. Tracy well knew the extent of his considerable powers, and, despite his protestations, Salières was in no doubt about the limitations of his either. As early as the previous April, while the colonel was still in France, the minister of war had made it clear to him that in Canada the lieutenant-general and the governor would have complete authority over all military matters, other than those of a purely routine nature.[41] Tracy's tart response, therefore, was no more than a reiteration of what the colonel already knew. Tracy had unquestionable authority on his side, and no matter how much it displeased him,

Salières, as an officer, could only bow to it. His protest achieved
nothing more than to place a strain on his relations with Tracy.
Almost as if it were a manifestation of that gentleman's displeasure,
the colonel was ordered to the Richelieu Valley to build still another
unit in the growing system of fortifications.[42] In reality the timing
of his departure from Quebec more likely had been determined by
the fact that the construction of Jacques de Chambly's fort was
sufficiently advanced for it to serve as a staging point and supply
base than by the general's pique.

By way of a postscript to the incident, Tracy must have reported
it, along with several similar episodes, to the minister of war, for
in due course the minister wrote to reassure him that he had acted
in strict accordance with his orders and that he did indeed speak
for the king on all military matters in Canada.[43]

The Marquis de Salières left Quebec for the Richelieu Valley on
2 September, ten days before the last eight companies of his regiment
sailed into port aboard the *Saint-Sébastien* and the *Justice*. It was
a pathetic body of men that straggled ashore from those two vessels
after 112 days at sea, battling adverse winds, mountainous seas, and
later scurvy. As many as 20 had died during the voyage, and over
130 were too weak to make their own way ashore at Quebec.
Hospital facilities in the town were totally inadequate for such an
influx of patients. The limited bed space at the Hôtel-Dieu was
quickly filled, as were the additional beds that had been set up in
the nave of the Ursuline Church so that the overflow had to be
accommodated in private homes.[44] Fortunately the indefatigable sisters, although few in number, did all they could to ease the suffering
of the men stricken with a disease whose cause and cure they knew
very little about. Thanks to their care and to the inclusion of fresh
produce in the meals they served, they inadvertently prevented an
emergency from deteriorating into a disaster.

The recuperating soldiers would have had few fond memories of
their recent ordeal to cheer them during their recovery. Their spirits
might have been raised by intense relief at being back on land, as
well as by heartfelt gratitude for the devotion of their nurses, which
in many cases had kept them alive. Small wonder, then, that they,
along with their more fortunate comrades who had escaped ending
up in hospital, turned to the church, much as penitents might,
convinced that the Atlantic fury they had recently faced was a sign
of divine displeasure at their past mode of life and a foretaste of
what lay ahead if they did not mend their ways. Huguenots abjured
without suasion, relapsed Catholics came willingly forward for confirmation, and a great many who were already in good grace hastened

to join the lay Brotherhood of Mount Carmel as an expression of their contrition. The entire eight companies were engulfed by a great wave of spiritual regeneration, which surged through the ranks as if to wash away every last vestige of sin and which gave the clergy in Quebec cause for considerable satisfaction.[45]

Before the end of the month, though, the crisis had passed. Thirty-five men had succumbed to their illness, and the rest of those who had been hospitalized had recovered sufficiently for them to be discharged and rejoin their companies.[46]

Thanks to more congenial travelling conditions than those that had prevailed on the lower decks, the lots of the new governor and intendant, Courcelle and Talon, proved to be more agreeable. Unlike the enlisted men who had been crammed into the ships' holds, they came ashore from the *Saint-Sébastien* in good health and were able to begin their duties immediately upon landing by assisting the Marquis de Tracy in his preparations for the coming campaign against the Mohawks – the timing of which rested very much on how soon the forts along the Richelieu River could be completed.[47]

By 25 September the Marquis de Salières and a detachment of seven companies reached that part of the river known as the Richelieu Falls, actually no more than series of rapids. There they trans-shipped from their boats to the canoes and shallops in which Jacques de Chambly's party of four companies had journeyed from Quebec two months earlier and which were better suited for navigating the shallower waters ahead. Unfortunately there were too few to carry the colonel's men and supplies in one trip; so it was not until the evening of the twenty-eighth that they reached Fort Saint-Louis, as Chambly's newly completed stronghold had been named, after a canonized king of France.[48]

Although this was the age of Vauban, the great French military engineer, there is nothing to suggest that any of the Richelieu Valley forts owed much to his theories of fortification. Some senior officers in the regiment might have been familiar with them, but they were of little practical use in a wilderness setting. Rather, the type of materials available on site, the shortage of skilled workers, and the need for all possible haste determined the forms the structures would take. So it was that Salières had only the sketchiest idea of where the site for the one he had been ordered to build was located and what method of construction he would use. By the time he left the next morning, though, he had learned as much as he could from Chambly, who had benefited from having a number of Canadian volunteers with him, able to give help and advice on the construction of his fort. Guided by the friendly Indians who had accompanied him from Quebec, he had also been able to reconnoitre along the river to the south and locate the site where the colonel was to build.[49]

Fort Saint-Louis was a source of information too, an object lesson in what was possible, given the limitations imposed by the men and materials available and by the site itself. The fort was roughly star-shaped and measured about fifty metres from side to side. Its palisade was probably between four and five metres high and had been built by the simple expedient of setting large logs upright in a trench and then filling it in to secure the logs in place. The fort was not much more than a hastily built stockade enclosing a courtyard wherein a number of crude huts and lean-to sheds provided shelter for the garrison. Considering that its shape was unlike that of any of the others, it was likely Chambly's own design. The instructions that he and the other fort builders received must have been very general and have consisted of little more than the overall dimensions of the structures. They appear to have been free to decide on the shape of the buildings, within the limitations imposed by the nature of the site and by the height, girth, and species of trees growing on or near it.[50]

Those limitations, however, were unlikely to have been uppermost in the colonel's mind as he left Fort Saint-Louis on 29 September. His immediate worry more likely was the possible consequences of the inadequate protection provided by his men's clothing against the inclement weather in the Richelieu Valley that year. It was a wet September, and rain driven by blustery winds often penetrated the soldiers' jackets and jerkins, soaking them to the skin. Coughs and colds were already evident in the ranks and would likely spread. Even so, the fear of that happening did not prevent Salières from marching out to follow the river upstream for twelve kilometres to a point of land that jutted into it, the site for his fort.[51]

There the colonel was finally obliged to confront his problems. To start with, neither he nor his officers knew any more about building forts in the Canadian wilderness than what they had learned during their overnight stay at Fort Saint-Louis. Then, he did not have the assistance of skilled workmen, who might have advised him and instructed his men; furthermore, the few tools he had been provided with were of inferior quality and unsuited to the required tasks. To make matters still worse, he had no cooking utensils to prepare hot food. Finally, as the wind and the rain persisted, the grippe took a tighter hold on his party, rampaging through its ranks so that each day saw its effective strength further reduced. Both officers and enlisted men fell victim, and those who did remain healthy must have festered with unhealthy thoughts as they huddled in miserable, rain-sodden groups under the arch of the forest.[52]

The problems over both the tools and the cooking pots, which, incidentally, Jacques de Chambly and Pierre de Saurel must also have experienced, could easily be attributed to the fact that the supply ship carrying most of the regiment's equipment, the *Jardin de Hollande,* did not reach Quebec until sometime after Salières had left for the Richelieu Valley. He would have had to manage with whatever the seven companies in his detachment had brought aboard the *Aigle d'Or* and the *Paix* or had been able to procure locally in Quebec. That hypothesis, however, falls apart when the itemized list of the stores and equipment supplied for the regiment as a whole is taken into account – items that presumably were aboard the *Jardin de Hollande.* The only articles it mentions that might have been of use in either fort construction or large-scale cooking are twelve pit saws, two large ripsaws, eighteen adzes (six of one size and twelve of another), ten small axes, four copper cooking pots, and four copper pastry bowls (see appendix A, table 3). Those few items are barely enough to equip one company adequately, never mind seven, or even twenty.[53]

The deficiencies may have been due to deliberate negligence on somebody's part, but that supposition is not very likely, for every company had been subjected to rigorous inspection before embarkation and, as recently as 19 August, to the Marquis de Tracy's scrutiny at Quebec. On both occasions the troops had been found to be equipped properly. The likeliest explanation for the deficiencies is no one thought that the troops would need lumbering and excavation tools or cooking pots. In Europe infantry regiments were not called upon to erect wooden forts in the wilderness, and they seldom needed cooking pots, because troops on the move in France were fed in staging camps along the line of march or were provisioned by the towns and villages through which they passed.[54] What everyone seemed to have forgotten when readying the Carignan-Salières Regiment for service in Canada was that in that country the main building material was logs, there were no staging camps, and there were only three settlements from one end of it to the other.

It would be very easy to point fingers of blame for that oversight, and for all the other deficiencies and inadequacies later revealed in the regiment's equipment, at the officials directly concerned, people such as the commissioner of supplies or Colbert de Terron, but to do so would be to lose sight of the real culprit – ignorance. An abysmal ignorance of the conditions under which the regiment would have to serve in Canada lay behind all those problems, and it extended from the king, to Colbert, to Le Tellier, and all the way down, through the intendants, the inspectors, and the commissioners, to the lowliest functionary involved with readying the regiment for action.

It was left for officers in the field to discover those conditions for themselves, often in moments of crisis, such as the one in which the colonel now found himself. Fortunately he was able to surmount the shock of realization, and his subsequent example of fortitude in the face of adversity prevented the pall of wretchedness that had descended on his men from deteriorating into anything more serious.[55]

Salières seemed to know instinctively that the only practical thing to do was to begin building the fort without delay. Initially he most likely got the work started by a direct order, couched in those colourful terms that flow so readily from soldiers' mouths. When it comes to stirring reluctant men to action, however, deeds often speak with a far more persuasive voice. It was he, therefore, who set the example by being the first to start work so that, by the afternoon of 2 October, only one day after arriving, site clearing was well under way and the position of the perimeter wall was staked out on the ground.[56]

The trees cleared from the site were mostly cedars, unsuitable for building because of the shortness of their trunks, but so long as the men did not mind a spark-spitting campfire, their branches made good fuel, good enough to cook by, and good enough to sit around in the evening and yarn, or grumble, the rest of the day away before sleeping. Already life had become a little more bearable.[57]

The logs best suited for building the fort needed to be about six metres long, straight, and between thirty and forty centimetres in diameter. The nearest stand of that description was on an island in the river, about two hundred and fifty metres away; however, before the trees could be felled, trimmed, and cut to length, men and tools had to cross the intervening water. For that purpose the trunks of the recently cleared cedars were put to good use. During the next several days they were lashed together to make a raft, which was able to carry up to twenty men at a time, thereby permitting logging operations to start. By 7 October dressed logs were beginning to reach the mainland.[58]

In the meantime, work on excavating a trench for a palisade was proceeding, a time-consuming and backbreaking task that necessitated hacking through matted roots and digging out tree stumps. Using only their bare hands and the few inadequate tools they had, the men took six days to complete the job, far longer than it would have had their equipment been better. Until the excavation was finished, the steady flow of logs coming from the island could only be stockpiled, except for a small number that were turned over to the sawyers for cutting into boards.

The holdup might have taxed the colonel's notoriously limited patience had he not been able to attend to another duty, that of gathering intelligence. Taking an escort of thirteen men in case of attack, he set out on 9 October to reconnoitre the area around another flight of rapids, about fifteen kilometres to the south. Returning to camp before dawn the following morning, he found the trench still unfinished. By the twelfth, though, the excavation was finally done, and he was at last able to see his fort take shape as the first logs were set upright in the trench. Three days later the outer wall was completed. The worst of the job was over, and it remained only to erect the buildings within the palisade that would house the garrison and its supplies. It was at that point that Fort Sainte-Thérèse, so named because it was completed, or nearly so, on the saint's feast day, welcomed its first visitors, an Algonkin hunting party en route to Lake Champlain.[59]

Salières took the opportunity to send out a second reconnaissance party, this one to explore south of the rapids he had just visited and into the lake itself. With a convoy of ten Indian canoes to escort his one, he was fortunate in that he could detail fewer men for the duty than he otherwise would have had to. Only ten men were sent, two of whom were officers, reserve Captain Des Portes and Lieutenant Mignarde of the La Colonelle Company.[60]

The expedition was away for six days, and during that time it went almost twenty kilometres down the river into Lake Champlain. The venture was successful for all concerned: for the Indians it yielded a good haul of beaver skins, as well as several bears and moose; for the enlisted men it provided a valuable object lesson on how to survive in and off the bush; for the officers it allowed them to acquire a good knowledge of the terrain around the northern end of the lake, particularly of the peninsula projecting into it from the north, a possible location for still another fort, which would be begun the following spring and named Fort Sainte-Anne.[61]

By the time the reconnaissance party returned, the fort had been completed, and it stood ready to serve as an outpost and a forward base. The finished structure was rectangular, about forty-five metres long and thirty-five wide, with a bastion at each corner. For some distance around it the ground had been cleared of all growth and anything else that could give cover, so that its defenders would have a clear field of fire should it be attacked. On the inside, about fifty centimetres above ground level, was a firing step, which ran around the palisade, and here and there within the compound were a number of log buildings, very much like those at Fort Saint-Louis, which would serve as barracks and storehouses for the garrison.[62]

Although the fort was rudimentary in design and Spartan in its accommodations, its completion in only three weeks was still a remarkable feat. That accomplishment was due, in no small amount, to the example and leadership of the colonel, who despite all the obstacles and setbacks, managed to inspire his men to work even though they might have been dispirited or unwell.

The garrisoning of the new fort was not long delayed. On the same day that the reconnaissance party returned from Lake Champlain, the new governor, Daniel de Rémy de Courcelle, arrived with the Du Prat, Rougemont, and La Colonelle companies, which, along with two already there, were to man it through the winter.[63]

One final task remained. A trail had to be slashed through the bush to Fort Saint-Louis, and for some reason the governor took personal charge of the undertaking. He detailed the Lamotte and Grandfontaine companies to start axing their way over the twelve kilometres. Fortunately that part of the forest was not particularly dense so that the job amounted to little more than clearing brush.[64] The so-called road, when it was finished, bore little resemblance to anything that might be termed a military highway, for it was just a cleared way through the bush, which barely warranted being called a trail. Even so, it was an essential part of a land-based line of communication planned to reach to the St Lawrence.

With the road completed, Courcelle was at liberty to return to Quebec. He must already have been contemplating an early foray into Mohawk territory, however, for he demanded that the colonel take him out to see the sort of country such a venture would have to traverse. It did not take him long to see all that he wanted to, and without even reaching Lake Champlain, he returned to the fort where he paused only briefly before hastening on to Fort Saint-Louis.[65]

On 26 October the Marquis de Salières handed Fort Sainte-Thérèse over to its first commander, Lieutenant-Colonel Du Prat. He too was now able to leave for Fort Saint-Louis and the St Lawrence, along with the La Fredière, Contrecoeur, and Salières companies, which were to winter in Montreal.[66]

At Fort Saint-Louis he again encountered the governor, who by then was more excited than ever at the prospect of a winter campaign and, consequently, was anxious to have a trail cut through the bush to the south shore of the St Lawrence, opposite Montreal. He summarily ordered the colonel to detail six officers and thirty-six enlisted men for the work of clearing a way through the intervening twelve kilometres of forest and marsh. Salières protested vigorously, arguing that his men were all tired and many were ill and that, in his opinion, the job could be carried out more easily if it was left until the ground was frozen hard. The argument was valid, and even though it showed an astute appreciation of the local conditions, it had no effect on Courcelle. He remained adamant: the trail would be cut. The exchange only further aggravated an already acrimonious relationship between the two, which persisted until 1668 when Salières returned to France.[67]

It seems unlikely that the enmity between the two could have been aroused in the few days they were both at Fort Sainte-Thérèse, the first time they were together since leaving France. The animosity had to have its roots in France, perhaps at La Rochelle during the weeks of preparations for embarkation, or maybe even further back, in some incident during their past army careers. Wherever its origins, the rift was wide enough to prevent the governor and the colonel from travelling together. Though neither delayed leaving Fort Saint-Louis, they left for Fort Richelieu separately. There the three companies of soldiers accompanying the colonel turned west for Montreal and winter quarters, while both he and the governor left for Quebec and, still separately, made all possible haste there, spurred on by an overwhelming desire to be the first to get Tracy's ear with his version of events.[68]

Salières was not willing to leave it at that either. Fearing that Courcelle would have the advantage in gaining the general's support, by virtue of his superior rank, Salières wrote directly to the Marquis de Louvois, Michel Le Tellier's son and understudy, at the Ministry of War, asking to be relieved of his command.[69] The move spoke eloquently of his fear that should Tracy, for any reason, be recalled to France before the regiment was, it would leave him at the mercy of a governor he knew to be ill-disposed towards him. At the same time it showed his dislike of the whole command structure in Canada, which, he felt, denied him the access to higher authority that had been the custom in France since 1661. Despite his fear and his disenchantment, however, the colonel continued to go about his duties – he was too good an officer to do otherwise – and as soon as his letter was on its way to France, he embarked for Montreal to take command of the garrison there.

He set out on that voyage on 6 November, boarding an open shallop with all the trepidation of a man in mortal fear for his life whenever he set foot in a boat. As it turned out, his fears of the horrors ahead proved to be well founded; for nine storm-tossed days, the party was buffeted by icy winds and battered by mighty waves, which turned each twenty-four hours into a thousand agonies. So great was his distress that, for those nine days, there could have been little room left in his mind for harbouring dark thoughts on the subject of the governor.[70]

CHAPTER THREE

Courcelle's Ill-fated March into Mohawk Country

Little is known of Daniel de Rémy de Courcelle's life before March 1665, when he was named governor of Canada, Acadia, and Newfoundland.[1] The few details that exist show that he had been a nobly born career soldier, who had distinguished himself sufficiently to attract royal notice and, thereby, to obtain an appointment as the king's representative in the government of the frontier fortress town of Thionville. The record is scanty too for his later career after his return to France in 1672 when he became the governor of Toulon.[2] His historical reputation therefore rests largely on the evidence of his seven years in Canada, narrow as that view of his life might be.

Courcelle was thirty-nine years old when he landed in the colony, and it immediately became apparent that there was an arrogance and a hotheadedness about him that were going to leave their mark on his governorship.[3] They could have been due to his relative youth and inexperience, or even to the ingrained prejudices of his class, but their effect was certainly detrimental both to the colony in general and to the Carignan-Salières Regiment in particular.

One of the more harmful manifestations of those traits was his jealousy of his authority to the point where he openly quarrelled with anyone he so much as suspected of encroaching on it – a practice that at times threatened to disrupt the smooth operation of government.[4] Another was to be seen in his actions that led to the many deaths in the regiment during the winter of 1666. That tragedy could have been avoided had it not been for his craving for the taste of victory and his unwillingness to listen to the counsel of those he considered his social inferiors. The only person in Canada who could exert any influence over him was the Marquis de Tracy, and he only because his own nobility, vice-regal status, and distinguished military career assured him of the governor's respect.

Those examples alone are sufficient to raise the question of Courcelle's suitability for such a position, and the related one of how he could possibly have been chosen for it by a king known for his skill in selecting able and dedicated men to fill the offices of state. By taking the few known circumstances of the appointment into account, it is possible to imagine how it most likely came about. The main clue, of course, lies in the very nature of royal government in Canada, which made the office of governor more of a military position than a civil one. Qualifications for it were thus very similar to those for a senior military position. Given the example of those Carignan-Salières officers who absented themselves from their duties as soon as the regiment was ordered to Canada, however, it is unlikely that the governorship attracted much enthusiasm. Under such circumstances, it is not hard to see how a relatively young and ambitious officer like Courcelle, who was willing to go to Canada, might have got the job, rather than one who was older and cooler headed. Without fully understanding the sort of man the governorship called for, the king would have evaluated Courcelle using military criteria, such as his aristocratic birth, his successful career in the army, his previously held position of some authority at Thionville, and the recommendations of influential friends at court.[5]

From the onset his governorship bore signs of his finally having found his true niche in life, that of a petty despot. As one of the three or four men who wielded most of the authority in Canada, Courcelle found himself in a position that gave him far more prestige and power than he had ever known in France. Accordingly, as befitted the military personage he considered himself to be, he surrounded himself with a considerable retinue and talked incessantly of war, boasting of what lay in store for the Iroquois when they came face to face with French troops, and always implying that he would be both the architect of victory and its triumphant general.[6] His whirlwind tour of the Richelieu Valley in the fall of 1665 attested to that implication, particularly when, after inspecting Fort Sainte-Thérèse, he demanded to be taken out to scout the country to the south. The sheer superficiality of that exercise tends to obscure its real significance – that he was already thinking in terms of a more or less immediate attack on the Mohawk villages.[7] By the time he returned to Quebec, which was still less than two months after he had landed in Canada, that notion had developed into a fully fledged plan of action. Thereafter he became increasingly impatient for Tracy to give it his approval.

So far as it can be pieced together from subsequent events, the plan was to marshal men and matériel at Fort Saint-Louis from where, guided by Algonkin Indians, he would move quickly to the south, pausing at Fort Sainte-Thérèse long enough to make any last-minute changes that were called for. Then it would be a fast approach to the Mohawk Valley and a devastating assault on the villages there, which would dispel for once and for all the cloud of uncertainty that had hung over the St Lawrence settlements for so many long years. Most likely because he was dazzled by the prospect of its brilliant outcome, Courcelle lost sight of two important variables in the strategic equation – the severity of the winters in those parts and the Indians' indifference towards rigid time schedules – while his own conceit blinded him to a third, his fallibility as a field commander. There were other contributory factors, but those three ensured the utter failure of his winter campaign.[8]

The final decision to permit that campaign to proceed was not made by Tracy until the first days of 1666. Until then Courcelle had to contain his impatience while the general engaged in peace talks with representatives of the Oneida and Onondaga nations, who also spoke for the Cayugas and the Senecas.[9] The first sign that any of the Five Nations might be interested in reaching a negotiated settlement with the French had been given on 19 November when a convoy carrying a delegation of Oneida and Onondaga chiefs had paddled into Montreal. Although the Marquis de Salières had arrived from Quebec to take command of the garrison just five days previously, nevertheless he had fully recovered from the miseries of the voyage and arranged for an appropriate welcome. The five companies of the garrison drew up on the waterfront, and as the canoes approached the shore, a welcoming volley of musketry crackled out to be culminated with a boom of cannon-fire. It was a most impressive greeting, one that also let the newcomers know that Montreal was no longer defenceless.[10]

As the smoke from the powder cleared away, it was possible to see that one of the occupants of the canoes was a white man. He was quickly recognized to be Charles Le Moyne, a Montrealer who had been captured while out hunting a few weeks earlier.[11] His presence could be taken as a token of the pacific intentions of his captors and also as an indication that they anticipated some hard bargaining and needed any extra leverage his release could give them.

Sixty-six men in all clambered out of the canoes, thirteen of them chiefs led by the great Onondaga leader, Garakontié, whom Marie de l'Incarnation had described as "a good friend of the French." The colonel greeted them all with dignity and then conducted the chiefs to his quarters where he regaled them with the contents of his pantry, tobacco jar, and wine cellar. They settled down to four convivial days before any thought of moving on to Quebec crossed his guests' minds. When they finally did decide to continue their journey, the marquis, despite his, by then, cordial relations with them, was still wary enough of their intentions to send with them an escort of twelve soldiers. The remaining members of the party stayed on in Montreal for seventeen more sybaritic days, mostly at the colonel's expense, before some returned to their tribal homes and others left to go hunting.[12]

It was not by chance that Garakontié and his fellow chiefs came seeking peace when they did. Although the thrust of the new forts was directed against the Mohawks, their significance was not lost on the rest of the Confederacy. While the outposts did not pose a direct threat to the other four nations, they did indicate a new capability on the part of the French, one that enabled them to move out from their enclaves along the St Lawrence to carry the initiative to their enemies' doorsteps. That position was in sharp contrast with their former plight, which had seen them kept tied down in their settlements by relatively small Iroquois war parties. By fortifying the Richelieu Valley, Tracy had served notice that he could do the same on the upper St Lawrence, as well as along the shores of Lake Ontario, and thus could hinder access to those waterways by any Indian nations that remained hostile.

Other considerations played a part in taking the delegates to Quebec, including those resulting from the long-term effects of the recurrent epidemics, all of European origin, that had plagued their peoples since the 1630s. Smallpox and scarlet fever had been by far the most prevalent, and the most lethal, of the diseases, closely followed by measles and influenza, and their combined effects had been to reduce the fighting strength of the nations of the Iroquois Confederacy to a fraction of what it once had been. Their weakened position was of particular concern to those involved in the Susquehannock War. The prospects of bringing that conflict to a successful end with only the dubious support of the Mohawks, and with the threat of a suddenly powerful and aggressive Canada in their rear, were not very good.[13]

The deliberations at Quebec were rich with all the ritual and rhetoric of such meetings. Gifts were exchanged, prisoners were bartered, and the air was thick with extravagant promises of future peace under the omnipotent hand of Louis XIV. Unfortunately all the peaceful gestures and protestations, sincere as they might have been, were made only on behalf of the four western members of the

Confederacy. The Mohawks chose to ignore the whole affair and gave not the slightest hint of wanting to negotiate with the French or anyone else.[14]

Tracy perceived the Mohawks' absence as nothing short of intransigence and, by so doing, blinkered himself to the possibility that it might not have been a boycott directed at the French, but at their partners in the Confederacy, whose representatives were in Quebec. For many years the Mohawks, by virtue of the proximity of their homeland to both the French and the Dutch settlements, and of their superior weaponry, had been able to control the trading practices within the Confederacy and had successfully prevented the flow of furs to the St Lawrence at the same time that they had facilitated it towards the Hudson. It was a position of some arrogance, which, although it had been grudgingly accepted by the Cayugas, Senecas, Onondagas, and Oneidas, was generally resented by them. The change of regime at Fort Orange, where the English had recently replaced the Dutch to put former trading arrangements in some doubt, together with the arrival of the Carignan-Salières Regiment, which made the French the most powerful European presence in the area, could have been all that was needed to push the other four confederates into making a move to challenge the Mohawks' self-appointed regulatory role in the Five Nations' access to European trade goods, particularly to guns. If that were so, the Mohawks could well have interpreted the presence of the delegation in Quebec as a brazen attempt to take advantage of their predicament at a time when the two colonial regimes, which alone gave their commercial hegemony meaning, were themselves undergoing changes that could alter the whole structure of relationships and arrangements upon which it rested.[15]

Tracy steadfastly refused to consider any of that argument or any explanation of the Mohawks' absence from the talks other than that they were neither intimidated by the presence of the Carignan-Salières Regiment in Canada nor by the Richelieu Valley forts and, as a consequence, had no intention of treating for peace. Finally giving up on negotiations, Tracy authorized Courcelle to prepare to launch his attack.

In some ways it was a surprising decision. Not only did it run contrary to the European tradition of not campaigning in winter,[16] but it also indicated an impatience that had not been evident over the preceding five weeks of the negotiations with the Onondaga and Oneida ambassadors. One cannot avoid wondering whether someone or something had intervened to effect such a change of heart, which saw him committing troops to a more or less immediate attack on the Mohawks. Of course it is not entirely beyond belief that Courcelle played some part in bringing about the change, but there is no evidence to that effect.

On 6 January 1666 the Marquis de Salières received his instructions over the signatures of both Tracy and Courcelle. He was to have eighty enlisted men, two captains, three lieutenants, and three ensigns ready to leave for Fort Saint-Louis on the twenty-eighth and to see that they were prepared for three weeks in the field. Similar orders would have gone to the garrison commander at Trois-Rivières, while at Quebec the governor himself took charge of readying the detachment there, which he led out on 9 January over the river ice and the snow to the rendezvous.[17]

Rather surprisingly the soldiers were to make up only a little over a half of the total party. The remainder was to consist of a number of friendly Indians and about two hundred Canadian volunteers.[18] It can be assumed that the Indians, who were to serve as guides, had all accepted Christianity, since they were the only natives the French were prepared to issue with firearms.[19] As for the Canadians, it is reasonable to believe that they were not entirely without military training, since a good many, if not all, would have received some such instruction as members of the militia companies in the colony. Events were to prove that Courcelle was indeed lucky to have them, for as Dollier de Casson has observed:

It is impossible to give any idea of the extraordinary difficulty he [Courcelle] had on this journey on account of the lack of experience of our French soldiers at that time ... Accordingly, I can only remark that M. de Courcelle had seventy Montrealers with him on this expedition under the command of M. Le Moyne, and that as the Governor knew they were the most practised in this kind of warfare, he did them the honour to give them the van in going and the rear on returning.[20]

Despite that recognition, though, it is improbable that the governor would have immediately shown so much confidence in his volunteers. As a professional soldier, he was far more likely to have resented than to have welcomed so many irregulars in his little army. Their inclusion must initially have been due to local pressures rather than to his own wishes. Those pressures would have had to come mainly from the volunteers themselves, who having been on the defensive against the Iroquois for so long, finally saw an opportunity to strike back and rallied behind their community leaders to petition Tracy or the Conseil Souverain to be allowed to join the venture. They very soon proved their worth, being familiar with the methods of

Indian fighting and with the skills needed to survive in the bush in winter. It could have been only after they had so proven themselves that Courcelle overcame whatever resentment he had for them and, thereafter, "relied a good deal upon them, exhibited a very special trust in them, and made a great deal of them."[21] On the two subsequent expeditions, those of Pierre de Saurel and of Tracy himself, their inclusion was a matter of course.

The number of volunteers who took part in the three campaigns against the Mohawks was considerable, particularly so in Tracy's, in the autumn of 1666, when as many as six hundred are known to have participated.[22] The magnitude of such a contribution can be properly appreciated if it is considered in the context of an estimated total of between thirteen and fifteen hundred adult males in the population of Canada at the time.[23] That means that up to 40 per cent of them accompanied the Carignan-Salières Regiment on the three expeditions against the Mohawks – a truly remarkable rate of participation.

Also remarkable is that, with the exception of the Marquis de Salières, no one connected with the regiment is on record as having expressed any misgivings about the wisdom or the organization of the proposed winter campaign. It was almost as if everyone concurred with the decision to launch it and was quietly confident that, with the Indians to guide the soldiers and to hunt for food along the trail, all would be well. Even the colonel, who normally had nothing good to say about the governor, supported the concept of the venture but, no doubt with the memory of his own recent experience in mind, was concerned that it be adequately equipped. He made a point of bringing that concern to Jean Talon's attention, choosing, perhaps, an inopportune moment when the intendant was occupied in trying to find sufficient lamps for the expedition. Under those circumstances, the intendant's reply might not have been sufficiently reassuring to have allayed the colonel's fear over the matter.[24]

Before proceeding to judge whether he had grounds for continued concern, we must first consider the reliability of the evidence upon which that judgment will have to be based. There are five known contemporary accounts of Courcelle's expedition: "Vers burlesques sur le voyage de Monsieur de Courcelles gouverneur et lieutenant général pour le Roy en la Nouvelle France en l'année 1666," by René-Louis Chartier de Lotbinière; "Le Livre de raison de François de Tapie de Monteil, capitaine au régiment de Poitou (1661–1670)"; "Mémoire de M. de Salières des choses qui se sont passées en Canada les plus considérables depuis qu'il est arrivé, 1666"; *The Jesuit Relations and Allied Documents*; and "Relation of the March of the

Governor of Canada into New York," in *Documents Relative to the Colonial History of the State of New York*.

All the works agree, more or less, on the basic points of the chronology, the numbers of men involved, the general sequence of events, and so on, but there is disagreement in two important areas, both of which have a considerable bearing on any analysis of what took place. The first is whether the men were equipped with snow-shoes, and the second is how many died during the expedition. The two questions are clearly interrelated: the fact of having or not having snowshoes could reasonably be expected to affect a man's chances of surviving the ordeal, considering that he had to contend with snow in excess of a metre deep for much of the way. For that reason it is important to chart a cautious way through any conflicting evidence before deciding on the likeliest course of events.

Of the five sources mentioned, "Vers burlesques" and "Le Livre de raison" provide first-hand accounts of the events, "Mémoire de M. de Salières" gives a part first-hand and part second-hand descrip-tion, while the other two are both totally second-hand versions of what took place. It has to be assumed that first-hand accounts are more likely to be accurate than second-hand ones, even if some bias is suspected, as in the case of the Marquis de Salières who is known to have disliked Courcelle. On the snowshoe issue, however, when the author of "Vers burlesques" wrote about a dejected soldier on the homeward march who lamented the feats of arms that would have been possible, "if we had had snowshoes,"[25] he was reiterating what the colonel had written in his "Mémoire," and Chartier de Lotbinière had no reason for misstating the facts.

The Jesuits, on the other hand, maintained that the men did have snowshoes, but bias could have played a part. Their account of the march is in two versions, one contained in their *Journal* for 1666 and the other in the *Relation* for the same year. The *Journal*, which was a day-by-day record of events, makes no mention of snowshoes in its account of Courcelle's departure from Quebec, while the *Relation*, which was a sort of newsletter sent to France for the edification of superiors and patrons of the order, was at pains to state that "every man wore snowshoes, with the use of which they were unfamiliar," and then goes on to refer to them as "a very inconvenient kind of fetters."[26] Although the "Relation of the March of the Governor of Canada into New York" also maintains that snowshoes were used, it is demonstrably at odds with all the other accounts on a number of points, including its description of a skirmish near Schenectady and its assertion that the French used dogsleds; it must therefore be considered imaginative in part.[27] For want of a better explanation, it could well have been compiled from anecdotes gathered some time after the events it purports to describe, most likely from tavern talk around Schenectady.

On balance, the weight of probability seems to lie with Chartier de Lotbinière and Salières both of whom claimed that the soldiers had no snowshoes. The same, however, cannot be said for the volunteers. They lived in the country and knew what conditions to expect at that time of year; therefore it is reasonable to believe that they equipped themselves appropriately.

On the question of how many died during the expedition, only two sources give a figure. The Jesuits entered in their *Journal* that "many died of hunger; the number is not yet known but it was over 60."[28] François de Tapie de Monteil, who was on the march, was somewhat more specific when he confided to his notebook that "on this expedition which we undertook in the month of January we lost four hundred men who dropped dead from cold while on the march."[29] As to the reliability of his count, one thing the notebook reveals about its author is that he was a meticulous recorder of facts and figures. Reading it leaves the distinct impression that if he said there were four hundred deaths, then there probably were. Since he wrote solely for his own information, his account has a forthrightness and a precision that the *Journal of the Jesuits* lacks. The *Journal*'s shortcoming no doubt resulted because, in the first place, the chronicler was not on the expedition and had to rely, therefore, on hearsay evidence, and, in the second, because of reluctance to say more on the subject, once the real extent of the disaster became known, for fear of depicting the affair in an unfavourable light and thereby arousing official displeasure.

For the purpose of this account of Courcelle's tragic winter campaign, therefore, it will be assumed that the soldiers did not have snowshoes and that four hundred fatalities occurred.

To return to the drama of that campaign, on 23 January a dispatch for the Marquis de Salières arrived in Montreal from Quebec. It advised him that the date for the rendezvous at Fort Saint-Louis had been advanced by one day, to the twenty-seventh, a change that added a note of frenzy to the already feverish preparations under way. The river ice, tortured into misshapen peaks and crevasses by the currents of the water, and the snow on top, driven into a labyrinth of ridges and rills by the wintery nor'westers, had to be smoothed if troops and supply sledges were to cross safely to the south shore. From there the trail to the fort, which had been cleared through the bush just three months earlier, too had to be opened up, as it had vanished beneath deep snow and was impassable to men without snowshoes. The colonel sent a party of forty soldiers armed with axes onto the river ice to smooth a path, but the job of opening up the bush trail was beyond its capabilities. That task was left to fifteen snowshoed Montrealers led by Charles Le Moyne.[30]

Within two days they had the trail open, but before it could be used, the weather changed, and the twenty-sixth dawned to the howl of a storm, which whipped the snow into blinding clouds, undoing much of the previous clearing. The storm precluded any departure that day, and it was not until the following morning that the colonel felt it safe to lead his men over the ice.[31]

Once the men were across the St Lawrence, progress was slowed by the deep, fresh snow. Only the colonel and the volunteers, who all had snowshoes, were able to negotiate the trail with any ease. In spite of his advanced age, he raced ahead to Fort Saint-Louis where he expected to find Courcelle already waiting to move on. However, he got there well in advance of the governor, whose column did not begin to straggle in until the following morning, after a miserable night spent bivouacked in the bush.[32]

By then a pall of gloom had descended on the fort, for Captain Des Portes had arrived from Fort Sainte-Thérèse with the news that its commandant, Lieutenant-Colonel Du Prat, was dead. The Marquis de Salières was deeply moved by the tidings, for not only had Du Prat been his second-in-command, but he had also been a long-standing personal friend.[33] Soon after the shock of that news, Courcelle, also wearing snowshoes, arrived with the vanguard of his column, most likely consisting of the volunteers from Quebec, well ahead of the main body, which was still floundering through the snow. About that time the last of the Montreal contingent was also getting in, exhausted and wet.[34]

To the colonel, watching his men drag themselves into the fort, it was all too apparent that they were not well equipped for what lay ahead – not a snowshoe among the rank and file, nor any climbing irons to facilitate clambering over ice and logs. Although they had both mukluks and moccasins, they had nothing to change into once the snow saturated the ones they had on. As for outer clothing, there was nothing uniform about it. Most of the men wore some individual concoction of winter wear. Some had fur hats, others had fur coats and leggings, but as they were supposedly travelling light, they had very little else to protect them from the cold save a single blanket. They had no tentage for shelter, very few axes for cutting firewood, and only mess tins in which to prepare food. Even the rations were reduced to a minimum, with each man carrying his own supply of biscuits, since it was Courcelle's intention that the Algonkin guides, in addition to leading the expedition to its destination, would hunt for game to supplement the hardtack.[35]

At Fort Saint-Louis, however, there was no sign of any guides, nor was there any word of their imminent arrival – an added setback to an already luckless enterprise. What lay ahead held little promise too, a six hundred kilometre round trip, with the best that could be hoped for being less-frigid weather and fewer winter storms than usual.[36]

Moved by the worrying sight of the raggle-taggle band of foot soldiers trudging in, the colonel spoke of his fears to a group of officers and confided that, in his opinion, only a miracle could give the expedition any hope of success. One of the group, the Jesuit Father Pierre Raffeix, added that to his knowledge Courcelle had personally supervised all the preparations at Quebec, refusing to listen to the advice of anyone and even turning down a merchant's offer to supply fifty pairs of snowshoes for the men.[37] It is not difficult to imagine what the colonel's response might have been: anger at the foolhardiness of the governor, fear of its consequences for those fated to march with him, and vitriol as a measure of his personal opinion of the man. However, with thoughts of the death of his friend on his mind, together with the overcrowded conditions at the fort – more than seven hundred men were there – he held his peace.

The next morning, 29 January, the perturbed colonel had a parting word with his officers. He wished them well and exhorted them to be sympathetic to the needs of the men in whatever difficulties they might encounter and urged them to maintain good order and discipline even when morale was low and in the face of the enemy. He then left Fort Saint-Louis for Montreal where he had urgent business; he had to write to Tracy and recommend that half-pay Captain Des Portes be appointed to replace the deceased Lieutenant-Colonel Du Prat.[38]

Meanwhile, for those fated to follow Governor Courcelle, the Spartan comforts of Fort Saint-Louis were short-lived. They had no more than a brief respite from the rigours of the trail, for no sooner had Salières departed for Montreal than Courcelle decided to set out for Fort Sainte-Thérèse, without guides. After drawing upon the resources of M. de Chambly's garrison to replace those men who had still not recovered from the march, he gave the order to form up and head out.[39]

There is no documentary evidence to suggest why Courcelle left Fort Saint-Louis without waiting for his guides. It could be argued, for example, that he planned to wait for them at Fort Sainte-Thérèse, but the evidence shows that he did not remain there long. He arrived on the evening of 29 January, and undeterred by the number of men who were suffering from frostbite and exhaustion, he paused only long enough to replace them from the garrison. The next morning he was on the move again towards Lake Champlain and the unknown territory beyond.[40]

The two first-hand accounts of the expedition – those of Tapie de Monteil and Chartier de Lotbinière – avoid the issue of leaving without the guides altogether, mentioning only their part in the subsequent misfortunes. Perhaps rather than blame one of their own, who, by virtue of his nationality and his exalted rank, had to be considered beyond reproach, it was considered wiser either to ignore the question or to find a scapegoat who could be maligned with impunity. Even in 1666, it seems, the cliché of the drunken Indian was already well established in Canada, judging by the Jesuit annalist who, not to be outdone by Lotbinière's reference to "the Algonkin who was delayed by the bottle," wrote in the *Journal* that the whole debacle was caused by "the Algonkins, 30 in number whose drunkenness had detained them on the road."[41]

Other explanations might appear to fit in with the known facts: one could be that when the Indians failed to appear, Courcelle decided to rely on the local knowledge of his Canadian volunteers to guide him; and another, that he trusted his own sense of direction. Neither stands up to close examination. The first collapses in the light of the evidence that in 1666 very few Canadians had much knowledge of the terrain beyond Fort Sainte-Thérèse, and even less about the approaches to the Mohawk villages, for they seldom, if ever, ventured far from their settlements along the St Lawrence. Of the second, Courcelle's ability as a pathfinder could be expected to be no better than that of a man who had been in the country for less than five months.

In the absence, therefore, of any confirmable explanation for his action, all attempts to provide one can only be speculative. Of the myriad possibilities, just one seems as if it might be credible. It suggests that by the time Courcelle reached Fort Saint-Louis and found himself far away from any chance of vice-regal vetoes, his conceit and thirst for glory drove him unthinkingly ahead. As the candle flame entices the moth, so did the prospect of fame and glory entice Courcelle into the wilderness without guides.

Ahead lay no more friendly outposts where reinforcements were to be had, and where the wounds of the trail could be licked, only a snow-covered, frozen lake and the dark forest fringing its shoreline wherein even the trees were unfriendly, offering, as they did, cover for an ambush. The governor soon learned, though, that his immediate enemy was not a Mohawk war party. The winter itself was a far more relentless foe. Snow blindness, frostbite, and hypothermia stalked the serpentine column, taking a victim here and another there with frightful regularity, some while they slept, others while they paused to rest bodies wearied by struggling through the waist-deep snow.[42]

Courcelle could have known only that his destination was somewhere to the south and west, and the platoon of Montreal volunteers in the van of the column, his so-called "Blue Coats ... the boys of his right hand," knew very little more.[43] The result was that after crossing the length of the frozen Lakes Champlain and Saint-Sacrament (Lake George), they covered many futile and lethal kilometres, following half-baked hunches and ill-advised miscalculations, the corpses littering the trail witnesses to the folly of it all. Days were lost that way, each filled with the same monotonous routine – fifteen kilometres slogging through chest-high snow, utter exhaustion, a few bites of hardtack washed down with icy water, then fitful sleep in a tomblike cavity in the snow with but one blanket for a coverlet.[44] And so they wandered, day after day, realization slowly dawning that they were undeniably lost.

On 20 February, after three desperate weeks, some Indian cabins were sighted in a clearing ahead.[45] Unaware that they were on the outskirts of the Anglo-Dutch settlement of Schenectady, and without bothering to reconnoitre the area, Courcelle ordered an immediate attack, thinking it was a Mohawk village rather than just a few cabins. No sooner had the command been given than he must have regretted what he had done. His troops, half-crazed by the privations and miseries of the preceding three weeks and lusting for something on which to vent their pent-up rage, overran and ransacked the cabins in a frenzy of wilful destruction. Then, shedding the last vestige of any veneer of civilization, they turned to the occupants, a half-breed boy and a number of old women, and butchered two of them on the spot and seriously wounded a third. They herded the survivors at gunpoint into the clearing, and the wounded one, unable to move fast enough for the attackers' liking, was knifed to death even as she tried to drag herself to the door. A bestial climax to the ill-fated march from Canada for which no words of extenuation are possible.[46]

There was no way that such savagery could pass unheard in the nearby village. The crackle of the gunfire, the yells of the assailants, and the screams of their victims, all plainly audible there, soon brought out about thirty well-armed Mohawks to investigate. Visiting Schenectady to trade with the Dutch merchants, who still conducted business there, they had been negotiating for the purchase of arms and provisions when they heard the din coming from the cabins.[47]

There followed the only combat of the expedition when, from the cover of the trees, the Mohawks took on the French invaders in what was more of a skirmish than a full-scale battle. The casualties were relatively light on both sides, probably four Mohawks, one French officer, five soldiers, and a volunteer killed; and six Mohawks, three French officers, and one volunteer wounded. The French casualties mostly occurred in a single clash when an outpost, consisting of nothing more than a hastily built snow parapet around the base of a large tree, was cut off. Tactically, if indeed there were any tactics, the Mohawks had the advantage. Their highly fluid method of fighting, with men moving swiftly and easily from cover to cover on their snowshoes, enabled them to shift the direction of their attack whenever they pleased. The French regulars knew nothing of that kind of warfare. Their training had all been directed towards contending with an enemy who stood still, in full view, facing them. Against the will-o'-the-wisp manoeuvres of the Mohawks, all the formal, almost stylized, drills that had been perfected on the plains of Europe were useless.[48]

The fighting did not last long. It came to an abrupt end when the burgomaster of Schenectady arrived and formally informed Courcelle that he had strayed into the territories of His Royal Highness, James, Duke of York. If he wished to occupy the settlement, the burgomaster continued, there was nothing to stop him from doing so, for it was undefended.[49] That was the last thing Courcelle wanted; already he had seen how his men had behaved in the attack on the Indian cabins and their actions led him to fear that if they remained in the vicinity for long, he would never get them back to the St Lawrence. They would desert and vanish for good into the English settlements along the Hudson. There were other considerations too. One of those settlements, Albany, was less than twenty-five kilometres away, and there was no knowing the number of soldiers the English had stationed there, all of whom would be fit and fresh, unlike his own men who were half-starved and weak from the ravages of their march. Should he seize Schenectady, there was also the spectre of prolonged diplomatic wrangling to take into account, which could be the ruin of him. Ironically, however, England and France had technically been at war for more than a month, although nobody in North America knew about it until much later in the year.[50]

In the end, the talk of occupation was dropped, and the negotiations devolved into a discussion of the French need for provisions and of the fate of the prisoners taken in the cabins, particularly the Métis boy, whose uncle, a Hollander in Schenectady, demanded his return.[51]

No doubt the weather sped the talks to an earlier conclusion than would otherwise have been the case, for, the same evening, Saturday, 20 February, the rains started, adding a new dimension to the already miserable condition of the invaders. So apparent was their dejection that the burgomaster, who must have sensed a deal in the making, switched roles from that of an outraged public official to that of an accommodating purveyor of victuals. Indeed, he could let Mijnheer Courcelle have what little food he could spare from his own meagre resources, a little flour perhaps? How about a few sacks of corn and one or two of dried peas? A cask of good wine, too, and maybe two of beer, and all at a very reasonable price? How much? Well, every sou the French could raise between them on the spot would do very nicely. The price was high, but Courcelle paid without a murmur, for he had no choice if he had any hope of getting back to Quebec.[52]

Only the question of the prisoners remained to be settled. The rains continued all that night and the next day, softening the ice on lakes and rivers, and with it Courcelle's resolution to prolong the negotiations much further. He was aware that once the ice went out, he would be stranded in hostile territory with a sadly depleted army and would be vulnerable to attack by both the Mohawks and the English. He procrastinated until ten o'clock that night and then capitulated, handing the prisoners over to the burgomaster. He ordered his troops to form up, and they marched off, in the dark, the way they had come.[53]

It is not difficult to imagine how many would have survived the return march on the provisions purchased from the burgomaster of Schenectady had not, early the next evening, a party of Algonkins appeared on the trail ahead. The guides who were supposed to have led the expedition from Fort Saint-Louis had finally arrived.[54]

The maxim better late than never was seldom truer than in this instance, because by then every man knew that the arrival of the Indians meant the possibility of surviving the return march. In the elation of the moment, therefore, no one really cared about the reason for the long delay. What did it matter if they had been carousing along the way, as some hinted, now that they had arrived? Whatever the cause of their tardiness, and there is no means of determining it, the truth of the matter remains that rigid time schedules are the invention of Europeans, who give them an importance that is often incomprehensible to other peoples. To the long-overdue guides, the whole expedition must have seemed an untimely venture in the first place and therefore ten days one way or the other would make little difference to its outcome at that time of year.[55]

The return journey took two weeks. During that time the Indians sustained what was left of Courcelle's expedition with fresh meat taken in the forest, as had always been the intention. They also taught the soldiers how to obtain a degree of comfort while sleeping in the open by simply making the best use of what nature afforded. Although a large food cache midway along Lake Champlain had been rifled, probably by a sergeant and several soldiers returning ahead of Courcelle, it did not turn out to be a vital loss because of the Indians' skills.[56] So it was that approximately one hundred men, all that remained of what had been a small army five times that size, arrived in reasonably good health at Fort Saint-Louis on 8 March, five and a half weeks after leaving that place. From there they returned to their winter quarters.[57]

The Montreal-based survivors of the ill-conceived enterprise arrived there on 11 March, and Captain Roger de Bonneau de La Varenne, the most senior officer with them, gave a detailed report to the Marquis de Salières, who, but for his sorrow at the tremendous loss of life, must have found some grim satisfaction in the knowledge that his prediction of the outcome had been deadly accurate.[58]

Of the five hundred men in the campaign, as many as four hundred lay dead along the trail – some struck down by hypothermia, others by starvation, and a few, very few, by Mohawks. That toll is the measure against which any accomplishments of the campaign have to be judged. In those terms the operation has to be considered a fiasco, and Courcelle, its instigator, should have shouldered the blame, but he did not. He accused the Jesuits of responsibility for the debacle, specifically Father Albanel, the chaplain at Fort Saint-Louis, for having delayed the Algonkin guides.[59] Of course, the charge was as valid as the man making it was willing to accept the fact of his own incompetence. His intention was the shabby one of trying to blame an acceptable scapegoat, the Society of Jesus, which he certainly knew not to be in the best of favour with the king and his ministers.[60]

At first both Tracy and Talon supported Courcelle in that stance, but before long Tracy modified his position to the point where he declared himself to be completely satisfied with the outcome of the expedition and to have found that the Jesuits played no part in any of the misfortunes. Moreover, shortly afterwards, he went even further so that the Jesuit annalist recorded in the *Journal*, "Monseigneur de Tracy assured me that Monsieur the Governor had completely altered his opinion respecting us." The general, it seems, had acquired more of an eye for the political realities in the colony than had the governor. Tracy realized that any settlement of the Iroquois problem would require the help of the Jesuits, who were held in considerable awe by the Five Nations of the Confederacy. As for Courcelle, after some initial misgivings, he decided to make his confession, upon returning to Quebec, to Father Pierre Chastellain, a Jesuit.[61]

What was the real significance of the expedition with its trail of unmarked graves stretching through the forest from Fort Sainte-Thérèse to Schenectady and back? Considered in the narrow context of colonial North American history, it amounts to a reiteration of the fact that, with the coming of the Carignan-Salières Regiment, France had become a presence to be reckoned with on the continent, and that anyone contemplating making war, or changing trading patterns and alliances, in the catchment areas of the St Lawrence and the Hudson rivers had better be aware of it. Taken against the broader panorama of world history, however, that aspect of it is lost from sight as the event merges with a thousand and one similar bunglings to help proclaim the undeniable truth that military incompetence has been around for a long time.

CHAPTER FOUR

Questions of Peace and War

By the time the men returning from Courcelle's expedition rejoined their more fortunate comrades who had remained in winter quarters, there were hints of change in the air. The changes that were occurring, the result of the interaction between the soldiers and their Canadian surroundings, would affect the tenor of life in the colony. They can be broadly categorized according to whether they were of military, economic, or social significance.

The most obvious change that had military significance was seen in a civilianization of the troops' daily routine. In the settlements, the normal activities of sentry duties, patrols, and drills were augmented by such nonmartial occupations as working in the fields, cutting wood, hauling water, and the like, all carried out on behalf of the habitants on whom the soldiers were billeted.[1] In this manner did military and civilian patterns of life in Canada begin to overlap and to merge.

At the same time, in the Richelieu Valley forts where billeting was not a factor, a similar civilianization was taking place, although the manner in which it occurred was somewhat different. There, besides patrolling the surrounding forest and manning the bastions around the clock, the soldiers also spent time improving the defences by adding new buildings within the palisades and by clearing more ground outside them to give those on watch a larger field of view. It did not take long before the idea of using the newly cleared ground for agriculture occurred to two of the commanding officers. As early as 1667, their first crops were in the soil, and farm animals were introduced into what would eventually become the seigneuries of Sorel and Chambly. The success of those developments, of course, depended almost entirely on the members of the garrisons devoting part of their time to purely agricultural activities, thereby presaging what it was hoped would become the pattern for the settlement of the Richelieu Valley after the pacification of the Iroquois.[2]

The second change that had a military significance arose directly from the manner in which the Iroquois waged war. Soldiers, who might at first have thought that carrying out agricultural and domestic chores was unbecoming, very soon discovered an unanticipated element of risk. In Canada at that time, the threat of attack was ever present so that even the simple act of going out to work in the fields could be tantamount to entering a potential no-man's-land, and foolish were those who ignored the fact. Because of their location, Montreal and Trois-Rivières were more exposed to Iroquois attacks than was Quebec. For that reason they were more like forts than towns, with their buildings huddled within the confines of palisades for greater protection. Around them some of the land had been cleared for agriculture, but beyond it lay the forest where Iroquois war parties could lurk at will, waiting to pick off incautious individuals who got too close without the protection of several others.[3] The troops did not even begin to learn about the nature of Indian warfare until a number of them had been killed under such circumstances, which provided a gruesome object lesson for their surviving comrades. It was a lesson difficult to learn for men trained to believe that war consisted of set-piece battles, fought on open ground with the enemy clearly in view. Of that Dollier de Casson observed:

Although Montreal was considerably strengthened this year by the arrival of the troops, amongst whom there were both brave soldiers and fine officers, nevertheless these wanted to apply the methods of defence used in Europe, which were most unsuitable for this country, to whose experiences in the art of war they attached too little attention. The result was that the enemy did not cease to kill numbers of our men as before.[4]

As the Iroquois tactics came to be better understood, therefore, the traditional military view of warfare was eroded.

Of the economic changes, one is to be seen in the operation of the fur trade after officers from the regiment began to participate in it. When Dollier de Casson deplored the deteriorating moral tone of Montreal after the arrival of the troops, not all his complaints had to do with unseemly behaviour on the part of the soldiery. He was also expressing concern over the practice, adopted by some officers, of dealing directly with the Indians for the purchase of furs. By diverting the trade from regular channels, those officers were contributing directly to the impoverishment of the local residents, who looked to that traffic for a part of their livelihood. The result, he contended, was that it became "impossible for people to live here without any means of buying implements or tools, with nothing with which to buy linen or cloth, or anything required for their maintenance."[5] Other officers, particularly those younger captains who were not interested in the fur trade, were not averse to transacting a little business either. If they could turn a profit by selling any consumer goods they had at their disposal, they were quick to take advantage of the opportunity – there was always a good demand for a keg of brandy or wine, knives, hand tools, and, especially, guns.[6] In these ways established patterns of commerce, particularly in the fur trade, were disrupted by the regimental officers participating in it.

There was also a dramatic change in the manner in which business was transacted in the colony that was due exclusively to the arrival of the troops. Previously, for want of currency in Canada, many business transactions had to be conducted more or less on the basis of barter, or of promissory notes. With the coming of the Carignan-Salières Regiment, which paid for the goods and services it received with cash, large amounts of ready money were injected into the economy. The magnitude of the amount the regiment put into circulation can only be guessed at, but a rough idea can be gained from the size of its payroll, which in 1666 alone amounted to more than 150,000 *livres*.[7]

Other expenditures too were made on the unit's behalf, mainly by the intendant, and they would have put several more thousand *livres* into circulation each year, all of which led Marie de l'Incarnation to explain to her son that "money, which was rare in this country, is now very common, these gentlemen having brought a great deal with them. They pay for everything they buy with money, both their food and their other necessities, which suits our habitants very well."[8]

Unfortunately the social changes that occurred as a result of the mixing of the military and the civilian populations are more difficult to pinpoint. The evidence is far from explicit and, moreover, is only fragmentary. Nevertheless it is possible to make a few general observations.

Although Dollier de Casson certainly complained of the soldiers' behaviour in Montreal, he did not specify what their various misdeeds were. When trying to estimate the validity of his complaints, one must remember that his judgment was probably based on the rather austere standards of conduct that had prevailed in Montreal throughout de Maisonneuve's governorship until he returned to France in

1665 and left the townspeople "in the hands of others from whom they could not expect the same disinterestedness [impartiality], the same affection and the same regard for the exclusion of vices which have, in fact, risen and grown here since that time."[9]

Of prime importance, in an assessment of social change, is the fact that the Canadian population was young. In 1666 the average age was just under twenty-five. It seems likely, therefore, that it would have been more receptive to change than it would if an older group had been predominant. It also would have had a considerable amount in common with the troops, whose average age, so far as can be determined, was about twenty-six.[10]

Another feature of the Canadian population was its overwhelming proportion of males, 63 per cent, versus only 37 per cent females. That demographic imbalance became even more pronounced when the Carignan-Salières Regiment, and the four companies that Tracy brought from the Antilles, added a further twelve hundred men so that in 1666 about two-thirds of the population was male, and one-third female.[11]

One possible effect of the predominance of males, and youth, in the population can be seen in the number of volunteers who eagerly joined the several military operations undertaken by the regiment. Young men, many of whom could have been no more than adolescents, saw the rough and tumble of the soldier's life as an exciting alternative to the daily round in Quebec, Trois-Rivières, and Montreal.

Even so, there can be no doubt that the euphoria of the early days after the regiment's arrival in Canada did not last long. It must have faded as soon as the realities of the situation dawned on the people – alleviating the pressure caused by the influx of troops was one reason, albeit a lesser one, for Tracy's move to send as many soldiers as possible to the Richelieu Valley. After that, the soldiers and civilians began to develop a modus vivendi in which each must have made some concessions to the other's interests, for there are no reports of communal strife resulting from the mixing of the two groups.

Whatever other changes these factors brought about in the social patterns in the colony, it is safe to say that they were of two sorts, those that contributed to friction between the military and civilian segments of the population and those that promoted harmony. It is certainly true that the participation of members of the regiment in the business life of the colony must have generated some hard feelings, but the influx of cash they brought into the economy was generally welcomed. Similarly the help provided by the soldiers in domestic chores and agriculture would have been welcomed too. It would be naive, however, to think that the rather staid lives of the habitants would not have been disrupted and that drunkenness and disorderly behaviour did not increase with the coming of the soldiers. Nevertheless, on the whole, although the relations between the troops and the settlers never did return to what they had been during those first wildly ecstatic days in the summer of 1665, there is no evidence to suggest that they ever deteriorated to the level of hostility and confrontation that was the norm in France. Perhaps the aptest description of the situation is that, with one or two exceptions, which did not show up until later, the troops were generally tolerated by the Canadians and vice versa.

The adjustment made by the soldiers and the settlers to each other's ways helped shape the mould in which Canada's society would be cast for almost a century to follow. In the immediate future, though, that long-term significance went unnoticed as the events of 1666 started to overshadow anything less momentous.

Essentially those events had to do with questions of peace and war, some resulting from Courcelle's recent venture and others from events on the other side of the Atlantic. They began on 16 March 1666 when twelve Seneca chiefs reached Montreal on their way to Quebec, but the still-frozen river gave them a pretext for delaying any further progress. The Marquis de Salières, diplomatically, made them welcome, and for two weeks entertained them to the best of his ability and provisions. He did, however, take immediate steps to inform Tracy of their arrival by dispatching Captain de La Varenne and a runner to Quebec. Although most of his guests left to go hunting, two stayed behind in Montreal. One was so critically ill it was considered essential that he be baptized so that he could receive the last rites of the church. The hastily arranged ceremony was performed at the man's bedside in the colonel's quarters. Jeanne Mance, the superior of the Hôtel-Dieu, and the colonel were pressed into service as godparents, while the officiating priest, for want of an appropriate baptismal name, christened the man Henri, after his godfather. The experience of nearly dying must have had some effect on the Seneca, for by the time the first of his comrades returned from the hunt, six days later, he had been restored to robust good health.[12]

By the beginning of May the ice was out on the St Lawrence, and navigation was again possible. The rest of the hunting party returned to Montreal at that time, and after ten more convivial days at the colonel's expense, the delegation, escorted by a lieutenant and twelve soldiers, departed for Quebec aboard a barque.[13]

Despite the peaceable intentions of the Senecas, it seems that not all the Confederacy was of like mind. At least one of the Five Nations still remained openly hostile towards the French, a state of affairs that was evident in an incident just four days after the departure of the delegation for Quebec. It happened while the Marquis de Salières was conducting Mgr de Laval around the settlement on a tour of inspection. Their party was suddenly halted by a distant cry of "To arms!" followed by a burst of gunfire. Two soldiers out shooting pigeons had been surprised by an Iroquois war party. One soldier ran for the shelter of a nearby cabin and managed to reach it safely, but the other was less fortunate. Before help could reach him, he had been felled by two bullets, scalped, and his skull smashed by repeated blows from axes. Both the colonel and the bishop were horrified by the incident, but they were unable to identify the assailants because they were too far away.[14]

The incident was followed a few days later by another in which a habitant, cutting wood in the same general area, was ambushed and captured and, a week later, by one in which two more soldiers were attacked and killed in a wooded area that the colonel had declared out of bounds as a precautionary measure aimed at reducing the perils to which his men were exposed.[15]

Such sporadic attacks were not restricted to the Montreal area. Similar occurrences took place elsewhere in the colony, and altogether they added up to a sign of increased Iroquois aggressiveness, which in turn led to a heightened state of nervousness among the troops.[16] Their unsettled state is well illustrated by an incident that had occurred a few months earlier at Quebec. As Marie de l'Incarnation described it:

A lieutenant who, not being able to be present at the assembly to recite his rosary, withdrew into a thicket to do so in private. The sentinel, who could not clearly discern him, believed it was an Iroquois hiding there, shot him almost point-blank, and immediately leaped upon him, expecting to find him dead. He should indeed have been so, the ball having entered his head two fingers above the temple. The sentinel was stunned to find his lieutenant on the ground all covered in blood instead of an Iroquois. He was arrested and his trial begun, but the one that was believed dead rose, saying that he asked pardon for the sentinel and that his injury was of no account. He was indeed examined and the ball was found buried in his skull but the man himself quite safe, which has been confirmed to be a miracle.[17]

Despite any ill intentions on the part of their fellow confederates, by 22 May the Senecas had completed their negotiations with Tracy and had signed a treaty of mutual friendship with France. In it they agreed to be loyal subjects of Louis xiv and asked for Jesuit missionaries to instruct their people in the Christian faith, a request that underlines the importance of the Black Robes in reaching any settlement with the Iroquois. Although such a request was a common feature of treaties made between members of the Confederacy and Canada, in this instance, however, there was a little more to it. The treaty contained a clause in which the Senecas undertook to protect the Jesuit fathers, as well as any other French settlers in their territories, from the Susquehannocks with whom they were at war. The inclusion of such a commitment in the document would seem to imply that the French were interested in establishing, at some future date, a presence among the Senecas, the most westerly of the Five Nations. If that were indeed so, it indicates that a possible expansion of Canadian influence was already being contemplated as early as 1666. Apart from that condition, however, the agreement was more like an imposed settlement than a pact between equals. The Senecas agreed to it for two very good reasons, the first being a recognition that the French possessed the military might to enforce any conditions they pleased, and the second that that nation urgently needed peace with Canada to leave it free to deal with the Susquehannocks. Under those circumstances Tracy had little difficulty in securing concurrence with his terms, imposed or not.[18]

On 11 June the homeward-bound Senecas reached Montreal, stopping over just long enough to assure the hospitable colonel that they would be back at the end of July, for apparently some cordiality had developed between him and his guests. Whether it emanated from a shared interest in the nature of warfare discovered during weeks of fraternizing is impossible to say, but on the face of it they had nothing else in common, except perhaps a palate for French brandy.[19]

On 6 July another delegation, this one from the Oneida nation, reached Quebec in search of peace. Somewhat larger than the Seneca mission, it consisted of twelve chiefs, twelve women, and two prisoners, who had been brought along as a token of good intent. One prisoner was a six-year-old child, and the other a surgeon, who had been captured the previous May near Fort Sainte-Thérèse and mutilated, three of his fingers having been hacked off.[20]

In less than a week agreement had been reached to a treaty very similar to the one with the Senecas, and by 14 July the Oneidas were returning to their villages. The Jesuit Father Thierry Beschefer, whom they had agreed to conduct to the Mohawks and the Onondagas, accompanied them as an emissary to try to persuade the chiefs of those nations to also come to Quebec and make peace with the French.[21]

The concluded treaties seem to suggest that, unlike Courcelle, Tracy was no warmonger at heart and was willing to reach peaceful settlements with the Iroquois nations, apparently only considering military alternatives as a last resort. Even so, he was realist enough to take the precaution of holding four Oneida hostages, three men and a woman, at Quebec as insurance against Father Beschefer's safety during his mission.[22]

The Oneidas were barely out of sight when word arrived that a hunting party, consisting of soldiers and volunteers, had been surprised at the northern end of Lake Champlain, near where Fort Sainte-Anne, the fourth in the defensive system begun the previous autumn, was nearing completion. Seven men had died in the attack, including two officers and the regimental quartermaster, Chamot. In addition the raiders had carried off four prisoners, one of whom was Tracy's cousin, Lieutenant Louis de Canchy de Lerole of the Monteil Company, detached from the Poitou Regiment.[23]

Outraged by the attack, and still further incensed by the capture of his relative, the general immediately sent Captain Arnoult de Broisle de Loubias with a party of soldiers to Trois-Rivières to intercept the Oneida peace delegation and bring it back to Quebec. There it was locked up with the original four hostages while Tracy set in motion preparations for a punitive expedition into the Mohawk country under the command of Captain Pierre de Saurel.[24]

Even at that dire juncture, though, Tracy continued to regard peace as his best option and chose to consider the ambush as the work of an isolated raiding party. As it happened, he was probably not far from the truth, for it was a feature of Iroquois political life that for every contentious issue there were two well-defined factions, one on either side of it, which enabled a nation to take simultaneously opposing positions on any such question.[25] It can therefore be assumed that within the Mohawk nation there was both a pro-French and an anti-French party of whose existence Tracy could have been well aware from his talks with the other four nations in Quebec.

On 22 July he released an Oneida hostage to guide and accompany Guillaume de Couture (Cousture) to Albany where he was to deliver a letter expressing French displeasure to the English administration, which, the general contended, should have had its allies under better control.[26] Tracy's gambit could not have been based on anything more than a wild guess. He could not possibly have known for certain the precise relationship between the governor of New York and the Mohawks at that time, except that, after the Courcelle winter campaign, he may have strongly suspected that an arrangement between the two existed over the continued harassment of the settlements and forts along the St Lawrence and Richelieu rivers.

Couture's mission, Tracy explained in a letter of introduction to the administrators at Albany, included securing the custody of the perpetrators of the attack near Fort Sainte-Anne and bringing them back to Quebec, but the governor of New York, Colonel Richard Nicolls, avoided meeting Couture on the pretext that he had urgent business elsewhere. Despite that implied snub, though, Couture's mission was successful. He not only secured the custody of the leader of the raid – a former member of the Neutral nation, who had been absorbed into the Mohawks – but he also managed to persuade the Flemish Bastard, a most astute diplomat and probably the spokesman for the pro-French faction within the nation, to accompany him back to Quebec.[27]

Of course the knowledge that a few days' march behind Couture was Saurel's punitive column, made up of a hundred soldiers augmented by two hundred volunteers and Indians, could possibly have had a bearing on the Mohawk decision to cooperate. Nevertheless Couture's accomplishment was considerable.

Tracy's penchant for keeping diplomatic doors ajar was well illustrated during the months immediately after Courcelle's winter expedition. During that period he was almost constantly ready to explore any avenue that might have led to a peaceful solution of the Iroquois problem, only turning to the use, or the threat of, force as a last resort. Even then, as with Couture's mission, he continued to give diplomacy a chance. But all that changed at the beginning of August when the first ship of the year arrived from France. It brought him the news of France's declaration of war on England and instructions on how to proceed. From that time on, whether he liked it or not, Tracy was committed to a military solution of the Iroquois problem.[28]

Meanwhile, two days' march from the Mohawk villages, Saurel met up with the Flemish Bastard and, according to the entry in the *Journal of the Jesuits* for 28 August 1666, three other Mohawks, all of whom, along with the prisoners taken in the raid near Fort Sainte-Anne, were on their way to Quebec. The encounter immediately gave rise to a very tense situation that persuaded the captain to turn around and return to Quebec. That change was forced upon him when the approximately one hundred Algonkin Indians in his party became hostile and demanded that he turn the Bastard and his fellow Mohawks over to them to deal with. Saurel, with two hundred soldiers and volunteers to back him up, denied the request but at the same time realized that responsibility for the safety of the delegation lay entirely with him. He therefore gave the order to turn about to escort it back to Quebec.[29]

There, in the aftermath of the Fort Sainte-Anne raid, the normally self-assured Tracy had started to show signs of disquiet. A day or so after Saurel had left with his force, he sent Major Balthazard de La Flotte de La Fredière, along with a detachment of soldiers, to Fort Saint-Louis with orders to build two redoubts, one at the foot, and the other at the head, of the flight of rapids between that fort and Fort Sainte-Thérèse, and to clear a seven-metre-wide trail between them.[30] His reason for doing so is not known, but he may have been worried over what the actions of the governor of New York might lead to. Tracy did not want the garrisons of his Richelieu Valley forts to have to fight a rearguard action without some additional defences in the event that the English in New York combined with forces in Massachusetts and Connecticut, as well as with the Mohawks, to launch an all-out attack on Canada from Lake Champlain.

Up until that time, despite all the diplomatic activity in Quebec, not a word had been heard from Governor Nicolls. Since he was responsible for the territory that had been violated by Courcelle, it is reasonable to expect that he would have expressed his displeasure, but he had not. So far as can be determined, he made no personal attempt to communicate with his counterpart in Quebec before August 1666. It is not that the governor of New York was unconcerned over the events at Schenectady, but, more likely, that he just did not know the best way to exploit them until he received news of developments in Europe.

Without going into the convolutions of the question of the Spanish succession, which were to dominate Louis XIV's European policies for the next forty-seven years, suffice it to say that although France was technically at war with England in 1666, it was not actually involved in any open warfare. So far as North America was concerned, however, the king instructed Tracy to consider two possibilities concerning the English in New York – either making war on them or, alternatively, securing their neutrality.[31] As it transpired, neutrality was the last thing the English governor had in mind.

It is not clear when Colonel Nicolls learned that England and France were at war, but he certainly knew about it early in July 1666 when he took two steps in response to the news. The first was to encourage the Mohawks, presumably the anti-French faction among them, to continue making raids into the Richelieu and St Lawrence valleys; the second was to try to persuade the colonies of Massachusetts and Connecticut to join with him to defeat the French troops. On 6 July he wrote to the Council of Massachusetts:

Received letters yesterday that the French were marching (in number according to the Indians' computation about 700 men) towards Albany. I presume they will not openly profess themselves enemies to us till they have either vanquisht the Mohawks or made peace with them. However I have strengthen'd my garrison at the Fort, to withstand their attempts ... & cannot imagine any reason to the contrary why so faire an advantage against the French, should be let slip ... and truly if from your Colony a speedy force of horse and dragoons not exceeding 150 would march and joine with a proportionable number of Conecticott Colony; in all probability few of the French could returne to Canada, whose whole strength is now so farr ingaged from home, and by consequence the rest of the French will not be able to make any considerable resistance.[32]

The letter could not possibly have been referring to Saurel's punitive expedition, which did not set out until 24 July, and then at extremely short notice. Colonel Nicolls therefore must have anticipated Tracy's decision to embark on an invasion of the Mohawk lands some time in late summer or early fall. It was not too difficult for someone with a military background to make such a prediction, especially if he knew that the Mohawks would continue their raids on Canadian targets and would not likely hurry to Quebec to sue for peace.[33]

It should be noted that there is an uncanny similarity between Colonel Nicolls's fear that after dealing with the Mohawks, the French might attack the colony of New York, and Louis xiv's instructions to the Marquis de Tracy about the actions he should take if he felt that securing the neutrality of the English there was either impossible or unwise. In part the king said: "But as I know the English are very weak in that country, especially in New Holland, you will carefully assess whether you would be able, with my subjects and with my troops, to be stronger than the English and to put yourself in a position to surprise them, to drive them from the country and to establish the French there."[34]

Could the similarity be purely coincidental? If not, how might it have come about? As it happens, the questions are academic because Tracy never did invade New York and both Massachusetts and Connecticut declined Nicolls's invitation. The colonies cited various reasons, including the fact that the approaching harvest was making great demands on their available manpower, and the following:

As the case is circumstanced wee find noe small difficulty, viz[t] because the Mohawkes upon whome the French are now warring, have bin a long season inveterate enemies to the Indians round about us, which will in reason engage them wth the French (whoe are their great friends) against the Mohawkes, and against us allso, if wee should warr wth the French. And your Honour well knowes the hazard of an intestine enemie. Your Honour allso (as you writte) hath so far engaged wth the Mohawkes, as to encourage them in the warr against the French, and notwithstandinge those treaties that have bin with the Mohawkes for peace with the Indians about us, they yet with great force manage their warr with the sayd Indians, and they have very lately killed and taken nine or tenn of the sayd Indians, and yesterday there was a party of the Mohawkes at Podunck (a place between this town and Windsor) whoe were discovered by the Indians, and as sone as discovered they fled. These things considered, (wth the number of Indians that are round about us) makes it difficult to us to part with any of our strength from hence, untill there could be an agreement or at least a cessation of warr from som sett time concluded upon, between the Mohawkes and our Indians.[35]

Unlike New France, the English colonies were not under the direct rule of their king, but were the private domains of chartered companies, as were Massachusetts and Connecticut, or of individual proprietors, as was New York. Corporate or personal ambitions thus determined the direction of the policies followed by the colonies. Consequently their loyalty and obedience to King Charles II were more token then real, and the obligations they owed to their neighbours were few.

The rejections of Colonel Nicolls's advances by Massachusetts and Connecticut forced him to consider an alternative course of action and directed his attention towards Canada. If the French could not be humbled, then they would have to be humoured, and, with that thought uppermost in his mind, the governor wrote to the Marquis de Tracy.

His letter, written on 20 August, stated his surprise at learning that Courcelle had penetrated into New York without permission, but he refrained from dwelling on the matter unduly, preferring to remind the general of what good neighbours his people had been, were, and, given the chance, would be in the future. He protested that it was unfair to even suggest that he, or his subordinates, might have colluded with the Mohawks over the raid near Fort Sainte-Anne, and then came the pertinent part of the letter:

Upon notice that you had employ'd a person of honour with your letters to Albany, I made all the hast possible from New Yorke personally to discourse with him, but unfortunately he is gone in pursuit of a business which may detain him longer than I can attend his return. I must content myself with the loss of this opportunity to have inlarg'd myself to the Sieur de Couture, and by him to your self, with how much integrity I shall constantly embrace the European interest amidst the Heathen in American, as becomes a good Christian, provided that the just, and well knowne bounds and limittes of his Maties American Dominions be not invaded; or the peace and safety of his Maties subjects interrupted and endangered by your forces.[36]

It was a most conciliatory letter, especially since the writer and the recipient were enemies, but it has to be considered in conjunction with Colonel Nicolls's recent correspondence with his counterparts in Massachusetts and Connecticut. In that context it indicates that the governor of New York was just as apprehensive about the presence of the Carignan-Salières Regiment in Canada as were the Iroquois nations, which continued to send delegations to Quebec seeking peace.

The latest of those visitations had taken place on 31 July when two Cayugas reached Quebec in advance of a huge delegation representing the whole of the Confederacy with the exception of the Mohawks.[37] Its object was to negotiate a comprehensive peace treaty, but the main party, consisting of 108 men, women, and children, was delayed along the way and did not reach Quebec until 28 August. By that time Pierre de Saurel and his column, which was escorting the Flemish Bastard and his party, were also on the point of arriving.[38]

Thus, it finally looked as if meaningful negotiations with the entire Confederacy might at last become a reality. At least it appeared so on 31 August when, following the formality of an impressive opening ceremony in the Jesuit Park, the grand peace conference got under way. The initial optimism, however, quickly degenerated into pessimism and frustration as the talks dragged on inconclusively. After eight days, the Flemish Bastard had heard enough. Somehow he seemed to know that the conference was futile, and he showed his dissatisfaction by walking out of the proceedings and refusing to take any further part in them.[39]

His interpretation of the situation was, of course, correct; the conference was nothing but a facade. Tracy had been using it as a screen for his real intentions while he actively prepared for war against the Mohawks. Had France not declared war on England when she did, he might have accomplished their pacification without the need to invade their lands in the autumn of that year, but since she had, he was left with no choice in the matter.

The letter from the king advising Tracy of France's declaration of war, which could not have reached him before 2 August, when the

Paon de Hollande, the first ship of the year reached Quebec from France, docked, did not mention the Mohawks.[40] The two options presented on dealing with New York, however, would affect them to a lesser or greater degree. The one seeking an undertaking of neutrality from the governor of New York would certainly have required him to cease encouraging the Mohawks to engage in offensive actions against the French, while the other, that of marching on Albany and beyond to annex the territory for France, became possible only once the Indians had been subdued so that they could not pose a threat to the rear of any such operations.[41] Tracy never seems to have considered the neutrality option, and since the annexation alternative was premised on the prior subjugation of the Mohawks, which would involve the deployment of a considerable army, he chose to get an other than military opinion on the proposal before finally committing himself to it.

Although the king's instructions to Tracy stipulated that he confer with Courcelle and the senior officers of the Carignan-Salières Regiment when deciding on a course of action, they made no mention of consulting the intendant.[42] That was the general's own doing. Knowing that the operation, as envisaged, would call for a considerable amount of civilian involvement as volunteers, he must have felt the need for some reassurance that his proposal would be acceptable to the populace as a whole. No one was better qualified to give him such an opinion than Jean Talon was. He was intelligent and efficient, and, most important, his duties as intendant kept him in close touch with the general population so that he knew, probably better than anyone else in Canada, where its sentiments lay. The report he produced, therefore, is perhaps more interesting for its glimpse of the contemporary Canadian view of the problems that faced the colony in 1666 than it is for its rather one-sided analysis of the political, strategic, and tactical implications of those problems.[43]

The report is divided into two parts, the first consisting of arguments in favour of war and the second, those favouring peace. Talon made no attempt to be impartial. His views on the subject were left in no doubt even before he got past the preamble to his case for making war. In it he asserted that "a lasting peace cannot be made with this nation [the Mohawks] which never keeps it unless it is useful to it, or that in breaking it believes it will not be punished." And if there were still any lingering doubts about his opinion, he added, "I think that war is more advantageous than peace for the following reasons," and then went on to detail his case.[44]

By taking that firm position from the outset, Talon successfully negated his own arguments in favour of peace before he even stated them, thereby giving the impression that they were of token value only. He added to that impression with his almost nonchalant remark towards the end of the report that "I have no doubt that peace could be supported by other reasons than these," which seems to cry out for the addition of the words "but do not ask me to provide them."[45]

In the main body of the report, Talon set out the case for making immediate war, basing his position on the following arguments.

1. The enemy was the Mohawk nation, not the entire Iroquois Confederacy.
2. The Mohawks were a barbarous, untrustworthy, and intractable people, and the only way to ensure peace was to defeat them on the field of battle.
3. The Mohawks were the allies of the English and were, therefore, fighting England's battles as much as they were their own.
4. Unless deterred, the English colonies to the south could combine to defeat the French.
5. The defeat of the Mohawks would open up the way for invading New York.
6. In the event of an invasion of New York, the Dutch settlers there would support the French in retaliation for their recent defeat by the English.
7. The troops and supplies needed to inflict such a defeat on the Mohawks, and to invade New York afterwards, were ready at hand.
8. Such a famous victory would add much glory to the king's reputation.
9. The time was propitious for such an enterprise because *(a)* the Mohawks would be off their guard with the peace talks actually in progress; *(b)* if it were left until spring or later, the chances of success would be diminished since supplies might be less available owing to shipping delays and losses; and *(c)* in spring the English might be less vulnerable, having received reinforcements during the intervening months (the port of New York was open for shipping year round).[46]

Tracy must have concurred with all those arguments, for he made no marginal comments, which cannot be said of those favouring the opposite point of view. For every one of them he wrote a rebuttal, a task, however, that could not have made any great demand on his analytic powers. Unlike his case for making war, Talon's reasons for a peaceful settlement lacked both conviction and logic. They consisted of six flimsy and disjointed arguments based mostly on conjecture, and, judging by his comments, Tracy found no appeal in them.

1. Because the English might already be attacking French ships in the St Lawrence, committing troops to attacking the Mohawks and New York would leave Canada defenceless. Tracy's rebuttal: An attack on Canada was unlikely since the English had neither the ships nor the artillery to besiege Quebec in the winter.
2. The harvest would deplete the number of Canadian volunteers available. Tracy's rebuttal: War had to take precedence over domestic needs, such as harvesting.
3. The Algonkins could not be relied upon since the Saurel expedition when they had been denied custody of the Flemish Bastard's party. Tracy's rebuttal: If need be, the Algonkins could easily be induced to join the expedition by means of gifts and direct orders.
4. The Mohawks seemed to be sincerely seeking peace; so why make war on them? Tracy's rebuttal: They should not be trusted. It would be far better to make war on them than to make an unreliable peace.
5. So far as is known, the English have not committed any hostile acts; so why make war on them? Tracy's rebuttal (which seems to have no connection with the point raised by Talon): The Dutch will join the French side once they have been made aware of the injustices they have suffered at the hands of the English.
6. Such an expedition would deplete the garrisons in the several forts and thus inhibit the movement of supplies. Tracy's rebuttal: A successful operation would mean that the forts needed fewer armaments and men. Even if one was captured, it could be readily retaken in the spring.[47]

Talon submitted the report to Tracy at the beginning of September, about a week before the Flemish Bastard walked out of the peace talks in Quebec. Whether he got some hint of what was afoot is impossible to say with any certainty, but it is not improbable that he could have done so from one or other of the notables with whom he associated during his stay in Quebec. That state of affairs caused Marie de l'Incarnation some unease, which she did not entirely hide when she wrote to one of the sisters in France: "The Flemish Bastard, who is a famous Iroquois, is treated at Monsieur the Intendant's table like a great lord; to honour him, Monsieur de Tracy gave him a fine suit of clothing for his use."[48]

Even if the Bastard had received some prior information, it would have made little difference. The secret could not have been kept for much longer because by that time the final preparations for war were well in hand and becoming increasingly obvious with every day that passed. The soldiers, and many of the young men in the settlements, were leaving the routine of their daily duties and work in the fields and the forests to turn their attention to getting ready for war. Care of the harvest and of preparing for winter was left to wives, children, and to the few older persons in the communities, freeing the menfolk to go and fight what their church told them was a veritable crusade against "the enemies of God."[49]

CHAPTER FIVE

Tracy's Splendid Victory Denied

Compared with Courcelle's catastrophic winter campaign, the one Tracy led against the Mohawks the following autumn enjoyed a modicum of success. It did reach its primary objective, the Mohawk villages, without mishap; it did destroy them; and it did return to Canada relatively unscathed. Where it failed was that it did not inflict a military defeat on the enemy and it did not go on to invade New York afterwards.

Those failures have often been overlooked, not only by recent commentators, but also by those of the day, if the views expressed by one of them are at all representative of contemporary public opinion. "Monsieur de Tracy," that account began, "returned then from this campaign with his triumphant army. The Indians who accompanied him speak of his valour, and of how he subdued the fury of the Iroquois."[1]

Such views helped give rise to the misconception that the last campaign of the Carignan-Salières Regiment in North America was an unqualified success, crowned by a splendid victory. In reality that so-called victory amounted only to a stand-off in which the opposing forces never confronted each other and nothing more deadly than a barrage of insults and a few futile, long-range shots ever passed between them.

For the Mohawks, however, the lack of direct confrontation could possibly have been seen as something of a victory, for they did avoid becoming embroiled in a pitched battle in the European style, a type of conflict they knew they were unlikely to win. The price they had to pay, however, was high. They lost their homes, as well as their stocks of food, and with winter not far off their immediate future looked bleak. The destruction of their villages was probably the most important outcome of the venture so far as the French were concerned, for it gave them a few years of relative peace in which they were able first to consolidate their foothold along the north shore of the St Lawrence and then to start expanding outwards.

The several components of the expedition began leaving their bases, in Montreal, Trois-Rivières, Quebec, and the forts, around the middle of September for a rendezvous at Fort Sainte-Anne on the twenty-eighth. The force was made up of about six hundred soldiers drawn from the twenty-four companies in the country, along with a similar number of Canadian volunteers and roughly a hundred Indians, who, as usual, in addition to serving as guides were expected to supplement the rations by hunting for game along the way. It was an army of about thirteen hundred men, all told, that set out to do battle with an enemy who, it was estimated, could put no more than three to four hundred warriors into the field against it.[2]

In Quebec the departure was the occasion for a great display of military might. Hoping to demonstrate what lay in store for those foolhardy enough to incur the displeasure of France, Tracy paraded the local contingent in full marching order past the heavily guarded Flemish Bastard, which gave rise to an affecting little scene between the Mohawk chief and the aging soldier setting out on what would be his last campaign. Marie de l'Incarnation described it in a letter to her son, and judging by the detail she was able to provide, she must have witnessed it herself:

When the army was drawn up ready to depart, Monsieur de Tracy had it pass before him and said to him, "Now that we are going to your country, what do you say?"

Tears fell from the Flemish Bastard's eyes at seeing such fine troops in such good array.

He replied, nevertheless "Onontio –" (that is to say "great chief") – "I clearly see that we are lost, but our destruction will cost you dear. Our nation will be no more, but I warn you that many of your fine young men will remain behind, for ours will fight to the end. I beg you only to save my wife and children, who are in such and such a place."

Monsieur de Tracy promised to do so if they could be found and to bring his wife and all his family to him.[3]

With the parade ended, the troops formed up by companies with the volunteers and the Indians to their rear, and, to the beat of the drums and the shrill of the fifes, they marched down the hill to the river to board canoes and shallops for the passage to the Richelieu River. From there they would continue from fort to fort until they reached Fort Sainte-Anne, the designated gathering place, before advancing on the Mohawk country.[4]

Four contemporary accounts of the campaign were consulted for this work. By far the most comprehensive is the one contained in Mère Marie de l'Incarnation's letter to her son on 12 November 1666. It is certainly not a first-hand description of the events, although it does have an air of immediacy. The reason for that is not hard to find: Mère Marie provides it herself when she reveals that her informant was Alexandre de Chaumont, Tracy's aide-de-camp, who accompanied him on the expedition. Given that none of the other principal figures involved in the adventure committed their recollections to paper, her letter, therefore, constitutes the nearest thing to an authorized version of the events.[5]

The second most complete account of the campaign is to be found in the *Jesuit Relation* for 1665–66. It is less detailed than Mère Marie's, most likely the result of editing by the Jesuits. It might be a first-hand account written by Fathers Albanel and Raffeix, both of whom travelled with the expedition, but they probably reported their stories to a third party, someone like Father Louis Mercier or Father Ragueneau, who stripped them down to their essentials when they were rewritten for inclusion in the *Relation*. The resulting digest retains enough detail to enable a reader to see that both accounts agree in the major events so that each more or less corroborates the other.[6]

A third account, one that is known to be first hand, is that in *A History of Montreal, 1640–1672*, by the Sulpician secular priest, François Dollier de Casson. He had just arrived from France six days before he left with Tracy's party from Quebec, and his presence on the expedition is confirmed by the *Jesuit Relation* for 1665–66, although the writer, or the original printer, misspelled his name as Cosson. Notwithstanding his having witnessed all the events, however, Dollier's account ignores the major occurrences and dwells on some of the discomforts, miseries, and mishaps suffered by himself and others present with him. For that reason it remains a useful document, since it supplements the two longer accounts, which sometimes provided few details of the travails along the way.[7]

The fourth account of Tracy's expedition is contained in the *Annales de l'Hôtel-Dieu de Québec, 1636–1716*. It is quite superficial and contributes nothing new to the story itself. Its importance lies only in its description of the exploits of Tracy and his troops as constituting a glorious victory, which is probably an accurate reflection of what many settlers felt at the time. Unfortunately, although history has showed that such an interpretation is quite erroneous, it has, nevertheless, managed to survive the passing of the years as part of the lore surrounding not only the Marquis de Tracy, but also the Carignan-Salières Regiment.[8]

To return to Fort Sainte-Anne, the late arrival of some of the troops brought about a delay and, perhaps, even an alteration in Tracy's plans. It is unclear whether he originally intended dispatching his army to the Mohawk villages in three parties, but that was what he ended up doing as a result of Courcelle's inability to contain his impatience to "gain the scene of action" until the entire force had been assembled. The outcome was that the governor moved off at the head of four hundred men several days before the main party. Tracy did not leave with that group until 3 October and was followed, four days later, by a rear guard under the joint command of Captains Jacques de Chambly and Alexandre Berthier.[9]

It may seem surprising that the Marquis de Salières was not put in charge of one of the three columns, despite his rank and seniority.[10] His age may have been the reason, but that explanation is unlikely, for Tracy himself was not much younger, being sixty-three years old at the time. More likely he had not been passed over, as it might at first appear, but Tracy, whose health was not good,[11] wanted to have a senior officer at his side as a deputy to relieve him of much of the burden of overall command, and thereby free himself to devote most of his time to the strategic and tactical aspects of the campaign. That explanation would account for the fact that there is no evidence that Salières complained about the assignment, as he surely would have had he felt unjustly treated, for in effect the move elevated him to the general's second-in-command.

As for the perennial thorn in the colonel's side, the impetuous Courcelle, he left Fort Sainte-Anne at the end of September and must have been well on his way down Lake Champlain before the rest of the army was ready to leave.[12]

None of the contemporary accounts explicitly give the route the expedition took to the Mohawk villages, but the two major ones do give a number of clues. A map contained in the *Jesuit Relations* shows what can only be taken to be two trails leading to them, one from the southern end of Lake Saint-Sacrement and the other from that of Lake Champlain. The shorter one, the one leading from Lake Saint-Sacrement, could well be the trail normally used by those travelling between the Mohawk villages and Canada via the Lake Champlain – Richelieu River corridor. The other could be an alternative route, or even the one followed by Courcelle on his ill-fated winter march. Sad to say, owing to its lack of topographical details, the map yields little more information, but one or two further clues provide a few more details.[13]

The *Jesuit Relations* add that Tracy found "there were many large lakes and rivers to cross." Assuming that he took the shorter of the routes, they can reasonably be taken to include Lakes Champlain and Saint-Sacrement and the Hudson River. The likeliest location for any more could be the southeastern part of the Adirondacks.[14]

Marie de l'Incarnation's description of the journey is a little more specific. She states that it was "necessary to ford several rivers and make long journeys by paths that are no wider than a plank and full of stumps, roots, and very dangerous hollows."[15] That account coincides very much with the Jesuits' and the map, and it also implies that there was a discernible trail of some kind. She then goes on to say that the men had to travel "a good distance through mountains and valleys and then to cross a large lake in skiffs that they built. After that they were on dry land till they reached the Iroquois,"[16] which appears to strengthen the case for the route passing through the Adirondack country. If it did, the presumption would have to be that it followed river valleys whenever possible. The only one that leads in the right direction, beyond the Hudson, is the Sacandaga, which leads towards the southwest until it reaches the area that today is occupied by the Great Sacandaga Lake, whereupon it veers north. The Great Sacandaga Lake, however, is a man-made reservoir of recent construction, but old maps reveal that it covers what was formerly referred to as the Sacandaga Swamp, a kind of catchment basin, or sump, into which a great many streams running off the Adirondacks drained to emerge ultimately as the eastern portion of the Sacandaga River, which flows into the Hudson.

The appearance of the swamp would have varied greatly from season to season. In summer it would have included a considerable amount of dry ground over much of which an army could have passed with ease. But when the spring run-off and the autumnal rains began, the streams carried a much greater spate of water into the swamp, swelling what had been lazy rivulets and still pools until they overflowed and merged so that, before long, the entire area would have been transformed into a large, shallow lake. In mid-October, when Tracy's men passed that way, the process would have started and would account for their having to "cross a large lake in skiffs." On the return trip, about a week later and after considerably more rain, things had changed and that same lake had become "so swollen it was impossible to cross it, even with machines," which, considering the nature and location of the swamp, along with the normal weather pattern at that time of year, was entirely predictable.[17]

The evidence therefore indicates that from Fort Sainte-Anne the troops would have gone southwards down Lake Champlain, by canoe, to somewhere near the site of the future Fort Ticonderoga; then, by portage, to the northern end of Lake Saint-Sacrement and, again by water, to its southern end. There the canoes would have been left, and the troops would have set out on foot in a generally southwesterly direction over the intervening watershed and into the upper Hudson Valley. They would have forded the Hudson, proceeded to its confluence with the Sacandaga, and followed that river to where it emerged from its namesake of a swamp. Keeping towards the southwest, taking as direct a route as possible through the swamp, they would have continued in that general direction until they reached the southern rim of the Adirondacks. There they would have descended into the Mohawk Valley, crossed that river, and followed its southern bank to their destination of the Mohawk villages (see figure 1). The four villages, each probably associated with a particular clan, were situated on the south side of the Mohawk River between Canajoharie and Schoharie creeks. Although their names are unknown, the most westerly was possibly called Tionnontogen.[18]

Tracy's hope was that the march could retain as much of an element of surprise as possible. To achieve that end he had three options. First, he could try to make a stealthy approach march to the Mohawk villages and hope that his army got close enough before its presence was detected; second, he could proceed with all possible haste, making no effort to avoid detection, and hope that he reached his goal before the Mohawks could prepare any effective countermeasures; or third, he could settle for a compromise, which would have him try to get to his destination quickly but without making his progress known with drum beating and other unnecessary noise.

In the end, the size of his army, the length of the march, and the lateness of the season led him to choose the third alternative.[19] It would have been unrealistic for him to think that thirteen hundred men could travel completely undetected for approximately two hundred and fifty kilometres, through territory where a vigilant and mobile enemy could roam at will. Also, with winter only a few weeks away, he would not have wanted to risk repeating Courcelle's fiasco, which could have become a real possibility if he had spent an excessive amount of time on the trail trying to keep his movements secret.

Despite its obvious merits, the compromise solution did have one

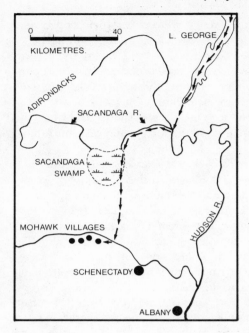

Figure 1. The probable route of Tracy's march to the Mohawk villages, 1666. Arrows indicate line of march.

major drawback. Since haste was an essential feature, the army would have to travel as lightly as possible, which meant limiting provisions and supplies to no more than what the men could carry on their backs without unduly restricting their mobility. From the highest to the lowest, civilian and soldier, officer and enlisted man, no one was exempt from carrying his share of the load, which included the particularly weighty burden of two small cannons, plus a supply of ammunition, that were deemed necessary to destroy any Mohawk defence works.[20]

Autumnal rains and winds began to plague the flotilla from the moment that it paddled out from Fort Sainte-Anne. While adding to the discomforts of the men, they had a more ominous effect as the surface of the lake was whipped into a torment of waves that not only threatened to capsize the fleet of canoes, but hindered its progress too. Conditions were not much better ashore. There creeks and rivers swollen into rampaging torrents meant that soldiers often had to be carried across on the backs of Indians, or of particularly burly comrades, but even that was not without its perils, as Tracy himself found out. While he was crossing such a raging river, the Swiss soldier who was carrying his considerable bulk stumbled and lost his footing, dumping his noble burden into the flood. Fortunately a young Huron grabbed the general before the current could carry him away.[21]

It was all too apparent that the French were experiencing problems. They were not accustomed to that sort of a march, through that sort of country. One volunteer was attacked and bitten by a bear, while Dollier de Casson discovered, to his discomfort, that "a scoundrel of a shoemaker had left him barefoot through a villainous pair of boots that had no longer any soles to them, which was most unpleasant in that country on account of the sharp stones in the water and on the banks."[22] Many other such instances must have gone unreported.

As the expedition got nearer to the Mohawk villages, the men began to become apprehensive and turned to their priests for solace. Dollier de Casson, like the rest of the clergy on the expedition, Fathers Albanel and Raffeix and the regimental chaplain, Jean-Baptiste Dubois d'Esgriseilles, found himself in great demand, not always at the most opportune time. He complained that "what exhausted him a great deal was the hearing of confessions at night and other spiritual labours which he had to perform whilst others slept." Even so, worse problems soon had to be faced.[23]

As the relative comfort of Fort Sainte-Anne receded, it became apparent that the supply of biscuit, which had been severely limited by the need to travel lightly, was going to be insufficient for the entire journey. Furthermore, to compound that shortage, the Indians' hunting prowess proved to be less productive than had been anticipated. The army was still some distance from the Mohawk villages when the consequences of reduced rations began to loom very large as men began to weaken for want of adequate food. Fortunately a bumper crop of wild chestnuts that year fed the men during the latter part of their outward march.[24]

The weather continued to be wretched, and fierce winds scattered leaves from the gaudy autumn forest in the way of the advancing column as it squelched over the last of the Adirondack foothills and into the Mohawk Valley. For some days the troops no longer attempted to hide their approach, ever since a Mohawk scouting party had skirmished briefly with some of the Algonkins accompanying the troops and quickly disengaged itself to hurry back whence it had come with word of the approaching French army. If Tracy still had any illusions of surprising the enemy after that incident, they would have been shattered as soon as he penetrated into the Mohawk Valley, where he was greeted by hoots of derision from lookouts posted on the surrounding hilltops. They fired off a few scattered shots, but the range was too great for anyone's life to have been endangered. All they did was to convince Tracy that the only hope he had left of retaining an advantage of surprise was to deny the enemy time to prepare a defence. Therefore the pace of his advance had to be accelerated to its utmost. On 15 October he ordered an overnight march, and in full view, with drums beating, he set off up the valley to his goal. Had he but known, his effort was wasted.[25]

The following dawn his army reached the first Mohawk village and found it deserted.[26] The trail-weary army must have marvelled at the sight. It was no encampment of primitive savages but a veritable fortress with sophisticated defences – a triple palisade at least six metres high with bastions at each of its corners. Within the fortifications were the longhouses, as many as twenty, elaborately ornamented with carvings and each one capable of housing eight or more, extended families. At one end each had a storeroom stocked with food, mostly maize and beans, in quantities such as had rarely, if ever, been seen in Canada, for although the Mohawks relied on hunting for their meat, they did have a well-developed horticulture, which provided much of their basic nutritional needs. One estimate was that the total amount of food Tracy found stored in all four Mohawk villages would have fed the entire population along the St Lawrence for at least two years. Even water was stored in casks, most likely for fire fighting should the villages be attacked. To the famished French invaders the food was like manna from heaven after days of subsisting on wild chestnuts.[27]

The second village, similar in plan to the first, lay fifteen kilometres farther west and Tracy hastened to it, hoping to find the missing Mohawks there, but it too was deserted. While the general, who had heard of only two villages, was debating his next move, an Algonkin woman follower approached Courcelle, whose advance party had rejoined the main force somewhere along the way, and told him that she had been a captive of the Mohawks several years earlier and recalled that there were two more some distance farther west. She grabbed a musket from a soldier with one hand, and the governor's arm with the other, and then, calling him to follow her, she pulled him towards the forest. Courcelle gave the order to follow, and off they all went, the woman, Courcelle, and a sizeable number of soldiers, civilians, and Indians. The woman's memory proved correct, and very soon afterwards the governor took possession of a third, and also deserted, village. In the hope of still finding the Mohawks, late in the day though it was but at the insistence of the Algonkin woman, they pressed on to the fourth, and the largest, of the villages. Unlike the other three, it was not completely abandoned. After a careful reconnaissance, the governor found four Mohawks: two old women, an old man, and a child. Other, more gruesome things were found too; near the ashes of what had been a large fire were the half-burned and mutilated bodies of some Indian captives, still lying where they had died, but of their torturers there was not a sign.[28]

The perplexing thing about the occupation of the four villages, and it must have crossed both Tracy's and Courcelle's minds when they entered them, particularly the fourth, was that at no time did the Mohawks make the slightest attempt to impede or attack the French invaders. A few derisive catcalls from the safety of high ground was the only expression of opposition they encountered. Tracy's army was allowed to do as it pleased, even when it totally destroyed the villages. Almost the entire Mohawk population had not only left their homes, but apparently had done so in great haste, leaving most of their belongings and provisions intact, all their water barrels filled, and the mutilated bodies of some of their prisoners unburied.[29]

There is no verifiable explanation for such an action, although three aspects are self-evident – the first that the Mohawks had no intention of facing the French invaders; the second that they could not have had much time in which to reach that decision; and the third that the decision must have been near unanimous, all factions within the nation agreeing whether they were pro- or anti-French. Anything beyond that is open to question. Nevertheless, it seems reasonable to suspect that the abandonment resulted in part from the fact that the Mohawk community was divided among four villages, which made it indefensible against such a large attacking force. With its villages separated from one another by as much as fifteen kilometres, it must have appeared impossible to prevent the French from taking them, one by one. Another factor to consider is that the Mohawks could not have reasonably looked to outside help at such short notice, for the time between their getting news of the invasion and the arrival of the French at the first village could not have been more than a week. As well, it is unlikely that the English at Albany had either the manpower or the desire to become involved in such a conflict, just as it was equally unlikely that any of the four western Iroquois nations would have been willing to come to the aid of the easternmost confederate. Everything seems to point to the conclusion that the Mohawks saw themselves as having just one simple choice: either surviving to fight another day, when the odds might be more favourable, or facing the humiliation of what looked like certain defeat. They chose the former.

Ironically, had they but known, the Mohawks could conceivably have successfully contested the invasion of their lands, for the French position was potentially more precarious than their own. The invaders were out of food, they were far from their bases, the weather was bad and, with winter in the offing, likely to get worse. Under those adverse circumstances, they would have been extremely vulnerable to sustained guerilla attacks. As it was, the Mohawks did what seemed best in the light of what they knew at the time. By abandoning their villages to Tracy, they ensured their survival as a force to be reckoned with and left him only a hollow victory to boast of when he returned to Canada.

Their empty conquest, however, did not prevent the French from taking formal possession, in the name of Louis xiv, of the four villages and their contents, as well as any crops still standing in the outlying fields. That duty fell to an officer of the Carignan-Salières Regiment, Captain Jean-Baptiste Dubois, the commanding officer of the La Colonelle Company, rather than to Tracy or Courcelle. Their responsibilities were essentially military, whereas civil and legal matters came under the jurisdiction of the intendant. As Talon's personal representative on the expedition, Dubois was therefore called upon to officially take over the villages.[30]

On the morning of 17 October, the entire invasion force was drawn up in review order before the westernmost village, and Dubois proclaimed all forts and settlements, their contents, and those of the adjacent lands to be the property of the French Crown. A cross and a marker post bearing the royal arms of France were erected near the main entrance. With that done, the cry "Vive le Roi" resounded, and then the ceremony ended with the intoning of the Te Deum and the solemn ritual of the Mass as an act of thanksgiving for the success of the enterprise, even though its prime objective, defeating the Mohawks, had eluded it.[31]

Significantly the formal take-over did not lay claim to any Mohawk lands. Annexation had not been part of the French plan, which had been to administer a blow to the Mohawks that would bring them to the peace table at the same time that it deterred them from harrying the rear of any incursion into New York. If territory was to be acquired, Louis xiv had let it be known that he was far more interested in the English colonies than he was in any Indian lands. In the context of mid-seventeenth-century America, the tribal lands of all five members of the Iroquois Confederacy were seen by France more as a potential sphere of influence than as territory to be taken and held.[32]

While Tracy's occupation of the villages might have been sufficient to bring the Mohawks under that influence, for a while at least, it had not impaired their military strength. The Mohawk force was undiminished and remained enough of a threat to place the question of an invasion of New York in considerable doubt.

Whereas the initial reason for sending the Carignan-Salières Regiment to Canada had been simply to secure the colony from Iroquois attacks, its presence there allowed Louis, after the outbreak of war with England, to combine the objective of attacking New York. By the time Tracy set out for the Mohawk Valley, both had become inextricably tied up with each other. The failure to neutralize the Mohawks by means of a crushing military defeat, therefore, jeopardized the proposed march into New York.

Being denied the opportunity to humble the Mohawks on the battlefield, Tracy could, however, diminish their ability to make war by depriving them of their bases and reserves of food. Consequently Dubois commandeered all the food, tools, and utensils that the French could carry, and Tracy ordered the complete destruction of the settlements.[33]

Sacking villages was no novelty to those veterans of the Carignan-Salières Regiment who had seen active service in Europe. They set about the task with a certain gusto and expertise, looting anything of value before the wooden structures were put to the torch. The sight of their homes and possessions in flames was too much for the two old women who had been found there. They broke away from their captors and threw themselves into the blaze, preferring a fiery death to ending their days in an alien society. Of the old man who had been taken prisoner with them, nothing more is known, but the child, on Tracy's orders, was taken back to Quebec.[34]

If the army was to push on to Albany and the Hudson Valley, it somehow had to engage the Mohawks in battle. Tracy first had to find them, and he had no idea where to start looking. It was possible that they had withdrawn to the northwest and found shelter in the villages of the Oneidas, but there was no way of knowing for sure. The prospect of sending thirteen hundred men there on perhaps a futile search, was not pleasant considering that the weather was deteriorating. The incessant rain, which raised the spectre of a repetition of Courcelle's unfortunate experiences, finally dissuaded Tracy from trying to find the Mohawks. Even though it meant an end to any thoughts of a march into New York, he reluctantly gave the order to turn around and begin the long trek back to the St Lawrence.[35]

On the return march, the three other Mohawk villages were dealt with in the same manner as the one they had come from so that all that remained were piles of smouldering ashes.[36]

The journey to their bases promised to be far from easy; ahead lay rain-sodden forests, flooding rivers, and brimming lakes. On one occasion it was only the chance discovery of some hidden Mohawk canoes that permitted the crossing of a flood-filled lake, which would have delayed their progress considerably had they been compelled to skirt its perimeter.[37] It was most likely a part of the Sacandaga Swamp swollen beyond recognition by the rains. Nevertheless, the expedition finally reached Lake Saint-Sacrement without any serious mishaps. At Lake Champlain, however, strong winds whipped the lake into such a fury of waves that they capsized two canoes. Their eight occupants drowned in the icy waters to become the only fatalities of the entire expedition.[38]

The rest of the return trip was accomplished without further losses, and, in the first week of November, the troops were back in their bases. On 5 November the flotilla of canoes carrying the Quebec contingent paddled into shore to disembark Tracy, Courcelle, and all those stationed there.[39] In the general climate of thanksgiving and rejoicing that greeted them, no one seemed to care that instead of humbling a recalcitrant enemy on the field of battle, they had only destroyed his villages and his stores. His military potential was unscathed, a fact which, combined with the inclement weather, had been sufficient to deter the general from embarking on an incursion into New York. To counter any thoughts along those lines, however, someone, Tracy, perhaps, but more likely Courcelle, let it be known that what the expedition had accomplished was more damaging to the Mohawks' ability to make war than an actual defeat in battle would have been. That rationalization must have been widely accepted, for it seemed to elicit extravagant talk of a "triumphant army" and of "the rout of the enemies,"[40] and even the Jesuits made use of it in their *Relations*.

As a result, those familiar with these Barbarians' mode of life have not a doubt that almost as many will die of hunger as would have perished by the weapons of our soldiers, had they dared await the latter's approach; and that all who remain will be forced by fear to accept such conditions of peace, and observe such a demeanour, as would have been secured from them with greater difficulties by more sanguinary victories.[41]

It was not a valid argument, though, for it implied that any deaths that might have resulted from starvation would have been restricted to the braves, whereas they would have been distributed throughout the entire nation. In any case, time has proved the contention to have no basis in fact, for there is no evidence that the privations suffered by the Mohawks as a result of Tracy's destruction of their villages had any major effect on their numbers. They seemed to have overcome their difficulties remarkably quickly, and at no great cost in lives, but by that time the warping of the story had served its purpose by transforming the event into a famous victory in the public's mind.[42]

As for the failure to proceed into New York, since that part of the plan never was public knowledge, there was no need to try to account for it. Had anyone raised the question, Tracy would have had a ready answer, since the king had given him two options on dealing with the English – he could either secure their neutrality or invade New York. Governor Nicolls, albeit unwittingly, had provided the answer in the conciliatory tone of his letter on 20 August 1666 in which he indicated his desire to maintain friendly relations with France and to remain neutral in her dealings with the Mohawks.[43]

Two things about the expedition stand out. First, whatever it did or did not accomplish, it gave rise to an air of optimism among Canadians. Suddenly they felt they could finally look forward to many years of peace and prosperity, so much so that one went so far as to write, "Hence there is no doubt entertained that soon we shall see well peopled cities in place of these great forests, and Jesus Christ worshipped throughout all these vast domains."[44] A somewhat visionary view, perhaps, but, nevertheless, it was an expression of the sentiment that prevailed along the St Lawrence in the weeks after Tracy's return from the Mohawk Valley. Second, even though the expedition did not achieve all its military objectives, it was a considerable feat in its own right. Those who made up the small army covered a distance of up to eleven hundred kilometres, at an average speed of twenty kilometres a day, and negotiated rough waters, rougher terrain, and raging rivers unspanned by bridges. All was done under conditions of constantly atrocious weather and, at times, inadequate food. Yet, despite those difficulties, very few of the men became casualties, and most returned to their bases in good order, good health, and good spirits, which was no ordinary accomplishment.

CHAPTER SIX

The Colony at Peace

Although celebrations, both religious and secular, highlighted the heady days after Tracy's return, behind the pomp and the euphoria serious business was afoot. Tracy was initiating courses of action designed to exploit the advantage he felt his military venture had given him; at the same time, the intendant was occupied with two matters of his own. The first was getting letters off to France to acquaint Colbert with the recent events, to outline his plans for the development of a colony at peace, and to suggest means whereby the king might still manage to acquire New York; while the second was gathering in all the flintlocks from the soldiers in Quebec and Trois-Rivières for shipment back to France.[1]

Colbert de Terron had requested the weapons be returned to the Naval Arsenal at La Rochelle, a move that was unquestionably dictated by the outbreak of war in Europe. When the king put his infantrymen in the field against his enemies, he wanted as many as possible to be armed with the best weapon available, the flintlock. It was the most advanced small arm of its day, far more reliable than the older matchlock, and capable of a much more rapid rate of fire. In 1666, however, they were far from plentiful, and those in the hands of the Carignan-Salières Regiment probably represented a sizeable proportion of the total Louis could call on.

Even so, Talon did not feel prepared to return all the weapons in the regiment's possession so soon after the destruction of the Mohawk villages. He left those in the garrisons of the Richelieu Valley forts and of Montreal because, in his own mind, there were doubts about whether peace was assured.[2] Although Tracy had administered a serious blow to the Mohawks, there had been no indication if, or when, they would come to Quebec seeking peace and, until they did, there was no way of knowing their intentions.

While Talon was attending to the guns, Tracy was providing the citizens with visible evidence of France's domination over the Iroquois and also impressing upon the hostages he held of the urgency of having their chiefs make a durable peace. The hostages were arraigned before him and harangued on the utter destruction he had inflicted on the Mohawk villages, a misfortune, he pointed out, that had been brought on by the insolent behaviour of some of their brother warriors in daring to attack the king's Canadian subjects and to prey on their fur trade. Then, almost as if he was the instrument of divine wrath, he had one of the Mohawk prisoners, most likely the Indian brought to Quebec by Guillaume de Couture, seized and summarily hanged. The idea was to intimidate the other hostages sufficiently to speed some of them back to their peoples, there to impress upon their chiefs and elders the absolute necessity of coming to Quebec forthwith to make their peace with France.[3]

It had the desired effect. Within a matter of days, not only was the Flemish Bastard on his way to locate his dispersed people, but similar missions were also en route to the other four Iroquois nations, sped on their ways by Tracy's parting words that the fate of the remaining hostages hinged very much on the dispatch with which they accomplished their errands.[4]

Tracy's actions helped to assure Canadians that the days when the Iroquois could attack them and their trade at will were finally over, but it had little effect on the soldiers, especially those who had recently returned from the Mohawk Valley. They knew that no decisive defeat had been inflicted on the Mohawks and that, wherever they were, they were probably anxious to avenge the destruction of their homes. The troops also knew that the ability of the Indians to do so was unimpaired, and if they were so disposed, they could still mount attacks on the Canadian settlements, as well as on the outlying forts in the Richelieu Valley. The result was that the soldiers displayed a marked reluctance towards venturing far from their fortified bases unless they were in a large party, which created certain damaging effects. One of the worst was to be seen in the plight of the garrison at Fort Sainte-Anne during the months immediately after the victory celebrations along the St Lawrence.

Unlike Fort Richelieu and Fort Saint-Louis, both of which were developing successful farming operations which made them less dependent on outside sources for their basic food needs, Fort Sainte-Anne had not had time to begin any such activities because of its recent construction. It therefore had to rely entirely on supplies from the St Lawrence settlements, a problem further aggravated by the reputed difficulty of gaining access to the fort. Owing to its location on an island at the northern end of Lake Champlain, the fort could be provisioned with ease, it was thought, only during May and June. For that reason, and for the reason that it would no longer be required after the defeat and subjugation of the Mohawks, Tracy had planned to abandon it in the fall of 1666. Having failed in that mission, however, he had been compelled to keep it in use beyond that time. Unfortunately that decision was made very late in the year by which time, because of the uncertainty of access to the fort and a reluctance among the troops to expose themselves to the danger of Mohawk attacks, only a minimum amount of food had been supplied. The result was that all the garrison had to see it through the winter was a little bacon, some spoiled flour, which was of little use for baking, and a keg of brandy, which was undrinkable because it had been adulterated with sea water in an attempt by the crew of the ship that had brought it from France to conceal the fact that they had consumed part of its contents.[5]

The effect of such a restricted diet soon became apparent when scurvy broke out among the sixty-man garrison, made up of men from the Lamotte Company of the Carignan-Salières Regiment and the La Durantaye Company of the Chambellé Regiment, one of the four that had accompanied Tracy from the Antilles. As the disease took hold, the garrison commander, Captain Lamotte de Saint-Paul, began pressing for relief in the form of additional supplies and a priest to help in ministering to the sick and the dying.[6]

The Sulpician Dollier de Casson was the priest delegated to go to the fort. He had just returned from the recent expedition, but getting to his new assignment was not easy either. Since the troops considered peace far from assured, especially at an outlying post like Fort Sainte-Anne, they were consequently somewhat reticent about providing an escort to accompany Dollier to his ministry. As he put it himself: "The officers here did not feel called upon to risk their soldiers and impose such a labour on them without definite orders from him [Tracy]."[7]

In the end Dollier had to make his own arrangements and attached himself to two soldiers who were returning to Fort Saint-Louis. Once there, he again ran into the reluctance of the troops to venture far from the safety of their stockades. Only persistent entreaties by the Sulpician persuaded the garrison commander to provide him with an escort to Fort Sainte-Anne, thereby enabling him to continue on his way in the company of an ensign and ten enlisted men.[8]

On reaching his destination, Dollier found things in a truly desperate state. Two men had already died from scurvy, and forty more – two-thirds of the garrison – were stricken with the disease in conditions that were far from conducive to any sort of a recovery, let alone a speedy one.[9]

At the best of times conditions at the fort were far from congenial. It had been built to meet a passing need, and neither time nor materials had been wasted on making it comfortable. The living quarters were nothing but a number of rudely constructed huts, divided into cell-like rooms with ceilings so low that a man could not stand erect. There were few windows so that a perpetual gloom pervaded the cramped quarters, and if they happened to house any of the victims of scurvy, the stench of their filth was heavy on the air, adding an odour of putrefaction to that of the eye-stinging smoke wavering upwards from open fires in the centres of the dirt floors.[10]

The priest had to implore Captain Lamotte to send a party of men to Montreal to seek the wholesome food that offered the only hope for recovery he knew of, and even then it was some time before the captain agreed and gave the order. Most likely he was deterred by the fear that reducing the number of able-bodied men in the fort would weaken its defences and make it vulnerable to any attack by a Mohawk war party. The only thing that could have persuaded him to take the risk would have been the prospect of an even grimmer alternative – the almost certain death of the entire garrison from scurvy.[11]

As it turned out, the mission was a success and the fort survived the temporary depletion of its garrison. When the party returned from Montreal, it brought several sleighs loaded with food, all consigned to the priest, who, despite pressure from Captain Lamotte to hand the victuals over to him, took personal charge of them and saw to it that they were fairly distributed to the sick. Happily, although he could not possibly have had any idea of either the cause of the disease or its cure, Dollier did resort to an appropriate regimen by dosing his patients with prunes and purslane, thereby giving them the vitamin C they needed to recover. Patients showing signs of recovery were loaded on the sleighs and taken to Montreal where their treatment could be continued under more favourable conditions in the hospital. Those who were untreatable were made as comfortable as possible to live out their last days at Fort Sainte-Anne.[12]

Thus a regular system of convoys, to and from the fort and Montreal, came into being. Every northward trip of the sleigh carried invalids to the hospital, and every return trip brought back those restored to health together with as much food as there was room for. The result was that the disease was gradually brought under control, thanks in no small part to the nursing care provided by

Dollier and the lone surgeon in the fort, a Montrealer by the name of Forestier.

The few healthy soldiers in the fort did not help much to ease the priest's burden. They mostly shunned the company of their less fortunate comrades, particularly those in the last stages of the illness, for fear of becoming infected. The sick therefore had to resort to odd stratagems in the hope of inducing their brothers-in-arms to spend some time with them as they lay dying. One such trick was to write out, or to have written out, elaborate wills, as if they had vast fortunes to dispose of, in which they bequeathed huge sums of money to any who were willing to sit by them in their last days. Such were the pathetic attempts of forlorn men, men who seldom owned more than the clothes on their backs, to save themselves from dying ungrieved and lonely deaths in a foreign place.[13]

Successful as the evacuation program proved to be, it was not without its cost. As a result of the depletion of his manpower that it entailed, Captain Lamotte was forced to consider allocating the defence of one of the fort's bastions to Dollier and his patients, although how effective they would have been is questionable. When a party of Mohawks was sighted approaching the fort, however, it looked as if they would have to take to the ramparts. Luckily it turned out to be a delegation, led by the Flemish Bastard, making its way to Quebec to sue for peace. The garrison commander took no chances, though. He ordered that large fires be lit within each hut so that their glow and smoke might give the impression that a great many men were on hand to defend the fort.[14]

That incident took place early in April 1667, for, by the twentieth of the month, the Flemish Bastard had reached Quebec, although not before having yet another brush with soldiers. His party came face to face along the trail with a column of men returning from Montreal to Fort Sainte-Anne, none of whom knew anything about peace delegations. Their immediate response, therefore, was to prepare to greet the Mohawks with a volley of musketry and to examine their credentials afterwards, when they were less likely to retaliate. The troops had already loaded their weapons and were about to fire when the Flemish Bastard, with the help of a Frenchman in his party, managed to convince the soldiers that his intentions were peaceful. It was a narrow escape, and it emphasizes the fact that, even five months after the end of Tracy's autumn campaign, the men of the Carignan-Salières Regiment were still very suspicious of any Mohawks with whom they came into contact.[15]

The Flemish Bastard was by no means the first to come to Quebec to sue for peace. He had been preceded by delegates representing the three western nations, the Cayugas, the Senecas, and the Onondagas, who quickly resumed the talks cut short when Tracy set off to make war on the Mohawks the previous September. They had assented to a comprehensive treaty as early as 13 December 1666, their haste in coming to terms no doubt reflecting their anxiety to be done with the matter so that they could concentrate all their attention on the nagging question of the Susquehannock War. The Mohawks and the Oneidas were, therefore, the last on the scene, and even when they did reach Quebec in April, Tracy refused to talk with either of them until all the prisoners they held were with them. They therefore had to return whence they had come so that they were not in a position to begin meaningful negotiations until they reached Quebec for the second time, three months later. As a result, it was 10 July 1667 before they finally made peace with the French.[16]

Not many details of the negotiations leading up to that agreement are known, except that the talks were brief, lasting only five days. The treaty itself, more or less imposed as it was by the French, had been conceived as providing the foundation for enduring peace in Canada. Like those agreed to earlier by the western nations, with which it was essentially identical, it would have been drafted by Jean Talon.[17]

The treaty provided for immediate peace between both parties and their allies too. Furthermore, to create an environment in which it could survive, it recognized that all the Indian nations in the region, whether they were Iroquois, Huron, or Algonkin, and whether they lived north or south of Lake Ontario, had specific territories they regarded as their traditional hunting and trading grounds, which should be respected as being inviolable. That condition was not only considered to be in the best interests of the Indians, but of the French too, for it contributed to the political stability of the entire Lake Ontario – St Lawrence basin, a necessary condition if the fur trade was to prosper.[18]

The main thrust of the treaty was towards facilitating that prosperity, which was to be accomplished at the expense of the Anglo-Dutch in New York, by way of establishing resident French traders in each Iroquois village. There they would be in a position to direct all the fur traffic that had formerly made its way to Schenectady or Albany towards the St Lawrence. At the same time, Jesuit missionaries were to be placed in the same villages, albeit at the request of the Indians themselves who saw the Black Robes as being the pro-Iroquois faction in Canada. Because their presence was valued, that of the French traders could only be enhanced by the association of the two in the minds of the Mohawk chiefs. It was a perception, nevertheless, that in reality did not have a lot of substance, for the Jesuits and the French fur traders were often at odds over the manner in which business should be transacted.[19]

The presence of both the Jesuits and the fur traders in the Iroquois villages, however, had the combined effect of expanding French influence as far south as the Mohawk Valley, and it was, therefore, of considerable diplomatic import. For that reason the peace treaties with all the Iroquois nations set out to protect their presence by instituting a system of hostages. Each nation in the Confederacy was required to send two of its leading families to live in each of the three main settlements along the St Lawrence. They would be provided with land and seeds and would have the same hunting rights as their French neighbours did. Ostensibly the goal was to improve relations and communications between their people and the French, but it is unlikely that anyone in Canada had any illusions about why they were really there.[20]

It was generally considered that the Mohawks were the most likely of the nations to break their treaty. To discourage that in a manner that made the fewest demands on military manpower, and called for the least expenditure of royal funds, Tracy proposed that the Richelieu Valley defences be rationalized by basing them on just two forts. Fort Richelieu and Fort Saint-Louis, which were fast becoming self-sufficient, would have their garrisons augmented, in the main by encouraging civilian settlement in their vicinity. In other words, they would become the nuclei for two new communities, which would in time grow to compare with the older ones along the north shore of the St Lawrence. Their expansion would ultimately permit the abandonment of the three most southerly forts – Sainte-Thérèse, the newly built Saint-Jean, and Sainte-Anne, which had proved so difficult to supply and sustain.[21]

By the summer of 1667, therefore, with the ratification of the several peace treaties and the plan for the reorganization of the Richelieu Valley defences drafted, the Carignan-Salières Regiment had technically completed its mission in Canada. Had the minister of war's original plan still applied, it would have been ready for repatriation to France. To have suddenly deprived the colony of its means of defending itself, before any alternative was in place, however, would have left it open to an early resumption of Iroquois raids. Consequently, until such time as other means of protecting Canada could be devised, the regiment remained where it was.[22]

CHAPTER SEVEN

Misdeeds, Marriages, and a Miracle

It has been said that the period immediately after the destruction of the Mohawk villages was one of increased rivalry between the civilian and military authorities in Canada. In practice, however, the two were indistinguishable.

The administration of royal government in the colony was very much in the hands of the Conseil Souverain, which at that time was dominated by Tracy, Courcelle, and Talon, two of whom were professional soldiers, and the third, a man whose responsibilities included many which were purely military. The so-called rivalry, which came to a head in 1667 over the question of who could and who could not discipline an officer in the Carignan-Salières Regiment, was nothing more than another manifestation of Salières's disgruntlement over Le Tellier's army reforms, which had deprived him of some of the autonomy he felt was rightfully his. Beyond that outburst, most of such rivalry – friction is a better word for it – occurred at a lower level in and around the three main settlements. Overcrowding there meant that soldiers and civilians were forced to live in closer contact with each other than either would have preferred, which led to certain unfortunate consequences. It is impossible to reconstruct a complete picture of all the incidents, for most of those that resulted in soldiers being charged with acts of misconduct were dealt with by their own officers, who left no records of their proceedings. The only offences that seemed to bring them into the regular judicial system were those that had been taken directly to a member of the Conseil Souverain, and they were very few in number.[1]

Even so, relations between the troops and the general public deteriorated in this period, but at a social level rather than a governmental one. The situation was aggravated by a feeling among the settlers that the soldiers had done the job they came to do and that there was no longer the need for so many of them to be stationed in places such as Quebec, Trois-Rivières, and Montreal. They were seen as occupying a privileged position in the settlements, which at times assured them of preferential treatment, such as that which led Marie de l'Incarnation to complain, "I have just refused seven Algonkin seminarians to my great regret because we lack food, the officers have taken it all away for the King's troops, who were short. Never since we have been in Canada have we refused a single seminarian, despite our poverty, and the necessity of refusing these has caused me a very sensible mortification."[2]

That sort of reaction from a person as compassionate and understanding as Mère Marie was an indication of the changed attitude towards the military. Those who might have closed their eyes to acts of high-handedness, disorderliness, and lawlessness in the anxious days of 1665 were inclined to be less tolerant in the more settled times after 1666.

Despite that increased vigilance, however, the evidence shows that most of the soldiers continued to lead inconspicuous lives, which were generally in harmony with those of their civilian neighbours. Their days were largely occupied with the routine of their duties, which often called for them to work beside the habitants in the fields, or clearing land for new settlements, and if they did err, it was usually during their off-duty activities. Even then they did not resort to roaming the streets in marauding bands and striking terror into civilian hearts.[3] More often than not, the trouble they got into was the result of intemperance and, in that, they were no different from most of the menfolk in the settlements along the St Lawrence where the incidence of drunkenness had grown out of hand, bringing with it the problems of sporadic violence and even of death. By the summer of 1667 the Conseil Souverain had become so concerned about the point it had reached in Trois-Rivières that it sent one of its members to investigate. It was an escalating problem that Talon proposed controlling by restricting the amount of liquor imported into the colony and then inducing the people to drink the beer produced from local ingredients in his new brewery instead.[4]

The soldiers' involvement in the problem was mostly that of allowing themselves to wallow in drunkenness, but, for a few, all officers of the regiment, there was a more pecuniary side to it. They knowingly added to the problem by increasing the amount of brandy and wine available on the market for any who had the price of it in his pocket.

The extent of their involvement can be no more than guessed at on the basis of the only figures available, those for the amount of potables brought into the country for the use of the soldiers during their first year in Canada. It consisted of 174 *barriques* of brandy (about 17,500 litres) and 53 1/2 *tonneaux* of wine (about 8,500 litres). Of those amounts, 76 *barriques* of brandy (about 7,600 litres) and 33 1/2 *tonneaux* of wine (about 5,300 litres) were earmarked for the use of forty-nine officers. The remaining twenty-five, or so, of them purchased unspecified quantities of "clothing, munitions, liquor and other refreshments" worth 13,523 *livres* before they left La Rochelle. It was all bought at royal expense and shipped to Canada with the rest of the regiment's supplies (see appendix A).[5] The many kegs of brandy and wine imported for the officers could not all have been consumed by them unless they had been in a perpetual state of inebriation. A considerable surplus remained, which they were happy to offer for sale in what can only be called a seller's market.

Captain François de Tapie de Monteil's notebook reveals something of the traffic in its mention of a few of his transactions. He wrote of having "delivered to Mademoiselle Amiot a *barrique* of brandy coming to forty *écus* in Canadian money ... to Monsieur Quoribon a *barrique* of wine coming to [amount illegible] of which he has given me six in Canadian money ... Also to Madame Lapointe, my laundress, a *barrique* of wine coming to seventy *livres* in Canadian money."[6] Those three sales alone would have brought him in about 380 *livres* in Canadian money, a considerable sum that was the equivalent of five months' income at a captain's rate of pay.[7] Traffic in spirits was not illegal at the time. Proceeds from it were considered part of an officer's remuneration, and so long as he adhered to the prices laid down by the intendant, all was well. Tapie de Monteil seems to have complied with them, although the same cannot be said of some of his colleagues.

Captain Lamotte, the builder of Fort Sainte-Anne, was one who contravened the regulations. He was arraigned before the Conseil Souverain, accused of having overcharged Antoine Pepin and his wife for two *barriques* of wine and Nicolas de Choisy, a cadet in the Maximy Company, for two *livres* of Brazilian tobacco. He had charged a hundred *livres* for each *barrique* of wine, although the prescribed rate was eighty, and six *livres* for the tobacco, when it should have cost only four. The Conseil found him guilty on both counts and fined him twenty-two *livres,* which he was ordered to donate to the poor in the Hôtel-Dieu in Quebec. It was a lenient enough penalty, for Lamotte had overcharged his customers forty-two *livres,* but yet he was fined only twenty-two.[8] It seems to imply that the Conseil was not without sympathy for him, and if that were so, it could only have been due to the fact that two of the most influential voices on it, Tracy and Courcelle, were both army officers, who would have appreciated the captain's predicament in having to rely on his business acumen to convert a recognized part of his income into cash.

A portion of a soldier's remuneration was often paid in kind, and so long as he could pass muster, the goods with which the Crown provided him as an emolument were his to dispose of as he saw fit.[9] He could sell them to whoever was willing to pay the price, no matter whether they were military men or civilians. As Captain Tapie de Monteil recorded in his notebook: "I received from Monsieur Beguan the sum of eleven hundred, or so, *livres*, this for my remuneration for the year 1666, he having sold the goods that His Majesty had ordered me to distribute." The kind of trade in which he and his fellow officers participated was not just limited to liquor and tobacco either. There was also a brisk demand for all manner of other goods, and he wrote of selling a musket to a Mademoiselle La Tellerie for twenty *livres* in Canadian money, two gross of knives to the Sieur Péré at twenty-eight *livres* a gross in French money, and two dozen more to a lady by the name of Madame Le Moisne de Champlain.[10]

The officers would all have certainly found their business ventures pleasantly profitable, but some wanted to become wealthy, and as quickly as possible, since those who intended returning to France knew that their days in Canada were limited. They took the profits they had made and used them as working capital to engage in the fur trade, purchasing furs from any one, French or Indian, who was prepared to sell them. Officers who engaged in the fur trade tended to use cash, for the French were forbidden to use alcoholic beverages as a medium of exchange when trading with the Indians. Those who contravened that regulation were subject to severe penalties ranging from heavy fines to floggings.[11]

Unlike the officers, the enlisted men had no such way to enrich themselves. They had nothing much they could sell, and their pay was insufficient for them to be able to afford any excesses beyond getting drunk, possibly on liquor that their own officers had sold. Two soldiers from the Saurel Company at Fort Richelieu, however, hit upon a scheme that offered great rewards for a very small outlay: if they did not have sufficient money to do what they wanted, they would, literally, make some. This enterprising pair were Paul Beaugendre, also known as Desrochers or Desroches, and Pierre de Gencenay, sometimes referred to as Jean Sendil.[12]

Either the counterfeit coins they turned out were very inferior copies of the real thing and were soon detected or else someone informed on them, for on 27 May 1667 Jean Talon issued a warrant for their arrest. They were taken into custody and held at Quebec while their alleged crimes were investigated. No details of the findings of the investigation remain, but they were both convicted and the Conseil Souverain imposed what it considered appropriate sentences. Desrochers must have been adjudged to have been the main culprit, for he was condemned to hang. His accomplice, however, got off far more lightly. Jean Sendil was sentenced to three years in the galleys, but on appeal even that was moderated when the Conseil agreed to let him spend the time in the Jesuit House in Quebec instead. No such clemency was in store for the unfortunate Desrochers though, and he paid for his crimes at the end of a rope on 28 June 1667.[13]

Hanging was to be the fate as well of two other soldiers the following August, and their story reveals a facet of seventeenth-century Canadian life that is often overlooked. It seems that whenever her husband was away, a certain lady in Quebec eked out a livelihood by catering to the sexual needs of soldiers in the garrison. Two of them, one known as Langevin and the other as Champagne, had become tired of the routine of military life and decided to desert. Being something of a womanizer, however, Champagne felt that the joys of freedom would be more joyful yet if he had his own personal doxy along. On the day the pair walked out on their military obligations, the lady was plying her trade as usual and had already serviced three men before the two seized her and hurried her off to the boat in which they intended sailing away to freedom. They did not get far, and were soon caught and taken back to Quebec to be charged, not only with desertion, but also with abduction for the purpose of rape, a crime that carried the death penalty.[14]

It was while they were in their cell awaiting their date with the hangman that the Jesuit Father Claude Dablon came to hear their confessions. Addressing Langevin, he said, "My friend, you and this Champagne are dead men for having raped that woman, but if you want to say to M. de Tracy that there was no impropriety between you, and then reiterate it before the Conseil, I will save your life." To that the soldier, although nonplussed at the proposal, replied, "I will say all that you want, but the truth is that this woman, not having her husband around, prostitutes herself to all the soldiers, however, since you want me to lie, I will do so in order to save myself." Somewhat shocked at what he had heard, the Jesuit rebuked the man saying, "Ah wretch! You will die if you speak like that to the Conseil. You must say that nothing untoward happened on the boat." Despite lingering questions about why he should have to lie to save his neck, Langevin agreed to do as his confessor had advised and apparently so did Champagne. They thus implied that the lady had joined them willingly and so had revealed herself to be a woman of immoral character. So far as can be ascertained, the Jesuit was as good as his word, for there is no record of either having been executed.[15]

The story has a humorous side to it in the ineptness and naivety of the two deserters. But perhaps more importantly it reveals that as early as 1667 prostitution did exist in Canada, and if one woman was engaged in it, there could well have been others.

Evidence to that effect is revealed in the case of Madame Marguerite Leboeuf, who was found guilty of keeping what, in another age, would be called a common bawdy house. Unable to pay the imposed fine, she asked the Conseil for three years' grace, supporting her request with a hard-luck story of how her husband, a cooper by trade, had impoverished the family with his business ventures. He had, she said, gone to France with a considerable quantity of goods – possibly furs – in the hope of selling them at a profit. Unfortunately he had suffered many misfortunes and setbacks during his travels and had returned penniless. Therefore, Madame Leboeuf explained, she found herself in such reduced circumstances that she was unable to pay the fine.[16]

Although she seemed to accept the Conseil's verdict, she never admitted that she had been running a brothel in order to survive. Assuming that she had, it is likely that her clientele would have included some of the soldiers in town and that her charges would not have been beyond their slender means, just as those of the lady who Messrs Langevin and Champagne allegedly kidnapped were not.

Perhaps the most startling aspect of both cases is that they involved married women whose husbands were, or had been, away, which seems to suggest that they were brought to prostitution by force of adverse circumstances. When their spouses left without providing for their support, they turned to the only saleable commodity they owned, their bodies, and for those they found a ready market among the unattached men, including the troops, who abounded in Canada.

Nevertheless, no more than a few of the twelve hundred soldiers could have found willing sex partners among the adult French women in Canada. Their numbers were small, nearly all were married and were the mothers of numerous children, and also, for the most part, they were faithful wives. There were, however, other communities in which different mores prevailed. These were the Indian encampments, often found just outside the major settlements and forts.

Among France's Indian allies – the Algonkins, the Montagnais, the
Ottawas, and the remnants of the Hurons – who were the main
occupants of those encampments, the custom was that unmarried
women enjoyed unrestrained sexual freedom.[17] As one French observer described it:

A young Woman, say they, is Master of her own Body, and by her Natural
Right of Liberty is free to do what she pleases ...
   The Young Women drink the juice of certain Roots, which prevents their
Conception, or kills the Fruit of the Womb ...
   The Savage Women like the French better than their own Countreymen,
by reason that the former are more prodigal of their Vigour, and mind a
Woman's Business more closely.[18]

Since the accuracy of that seventeenth-century observation is borne
out by more recent anthropological and historical research, it would
seem reasonable to suspect that at least some of the soldiers in the
Carignan-Salières Regiment made their way to those encampments
when looking for sexual favours.[19]

   Claude Maugrain, known as Le Picart, may have been one, but
in the spring of 1667 he met Ester Coindreau and immediately became
so enamoured of her that he sought out her company whenever
possible, not caring that she was a married woman with a home and
husband. On one occasion, when he was trying to entice her into bed
by telling her of prodigious feats of love-making, he boasted that he
had once deflowered a young girl. As if to dispel any of her doubts,
he proceeded to demonstrate how he had accomplished it by baring
himself and preparing to repeat the act with Coindreau's young daughter
by a previous marriage, Marianne de La Porte, who was about five
years old at the time. The mother and some others present pulled him
away and saved the child from coming to any physical harm, but that
did not prevent the matter from coming to the attention of the Conseil
Souverain. In the ensuing investigation, it was found that Maugrain had
indeed acted as the mother had alleged, and the Conseil sentenced
him to receive twelve strokes of the birch from the hands of the public
executioner. The sentence was to be meted out in the prison where
it was to be witnessed by the complainant, two other women of her
choosing, and her daughter.[20]

   Although Maugrain was a thoroughly unsavoury character, his
reputation for depravity might be surpassed by that of Major
Balthazard de La Flotte de La Fredière, should the whole story of
that officer's misdeeds ever become known. The reluctance to accord
the major recognition as the most despicable man in the regiment,

a dishonour that he probably richly deserves, comes not from any sympathy for him, but from the fact that so little is known of his sins beyond that he was unceremoniously sent back to France for them.[21] Of the evidence that could reveal them, very little has survived: one entry in the Registre du baillage du district de Montréal dated 10 September 1667, and accounts in volume 3 of the Abbé E.-M. Faillon's *Histoire de la colonie française en Canada*.[22] Admittedly the *Histoire* is a secondary work with a strong religious bias, but its historical content is based almost exclusively on documentary evidence, which gives it an air of authority. Its authenticity is reinforced, inasmuch as Major de La Fredière is concerned, by the direct connection between an entry in the register regarding an altercation between La Fredière and André Demers and Faillon's account of the subsequent events resulting from it. The Abbé's work is rich with details of that sort, the result of a meticulous and exhaustive examination of documents in Montreal, Paris, and London.[23] His accounts in the *Histoire* of one or two of the major's nefarious, extra-military doings will, therefore, be accepted as accurate in the absence of any evidence to suggest otherwise.

Physically La Fredière was a repulsive man, who viewed the world through just one eye, having lost the other earlier in his career. But, despite his unprepossessing appearance, he was considered a competent officer by his superiors. He was wounded in the skirmish outside Schenectady during Courcelle's ill-fated winter campaign; he was entrusted with building additional fortifications in the Richelieu Valley shortly before Tracy's march to the Mohawk villages; and he was appointed military governor of Montreal in the spring of 1666, a post he held until his disgrace the following year. Most of his wrongdoings took place while he was military governor.[24]

One of them was the illegal practice of trading brandy to the Indians in exchange for furs, despite the severe penalties prescribed by the Conseil Souverain for those caught doing it. The extent of his involvement can only be surmised, but since in the one year for which figures are known, at least three times as much liquor was brought into Canada on his behalf as on that of any other officer, it was probably quite considerable (see appendix A).[25] He engaged openly in the trade, for, as military governor of the settlement, he was, for all intents and purposes, safe from prosecution. Moreover, people were inclined to keep their knowledge of his activities to themselves because not only were they intimidated by his vile temper, but they were also afraid of suffering the effects of his vicious and vindictive disposition if they crossed him. André Demers found out what they were, much to his misfortune.[26]

Demers, a habitant at Montreal, took exception to the major's practice of hunting on his land, particularly when his crops were maturing. On one occasion he became so incensed about it that he took his gun, confronted the officer, and ordered him off his farm. News of the incident spread quickly through the small settlement, and when La Fredière learned that it had become known, he became only more intent on revenge. He very soon had Demers arrested on a trumped-up charge and, as military governor, sentenced him to a form of punishment known as the wooden horse, which was usually reserved for delinquent soldiers.[27]

The wooden horse was a device very much like a large, high trestle, which the victim straddled, his feet clear of the ground and with weights attached to them. The unfortunate Demers spent more than an hour on the thing with an incredible weight of 120 *livres* (over 54 kilograms) suspended from his feet. He survived the ordeal, but it is not known whether he suffered any injuries as a result.[28]

In addition to his viciousness and cruelty, La Fredière was also a lecher, ever on the lookout for an attractive woman to seduce, such as Anne Thomas, the young wife of carpenter Claude Jodoin. The trouble was that the husband was most attentive and rarely left her alone so that the major was unable to find an opportunity to have his way with her. Once again he abused his authority as military governor and arranged for Jodoin to be given a corvée, which would take him away from the settlement for nineteen days. He then proceeded to try to bed the wife. The records do not show whether he succeeded, but when the incident became known, the community was so outraged that it took a stand against the major's excesses in the only effective way open to it, that of bringing his misdeeds to the attention of the Conseil Souverain.[29]

The opportunity to do so came in the spring of 1667 when Jean Talon visited Montreal on business connected with his duties as intendant. One after another the habitants complained to him of the injustices, inhumanities, and illegalities inflicted on the settlement during La Fredière's term as military governor. His downfall had begun.[30]

Believing all he had heard, Talon returned to Quebec and reported it to Tracy and Courcelle, who reacted similarly. What to do about it was another matter. All three knew the extent of their authority in such a case, for two were long-serving soldiers and the third was the chief legal officer in the colony, and, as a result, they found themselves in a dilemma. They knew what ought to be done, but they lacked the authority to do it. Owing to the technicality that the regiment was considered of foreign origin, authority belonged to the Marquis de Salières. It could be argued that he had shown his indifference towards that prerogative by not raising any objections when Captain Lamotte had been brought before the Conseil charged with profiteering, and when the soldier Maugrain had been convicted by it for gross indecency, but the case of Major de La Fredière was different. He was the colonel's nephew, besides being a senior officer in his regiment, and there was no knowing the marquis's reaction if the matter was dealt with in open court. Most likely for that reason the affair was kept away from the formality of a hearing before the Conseil and was handled at an informal level where persuasion, rather than coercion, was used in the hope of getting the major to leave Canada voluntarily. With that in mind, he was counselled to take leave under terms which would require him to return to France to enjoy it.[31]

La Fredière was not to be removed that easily, though. He had no intention of returning to France if he could possibly avoid it, for he was attempting to make a fortune and wanted to complete the job. He knew all about the peculiarities of the chain of command as it applied to the Carignan-Salières Regiment, just as he knew all about his uncle – the colonel's hot temper and jealousy of his prerogatives; it is not surprising, therefore, that he referred his problem to his relative. Thus the affair was immediately transformed into a jurisdictional dispute in which the point at issue ceased to be the major's conduct in Montreal and became the one of who could, and who could not, discipline members of the regiment.

For the Marquis de Salières it was a heaven-sent opportunity to reopen the argument that had flared up soon after his arrival in Canada when he had questioned Tracy's authority in sending Captain Pierre de Saurel and his company to rebuild Fort Richelieu. The only difference was that, on this latest occasion, his argument had much more validity than his earlier one had.

The colonel stated his position in a letter to Talon on 1 September 1667, in which the question of his nephew's guilt or innocence was never broached. He devoted himself entirely to disputing Tracy's authority to send one of his officers back to France without having been ordered to do so by the king. The argument rested on the fact that the Carignan-Salières Regiment was of foreign origin, and, as such, jurisdiction in all criminal matters, with the exception of cases of high treason, rape, sacrilege, and arson, rested with its colonel.[32]

He was, of course, technically correct, for the regiment still retained its Savoyard connection, even if it was little more than a nominal one. In practical terms, though, after the army reorganization following the Peace of the Pyrenees, the entire cost of its upkeep had been assumed by the French Crown so that for most purposes it was just as much an element of Louis xiv's army as was, say, the Lorraine Regiment.[33]

There is no doubt that Tracy, Courcelle, and Talon did act arbitrarily, and did exceed their authority, but they had had little choice. If they had ignored the major's conduct, and had allowed him to remain at his post, they would not only have had the church clamouring for his removal, but the people of Montreal too. Moreover, La Fredière was the military governor of the settlement, and if he had been permitted to continue abusing his authority, it would have reflected very unfavourably on the three most important members of the Conseil Souverain, the body to which people looked for a fair application of the law. As well, it would have left the impression that the members used a double standard when meting out justice in the colony.

Of the options open to them, none was devoid of unfortunate side effects, and the one chosen appeared to have the least disagreeable consequences. Even though it triggered a jurisdictional squabble, and even though legitimacy was on the side of the colonel, Tracy did have his way in the end and La Fredière was compelled to leave Canada on the last ship of the year.[34] As for the more legitimate alternatives the general had open to him, they suffered from the uncertainty of having the desired outcome. If he had turned the case over to the colonel, there was no way of knowing his verdict in advance; if he had referred it to the king, a year would have elapsed before an answer was received in Quebec and by that time the major might have committed further crimes.

With La Fredière's departure, Talon wrote to the Marquis de Louvois explaining the reasons for the action taken and promising to provide greater detail the following year when he returned to France.[35] But, so far as is known, that was the end of the matter. As usually happens in confrontations between two levels of military command, the higher one seems to have prevailed.

Meanwhile, on a less sordid and contentious plane, the first marriages took place in 1667 between members of the regiment and daughters of families living in the colony. That development was displeasing to neither the king nor to his officials in Canada, such as Jean Talon, who saw it as having nothing but beneficial effects.

This country is starting to take on a whole new aspect from the one it had before the king's troops arrived. It is apparent in many places, and the decision of several officers to remain here will make no small contribution to its establishment. Already Messieurs de Contrecoeur and Dugué, both captains, and Lieutenant de Varennes are committed to it, even to the extent of marrying local girls, and four or five other subalterns are about to surrender to their mistresses. You will notice by the first reports from the king that this is agreeable to His Majesty, not only because of their remaining here, but moreso by their inviting their soldiers to do likewise. I reckon that a number of them will not be returning to France.[36]

The development was also seen as deterring any parents of the brides from returning to France to spend their latter years, thereby retaining their expertise in Canada. As the intendant put it in a letter to Colbert:

For all the good reasons that you pointed out in your dispatch, one cannot strive too hard to ensure that any girls of marriageable age are, in fact, married since, by becoming so, they will bind their parents to remaining in the land where they intend to establish their permanent homes; ... And you will not be displeased to know that among those who are tied to this country by the sacrament [of marriage] are three of the four shipwrights who Monsieur de Terron sent here.[37]

It is hard to say exactly what might have turned hard-bitten soldiers' thoughts towards matrimony, but it is unlikely that romantic love was as important a factor as it is today, particularly in cases like those of Captain de Contrecoeur and Lieutenant de Varennes.

Antoine Pécaudy de Contrecoeur, was seventy-one years old when he married the fifteen-year-old Barbe Denys, and so it seems hardly likely that the searing heat of youthful desire had brought them together. Despite the disparity in their ages, though, they seemed to get along well enough, and the young wife was not intimidated by her elderly spouse over whom she managed to have a moderating effect. As the Marquis de Tracy remarked, "The good fellow Contrecoeur is slightly inclined towards wine, but being married for a while to a girl of the country, and building a considerably sized house, I reckon he can be left in Canada."[38]

It was not the captain's first taste of matrimony, and if his previous marriage is any indication, his interest in entering into it for a second time, at his age, may have been motivated by the promise of material benefits accruing from a dowry and the possibility of receiving a seigneurial grant. Long after he married for the second time, he and members of his family in France were still disputing with his first wife's relatives over the disposition of her estate, which gives rise to that suspicion that he probably kept his eyes on the main chance when choosing a wife. The notion is further strengthened by the fact that Barbe Deny's father, Simon, was well-to-do by Canadian standards and was also a member of the Conseil Souverain, a position of considerable influence in the colony. On the other side, the captain may have proved attractive as a son-in-law to the Denys family because of his nobility, which could have been seen as adding lustre to their status in Canada. Nevertheless, the captain must have been a lusty old soul, and life with a young wife must have agreed with him, for the pair produced three children during the twenty years they spent together before he died, in 1688, at the venerable age of ninety-one.[39]

Practical considerations were also what brought Lieutenant René Gaultier de Varennes to wed Marie Boucher. She was the oldest daughter of Pierre Boucher, the governor of Trois-Rivières, and, at the time of her marriage to the thirty-three-year-old officer, she was only twelve. In her case, though, her father played the decisive part in bringing the marriage about. Boucher wanted to be rid of his duties as the governor so that he could devote more time to the fur trade from his seigneury at Iles Percées (Boucherville). The presence in Trois-Rivières, as part of the garrison, of several officers of the Carignan-Salières Regiment offered the opportunity if he could persuade one of them to marry his daughter. Varennes was attracted by the idea, but, even so, he struck a hard enough bargain with Boucher for the price of his cooperation. He required his prospective father-in-law to recommend personally his candidacy for the governorship to Courcelle and, in addition, to provide him and his wife with bed and board for the first six months of their life in Trois-Rivières. On that basis the wedding took place on 26 September 1667, and in due course Varennes was confirmed as the governor of the settlement.[40]

The third officer who Talon reported as having married was Michel-Sidrac Dugué de Boisbriand. He had all the makings of a fur trader about him, and although he received a seigneurial grant in 1672, he spent the greater part of his life either trading with Indians or fighting them whenever the need arose. Little is known about his married life, except that his wife was named Marie Moyen and that she was probably quite young, for she bore him nine children before she died in 1687.[41]

A fourth officer also married in 1667, but after the ship carrying Talon's dispatches had left for France. He was Roch Thoery de L'Ormeau who on 5 December married Marie-Rogère Lepage at Quebec. Once again, not much is known about the couple beyond the fact that she was a widow and that both she and her husband were thirty-six years old at the time of their marriage.[42]

At least four ordinary soldiers are also known to have married in 1667, and all to teenaged wives. It is likely that they were not local girls but were from the ranks of those sent from France by Colbert for the specific purpose of marrying in Canada. One of the men, Gabriel Gibaud, married the fourteen-year-old Suzanne Durand; a second, Bernard Delpesche, the sixteen-year-old Marguerite Jourdain; a third, Antoine Adhémar, the seventeen-year-old Geneviève Sageot:; and a fourth, André Poutre, wedded the nineteen-year-old Jeanne Burel.[43]

Out of all the soldiers in Canada, this total of eight who solemnized marriages might seem an insignificant number. Few as they were, however, those first weddings began the process of laying the ground-work for an expansion of the seigneurial social structure within which a growing colony could be both developed and defended. In the case of the officers, they marked a step towards providing Canada with a cadre from which future seigneurs might be drawn and, in that of the other ranks, with a pool of tradesmen and quasi-professionals to supply the increased services needed as new settlements opened up. Antoine Adhémar, for instance, became a notary serving the area east of Trois-Rivières, and André Poutre became a shoemaker, first at Fort Richelieu, then in the seigneury of Sorel, and finally, after 1681, in Montreal.[44]

That these marriages were unlikely to have been idyllic love matches is not out of keeping with the custom of the time in which practicality was the overriding principle. The couple often had very little opportunity for meeting socially and privately before they were married. There were few public occasions to meet, except for the church, and social events, such as balls, were rarer still, the first ever being held in February 1667. After three or four visits to the girl in her home, suitors were expected to start talking of their intentions to her parents, often with the parish priest keeping a watchful eye on the proceedings. The marriages in which local girls were the brides, however, had none of the haste associated with those involving the so-called *filles du roi*. Arrangements for the former followed a well-established route, with no vows being made before the marriage contract had been drawn up to everyone's satisfaction and signed. What is, perhaps, a little surprising is the extreme youth of some of the girls, but even that is not as extraordinary as it might at first seem. In seventeenth-century Canada, the moment a girl reached puberty, pressure was brought to bear, both on her and on her parents, to marry; that pressure originated in the need to increase the size of the population and thus contribute towards consolidating and defending the colony.[45]

Despite the pressure to marry, soldiers, especially officers, and Canadian women did have informal liaisons. Jean Talon gives a broad hint of such relationships when he advised Louvois that "four or five other subalterns are about to surrender to their mistresses," and, in somewhat more specific terms, informed Colbert that "one lieutenant and four ensigns are discussing it [marriage] with their mistresses, and I consider them to be already more or less betrothed."[46] Some support for that interpretation is to be found in Captain Tapie de Monteil's notebook in which he bemoans the "terrible uncertainty of love," and then goes on to wonder when the lady will deliver him from his torment. Unfortunately he neglected to date the entry or name his inamorata, and so it wants for some specificity. Nevertheless, the evidence of the notebook suggests that the captain's period of service in Canada was not entirely celibate and that the relationship was not permanent, for when he returned to France in November 1668, he was still a single man.[47]

Similarly unspecific is the evidence concerning an incident at the shrine of Sainte-Anne-de-Beaupré when Jean Pradez hobbled in on his crutches one day in June 1667.[48]

Generally speaking, the Carignan-Salières Regiment is not notable for its impact on the spiritual life of Canada, notwithstanding the view expressed by some that its men were nothing less than crusaders and their mission, a holy war. They undoubtedly carried out their obligations to the church – their priests would have seen to it, but otherwise they showed few signs of any great piety. Apart from what might be called institutional acts of worship, which included Te Deums to mark great moments and the sermons and celebrations connected with the abjuration of the Huguenots in the regiment, the records show that spontaneous outbursts of religious fervour involving any appreciable number of the soldiers occurred only three times. One was on their arrival from France when they showed their thankfulness at having survived the Atlantic crossing by joining in several acts of piety and worship; another was during Tracy's march to the Mohawk villages when, apprehensive about the future, they kept the accompanying priests awake at nights listening to confessions; and the third was at Fort Sainte-Anne, at the height of the outbreak of scurvy, when its victims sought to prepare themselves for death. Other than during those instances, the attitude of most of the soldiery towards the church was one of passive obedience, with some of the men taking a far livelier interest in things of the flesh than in things of the soul. Few of them, therefore, can be described as having been ardent religionists beyond the prescribed routine of their Catholicism.

Jean Pradez was one exception. He turned to the church out of desperation, and his faith was apparently rewarded. Some time during the winter of 1666–67 he was stricken with a paralysis in one leg so that he had to use crutches. He was examined by surgeons and declared incurable. At that juncture he must have turned to the church for help. The outcome was that towards the end of June 1667 he was taken to the shrine of Sainte-Anne-de-Beaupré, about forty kilometres northeast of Quebec, and there, according to an account of the event, he was miraculously cured. He abandoned his crutches and walked away unaided.[49] A genuine cure seems to have taken place, for there are two independent reports of the so-called miracle. Whether it was real or not, Jean Pradez's cure inscribed his name, and that of the Carignan-Salières Regiment, in the lore of the shrine.

CHAPTER EIGHT

The End of the Mission

With the peace treaties between France and the Five Nations of the Iroquois Confederacy in place, the Carignan-Salières Regiment had completed its mission in America and was ready for repatriation. The imminence of that event brought to the forefront the question of the future defence of the colony, since the Mohawk potential for retaliation remained unimpaired.

Even before the regiment had left France in 1665, the question had been considered. In his letter of instructions to Jean Talon, the king had indicated:

When the expedition against the Iroquois is over, the king wishes that the said Sieur Talon invite the soldiers of the Carignan Regiment, as well as those of the four infantry companies that first went to America under the command of the Sieur de Tracy, to remain in the country by giving them a small gratuity, in the name of His Majesty, to provide them with more of the means needed to establish themselves there.[1]

In one of his last acts before he returned to France himself, Tracy therefore drew up a plan designed to integrate the men who took advantage of the offer into a force dedicated to the defence of New France after the regiment had left.[2]

Working on the assumption that about four hundred of the troops would be willing to remain in Canada, he conceived the idea of a new body, made up of nine companies, with forty men in each. Before he could go very far towards detailing the organization and deployment of the companies, however, he first had to establish the number of officers available to command them. Already Jacques de Chambly and Pierre de Saurel were at an advanced stage of converting the land around Forts Richelieu and Saint-Louis to productive agricultural use, and Captains de Contrecoeur, de Froment, de La Tour, and Petit also looked as if they were putting, or were about to put, down roots in Canada.[3] He assumed therefore that they would all be willing to continue to shoulder the responsibilities of company commanders.

Tracy needed nine captains in all if his plan was to be viable, and to provide the other three, he proposed promoting three lieutenants who had shown an interest in remaining in Canada: his own cousin, Lieutenant de Lerole; Lieutenant de Lespinay; and Lieutenant de Varennes, who had recently married Pierre Boucher's daughter. He also counted on finding the eighteen subalterns he would need among the other lieutenants and ensigns who wished to stay on in the country. If any vacancies remained after tapping that source to its limit, suitable Canadians could be appointed.[4]

What the plan provided for was the creation of a loosely knit military formation made up of nine autonomous companies located at strategic points in both Canada and Acadia, and under the overall command of the governor, but it never worked out that way. It failed mainly because Tracy misjudged the effects of allowing the soldiers the option of leaving the service, if they so desired, and becoming settlers. The option was given, he argued, because without it "there would not be a hundred soldiers in Canada."[5]

The option also rankled with those captains who intended returning to France, who saw it as leading to the disintegration of their companies.[6] Particularly the older officers, such as the Marquis de Salières, were angered even more by the fact that the inducements offered to the men to remain in Canada infringed on their authority as company commanders and were an incursion into an area in which neither the king, nor his officials, had any right to interfere. And that was not the only complaint the officers had. They saw further violence being done to their already trampled rights when Tracy limited the number of men they could protect to form a cadre around which to rebuild their companies back in France. He left them with very little room to manoeuvre when he wrote, "I think I should accord to all the captains crossing the ocean only six men of their choice from each company who shall be corporals or anspessades or appointees, with the proviso that, if there are any of them who wish to remain in this country, the captains will be obliged to leave him and to take another soldier from his company."[7]

Tracy was not in Canada when all the weaknesses of his grand plan began to show. He sailed for France on 28 August 1667 and left the task of dealing with them to Courcelle and Talon.[8]

They very soon found out that, of the officers the general had selected to take charge of his nine companies, Chambly, Froment, and La Tour, as well as Lieutenant de Lerole, had all changed their minds and intended returning to France after all. Captain Petit let it be known that he was leaving the army altogether to enter the priesthood and he subsequently enrolled in the seminary at Quebec. Nevertheless, it was not a shortage of officers that wrecked the plan because seven captains, eight lieutenants, and eleven ensigns did stay in Canada, and so it would not have been difficult to have found satisfactory replacements for those who had left (see appendix B). The reason the plan foundered was that by the end of 1668 there were only enough men left in the army in Canada to make up four twenty-five-man companies.[9] It was not that the rest had returned unexpectedly to France, as some of their officers did, but that they had taken the option of leaving the service to become settlers. Many of the ordinary soldiers had possibly enlisted for only three years. If so, their engagement would have expired sometime in 1668, depending on when they had been recruited, and it would simply have been a matter of persuading them to take their discharge in Canada rather than in France.[10]

It is possible to arrive only at approximate figures on the number of soldiers who did and did not return to France in 1668. Of the original 1,200 to 1,300 officers and men, 446 (30 officers, 12 noncommissioned officers, and 404 ordinary soldiers) are known to have settled in Canada (see appendix B), and about 100 more to have remained in the army there.[11] In addition, and assuming that about two-thirds of Tapie de Monteil's estimate of 400 deaths during Courcelle's disastrous winter campaign involved soldiers, there were about another 350 who fell victim to disease, the climate, hostilities, and various mishaps.[12] It seems likely, therefore, that as many as 900 did not return to France.

If so, it follows that roughly 350 must have been repatriated, an estimate seemingly supported by the little evidence that remains. According to the Abbé Daniel's *Histoire de la milice françoise,* the several officers, sergeants, and soldiers who disembarked at La Rochelle with the Marquis de Salières consisted of about 200 men,[13] and if Tapie de Monteil's company of the Poitou Regiment is typical, the four detached companies took about 30 men each back to France with them.[14] The total number of repatriates seems therefore to have been between 320 and 350, which ties in very closely with the estimate of the number who never left Canada. Whatever the exact figures, they did give Colbert cause to observe that "His Majesty has been very pleased to learn that most of the soldiers of the Carignan-Salières Regiment have decided to live in this country [Canada]."[15]

What was it, then, that induced over four hundred soldiers to quit the army, to turn their backs on a well-established society in France, wherein they enjoyed several privileges, to settle in a colony that was remote, was cursed with numbing winter cold, and was barely at the pioneer stage of development?

There was, undoubtedly, the attraction of getting out of the army and receiving the "small gratuity" the king had promised. For sergeants, that sum amounted to 150 *livres* or, alternatively, 100 *livres* and a year's rations. Ordinary soldiers did not fare quite so well; they had the choice between 100 *livres* and 50 *livres* plus a year's rations.[16] Generous as such grants might have seemed to soldiers who had probably never before seen so much money at one time, they were not as great as they might have appeared at first sight, especially when they were considered beside the realities of settling in Canada. Marie de l'Incarnation drew a discouraging picture of those conditions in a letter to her son. "When a family commences to make a habitation, it needs two or three years before it has enough to feed itself, not to speak of clothing, furniture, and an infinite number of little things necessary for the maintenance of a house."[17]

It was, nevertheless, the kind of life to which the king wanted to attract the soldiers, and one thing that certainly helped a few make up their minds was the recollection of their outward voyage, as well as the realization that they would have to recross the same ocean to return to France. For most men, though, their decision to remain in Canada was based on more positive reasons.

When they considered the question from an economic viewpoint, the soldiers were able to turn to the experience they had gained from having been in Canada for three years. Many had toiled in the fields alongside the habitants so that they were acquainted with the difficulties they would likely encounter if they chose to stay in the colony, a knowledge that would have deterred them. If they took a purely emotional view, however, those deterrents were largely counterbalanced by the appeal of having a piece of ground to farm and a home nearby, even if it was nothing more than a hovel. That prospect would have been especially attractive to those soldiers who had belonged to the mass of impoverished and landless people in France.[18] It needed something more, therefore, to tip the scale one way or the other, and that proved to be the fur trade – the men had learned that it provided a cushion of economic relief during bad times.

The men would also have known that, despite the almost nomadic life it entailed, the métier of the *coureur de bois* offered freedom from the restraints of an austere society, as well as economic rewards. The prospect gained even more allure since the completion of the Iroquois peace, for the main danger had been removed, and the men were able to move freely without the fear of being killed or captured along the way by a marauding war party. As well, the same motivations that had led many to join the army may have drawn them to the life of the *coureur de bois*. Both involved a spirit of adventure and the possibility of overcoming poverty.

As a result of the combined effects of the conflicting influences that determined their decision to remain in Canada, many soldiers went on to lead what can only be called double lives in the colony. For part of the year they lived as farmers near one of the forts or settlements, and for the rest, as *coureurs de bois,* ranging the forests, paddling the waterways, and emulating the ways of the Indians, who often accompanied them on their expeditions in search of furs.[19]

One side effect of that pattern of life was that the soldiers were reluctant to marry. From the available evidence it seems that the number who married immediately after leaving the army was pathetically small. It was so small, in fact, that in 1670 the intendant became concerned, since it was not in keeping with his plan for the orderly development of the colony.[20] The lure of the fur trade was difficult, if not impossible, to counter, and although it is true that few ordinary soldiers from the Carignan-Salières Regiment became major figures in it, essentially because they lacked the working capital, they often worked on behalf of those who had. In return for a share of the profits, men such as their former officers were willing to finance their operations.[21] But, even in that dependent role, they remained attracted to the life of the *coureur de bois,* which allowed them the means to work on the land for the rest of the year, in an enterprise that by 1668 had not even reached a subsistence level of productivity.[22]

The unique pattern of life the former soldiers developed was well suited to their circumstances, but it was certainly not smiled upon by officialdom. Jean Talon went to the length of referring to them as "those willful individuals (of whom on my return I found considerable numbers literally pursuing careers as bandits)." To him their way of life contradicted all he wanted the colony to become, and, as already mentioned, one of its most disturbing features was that it inhibited the former soldiers from marrying. As a result, he ordered that if any was still unmarried fifteen days after the arrival of the next ships bringing girls from France, he would be barred from all hunting and trading activities. Well-intentioned as the rule might have been, it was unenforceable so it had little effect on the marriage rate among the former soldiers.[23]

The fact that some of the girls sent over from France were unsuitable as wives may also have deterred the men from marrying. One group, which arrived in 1668, was described as consisting of "Moorish, Portuguese and French women, and some from other countries." Another, which came the following year, was said to have "some among them that were very coarse and very difficult to manage." They were plainly not the well-brought-up girls from Parisian orphanages who had formed the first groups sent to Canada. With time it is likely that all such sources had been exhausted so that suitable candidates had to be found elsewhere. The effect was that, before long, the calibre of those recruited had deteriorated to the point where they were found to be so unsuited for a life as farmwives that it was deemed necessary "to ask henceforth for only village girls that are as fitted for work as men; experience shows that those not thus reared are not fitted for this country."[24]

A deliberate attempt was also made to include more refined ladies in subsequent groups, some of whom would have been suitable mates for the unmarried officers in Canada, but it was all to little avail. Despite every effort to increase the marriage rate, whether by coercion or by persuasion, it did not markedly improve. Many of the former soldiers probably lived out their lives as bachelors, a consequence of the time, the place, and the circumstances. Nevertheless, it was not without its ill effects on the colony. First, many of the military veterans never became attached to the settlements by the ties of marriage and family.[25] The dramatic increase in Canada's population after 1668 was more the result of unions between civilian workers and girls, both recently arrived from France, than any involving former members of the Carignan-Salières Regiment. Second, with so many leaving the army and then spending part of the year away from their homes, the defences of the colony were weakened. Third, the fur trade changed so that some aspects of it became marked by an unscrupulousness and a lawlessness that were not present before.

That regrettable development is well illustrated by an incident that occurred in 1669 some time after the ice had gone from the rivers. It involved several soldiers from the Carignan-Salières Regiment, an officer, and three enlisted men.[26]

The enlisted men, who were not strangers to the ways of the *coureur de bois,* set out from Montreal on an expedition to buy furs, having previously provided themselves with a good supply of brandy, purchased with money the officer had loaned them. Near Pointe-Claire they met a lone Iroquois chief, whose canoe was filled with moose hides, which the three soldiers immediately coveted. They plied the Indian with brandy until he became so drunk that he lost consciousness. Then they tied a large rock to his neck, loaded him into their canoe, paddled some distance from shore, and threw him overboard. Returning to Montreal with the moose hides, they sold them to the officer who had backed their trip, and after deducting the amount he had advanced them, he paid the soldiers, apparently without asking any questions about the circumstances under which they had acquired them.[27]

Soon afterwards, the rock used to sink the Indian's body came untied. The corpse floated to the surface and was discovered by some of his fellow tribesmen. They recovered it, identified it, and took it to Montreal where they claimed that their chief had been murdered by Frenchmen, since they knew of no Indians having been in the vicinity at the time. An official investigation ensued, but it could find no evidence to suggest who the culprits might have been.[28]

A short while later, the officer who had bought the skins used some of them to settle a business debt, and, in that manner, they became part of the currency of the barter trade in Montreal. Subsequently they passed through other hands until finally an Iroquois from the dead chief's nation noticed one and recognized the mark on it as being that of his murdered comrade.[29]

On the strength of the new evidence, the investigation was reopened, and before long the skin was traced back to the officer and from him to the three soldiers. They happened to be away on another fur-trading expedition at the time, and so, unaware that their connection with the crime had been established, they returned to Montreal and were promptly arrested.[30]

They were tried by a court martial, found guilty, and condemned to die. The three were tied to posts and shot, much to the amazement of a great gathering of Indians, both Ottawas and Iroquois, who had been summoned to witness French justice being meted out and who considered that three deaths for one was a most generous gesture on the part of the French.[31]

The incident, which could easily have triggered a renewal of Iroquois raids had it not been dealt with severely, illustrates the degree of ferocity some of the soldiers had introduced into the fur trade and also shows the lengths to which some of the *coureurs de bois* were prepared to go to turn a profit. The only necessities of their traffic were a cargo of brandy and perhaps a few trade goods to induce Indians to part with their furs at the least possible cost to the buyer. Notwithstanding all the appearances to the contrary, though, the practice did have a little merit from the Indians' point of view. It saved them the trouble of having to travel to one of the major settlements to dispose of their furs, but, other than that advantage, they generally came off second best in the deals they made. An obvious consequence of that change in the trading pattern was that an increasing number of the pelts crossing the counters of trading posts, particularly in Montreal, were not tendered by Indians, as they had been in the past, but by the "vagabonds" of the trade, as Talon called them, the self-appointed middlemen, and often former soldiers, who had come by them cheaply and possibly illicitly.[32]

It is impossible to say how many of the former noncommissioned officers and enlisted men of the Carignan-Salières Regiment looked to that kind of business for at least a part of their livelihood. The few surviving records are pitifully short on such details. All they show is the occupation of twenty-one of those who remained in Canada. Five were surgeons, four were licensed fur traders, three were notaries, two were shoemakers, and the other seven consisted of a builder, a churchwarden, a court clerk, a general merchant, a seigneurial steward, a servant, and a woodcutter (see appendix B).

A little more is known of the officers who settled in the country. At least five engaged openly, and therefore presumably legally, in the fur trade, and four became government functionaries (see appendix B). In addition, there is a strong hint that some at least encouraged others to participate in the shadier aspects of the fur trade, as appears to have been the case with the officer who financed the expedition in which the Iroquois chief was murdered.[33]

It had been erroneously assumed by everyone concerned, from the king down through Colbert, Le Tellier, and Tracy to Jean Talon that, whatever else they did, the officers and men from the Carignan-Salières Regiment would still constitute a military presence within the general population of the colony, which would stand ready to come to its defence. It did not, however, work out that way. Not only were the ranks of the remaining companies depleted by their leaving the service, but with so many of them roaming the forests in search of furs at some times of the year, their effectiveness as informal militiamen was greatly diminished. As a result, a dangerous situation was created, particularly in the Richelieu Valley where the new settlements were most vulnerable should the Mohawks attack. It was an uneasy period, made more so by incidents such as the one in which the Iroquois chief had been murdered for moose hides, or a similar one in which six Mahicans had been murdered by three Frenchmen. Either could have led to renewed warfare, as could have a bloody quarrel that erupted between France's Indian ally, the Ottawas, and the Iroquois, but peace was preserved, allowing time for the situation to be rectified.[34]

Luckily the remedy had soon been recognized. Someone, most likely Jean Talon on his return to France in 1668 at the end of his first term as intendant, managed to convince both the king and Colbert of the need to take steps to restore the advantage the presence of the Carignan-Salières Regiment had given the French in Canada. Consequently, by 1669 when the peace in the colony looked as if it was on the verge of collapsing, a plan for regaining that advantage was ready for implementation. Its contents were made known to Courcelle in a letter written on 15 May 1669.[35]

The plan called for two steps to be taken, each designed to supplement the other in restoring the military potency of the colony. The first was to reinforce the regular troops remaining in Canada by sending "six companies, fifty men strong, with more than thirty officers, or gentlemen, to establish themselves there." The second was to augment their effectiveness by establishing a first line of defence by the use of militia companies located in each of the settlements in the colony. As it was put to the governor:

You will learn from His Majesty's letters what he wants you to do in order to keep the habitants trained in the use of arms, and in military discipline, and you must consider this to be of the utmost importance, and the one thing that will contribute most towards maintaining, augmenting, and fortifying the colony so that it will be better able to beat off the attacks that might be made upon it, and to put down with all possible force any uprisings of the Iroquois, and of the other nations if that becomes necessary.

To gain the maximum advantage from the two measures, the Iroquois nations had to be apprised of them and to be made aware of their consequences. Therefore Courcelle was advised that the decision he had taken "to appear sometimes in Montreal fits in well with His Majesty's intentions, but he wishes you to carry this idea further, that is to say, you should venture into the Iroquois country with all the force you can muster every two years, or more often if you think it opportune."[36]

More than six weeks before Colbert had written that letter, if he indeed was its author, and soon after his appointment on 7 March 1669 to the office of minister of marine,[37] he issued orders for the raising of the six companies of soldiers referred to. They were to become the first Troupes de la Marine to be sent to Canada, although the four companies already there came under the minister's jurisdiction at about the same time and were, technically at least, the first in the country.[38] To some extent the change gave official recognition to the long-standing practice that subjected all traffic to and from New France to naval supervision, but it was not without political significance too. For one thing, it marked a small victory for Colbert in the power struggle within the king's entourage between himself and the Le Telliers, father and son. More importantly, from a Canadian standpoint, it ensured that all matters relating to the colony would be dealt with by the Ministry of Marine. All troops serving there were thus placed outside the jurisdiction of the Ministry of War, which thereafter concerned itself solely with the army in Europe. It might have been seen by some as a hollow victory for Colbert, since both the king and the Le Telliers seldom displayed much interest in naval and colonial affairs beyond the extent to which they affected the course of events in continental Europe, but the view was somewhat different from the Canadian side of the Atlantic. From there, the colony had clearly benefited by gaining a single, powerful, and largely sympathetic minister to look after its interests in Paris.

To some degree the advantageous position gained was evident in Colbert's selection of veteran officers from the Carignan-Salières Regiment to command five of the six companies he raised for the defence of Canada. Berthier, Chambly, Durantaye, Grandfontaine, and Loubias were all experienced in the conditions they would encounter in the country, and they all seemed eager enough to return there. They each gave a written undertaking to raise a fifty-man company, for which the Crown agreed to give them one thousand écus to equip, pay, and provision the men.[39] They reached Quebec during the late summer of 1669, when their disembarkation occasioned one observer to note: "The King has sent captains and officers back here and has given them forts, so they may settle here and marry."[40] As had been the case with the Carignan-Salières Regiment, the additional soldiers had not just come as much-needed reinforcements, but as potential settlers too. From Colbert's position, it made good economic sense, for the greater the number of veterans settling in the colony, the stronger would become the new militia units, which would reduce the need for further reinforcements and which, in turn, would save the Crown a considerable sum of money.

By the time the six companies had disembarked at Quebec, Courcelle would have received the king's instructions, countersigned by Colbert, on establishing those militia units. Adult males in every community were to be organized into them, and officers were to be appointed to oversee their training in musketry and other military arts. In locations more than a day's travel from the centres where the monthly training sessions would normally be held, the governor was authorized to subdivide companies into two or more squadrons, each consisting of forty to fifty men. Should that sort of an arrangement become necessary, he was cautioned to ensure that the entire company received training as a single unit one or two times a year. Furthermore, he was urged to keep a watchful eye on the training and also to make certain that every militiaman had sufficient powder and shot at all times to be ready for immediate action should an emergency arise. To ensure a uniformity of practices, as well as to give the men practical experience under active service conditions, the king further stipulated that all the companies in the colony assemble once a year for joint manoeuvres, which, ideally, would take the form of a massed march into the Iroquois lands. That tactic had the added advantages of maintaining a regular surveillance over the Five Nations and, at the same time, of keeping them in awe of French arms, thus discouraging them from nourishing any thoughts of resuming their raids on Canada.[41]

With time and training, Courcelle's militia became an efficient and formidable force, its ranks considerably strengthened by the presence of those veterans of the Carignan-Salières Regiment who spent at least part of each year in their home settlements. Moreover, those who were engaged some of the time as *coureurs de bois* brought new skills in bush craft to the companies so that they became extremely skilful and effective practitioners in the kind of combat needed against an Indian foe. It became, therefore, a force adept at a form of fighting totally different from the semistylized warfare practised on European battlefields. It could take strategic advantage of the forest, the rivers, the lie of the land, and even the climate, all things that had hindered the Carignan-Salières Regiment in its attempts to discomfit the Mohawks.

Finally, it remained for the seigneurial system to promote the development of the civil administration of the expanding colony, just as the militia companies had strengthened its defences, and, thereby, add another element to the mould that would shape life in the new settlements until the Conquest, and beyond. With so many new communities springing up along the shores of the St Lawrence and, to a lesser degree, in the Richelieu Valley after the Iroquois peace treaties, the need for such a development became more urgent by the day, but, even so, it took until 1672 before anything was done. At that time forty-six new seigneuries were created, twenty-four of them being granted to former Carignan-Salières officers.[42]

It was an attempt by Colbert to restore Canada to his own vision
of it as a compact, self-sufficient, and easily defended colony, one
that was able to pump wealth into the French treasury as a result
of its surpluses. Jean Talon, from his Quebec viewpoint, though,
had seen it differently. He had soon learned that the only profitable
pursuit for the colony was the fur trade. That led him to encourage
expansion, out along the waterways and into the heart of the
continent, one of the few policies over which he and Courcelle
were in full agreement. In 1672, however, Colbert was provided with
the occasion to try to counteract that trend. For one thing an
administrative changing of the guard was imminent in which both
the intendant and the governor would be returning to France. It
was a doubly propitious occasion, though. With Louis xiv deeply
embroiled in European affairs and war being inevitable, he was
reluctant, therefore, to divert resources for the maintenance of his
American colonies. The expansion of the seigneurial system was
Colbert's chosen counteractive measure. He saw it as a means of
concentrating and holding the increasing population along the shores
of the St Lawrence, thus putting a brake on further expansion. As
well, it would bring more land under the plough, thereby adding
to the colony's self-sufficiency and reducing its dependency on the
mother country.

Some historiographical accounts infer that the entire Richelieu
Valley was carved into seigneuries that were granted to former
officers in assertions such as, "The corridor of the Richelieu, the
invasion route of the Iroquois, was peopled henceforth by seigneurs,
veterans of the Carignan-Salières regiment."[43] In reality the defence
of the Lake Champlain – Richelieu Valley corridor continued to
depend very much on Forts Richelieu and Saint-Louis. Only six of
the twenty-four seigneuries granted to officers were located anywhere
near the Richelieu River and, of them, just four were in a position
to defend effectively the approach to the St Lawrence via that
waterway (see figure 2). The other eighteen were strung out along
the St Lawrence shoreline, from Ile aux Oies, more than seventy
kilometres downstream from Quebec, to Ile Perrot, twenty kilometres
upstream from Montreal.

As they settled on their seigneuries, the former members of the
Carignan-Salières Regiment can be said to have become well dispersed and assimilated into the larger population of Canada. They
were no longer discernible as being different from a great many
other settlers.

The same sort of anonymity awaited most of the officers and men
who returned to France with the Marquis de Salières in 1668. Although

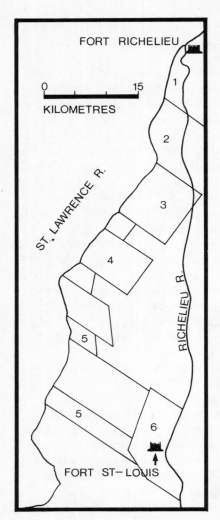

Figure 2. Seigneurial grants near the Richelieu Valley made to former officers of the regiment, 1672: *1*. Sorel seigneury; *2*. Saint-Ours seigneury; *3*. Contrecoeur seigneury; *4*. Verchères seigneury; *5*. Varennes seigneury (two parts); *6*. Chambly seigneury. The map is based on a plan drawn by Samuel Gale in 1774, which is preserved in the National Archives of Canada.

very little is known of them, some who chose to remain in the army would undoubtedly have been absorbed into the Soissons Regiment, a new sixteen-company unit that was the successor of the Carignan-Salières Regiment, while some others would have joined with their former officers to return to Canada as members of the Troupes de la Marine in 1669.[44] Still less is known of the personnel of what remained of the four detached companies. The rump of the Monteil Company of the Poitou Regiment, along with its captain, was posted to the garrison of the Château Trompette in Bordeaux, where the commanding officer was none other than the Marquis de

Tracy, who continued to serve as the governor of the fort until he died on 27 April 1670.[45]

The fate of the Marquis de Salières is better documented. He stepped ashore at La Rochelle in a very soured state of mind, which should not have been entirely unexpected at the end of a long sea voyage. He was thoroughly disgruntled over the treatment meted out to his men, his officers, and himself during disembarkation, about which he complained in an irate letter to the minister of war.[46]

His return to France was perhaps more noteworthy for the five Indians he brought with him to show off at court where they caused a great stir, especially among some of the noble ladies. Even so, the courtier's life was not for him, and despite his advanced age, he soon resumed his military career as the colonel of the newly formed Soissons Regiment. He did not finally retire from the service until 1676 at which time his son assumed the command of his company, thereby maintaining the family's link with the regiment until 1718 when he too retired from the army.[47] By that time, though, it was no longer the Soissons Regiment. In 1690 it had been renamed the Perché Regiment, and in 1744, the Lorraine Guards. Twenty-two years later it underwent yet another name change and became the Lorraine Regiment, a title it kept until the outbreak of the Revolutionary War in 1791 when it experienced its last transformation to become known by the prosaic title of the 47th Infantry Regiment.[48]

The Marquis de Salières died in Paris on 22 July 1680, at the reputed age of eighty-five years. He was buried in the Church of Saint-Sulpice in Paris, whose associations with Canada, particularly Montreal, made it a fitting last resting place for him.[49]

His death, in effect, symbolizes the end of the Carignan-Salières Regiment too, for by that time it had ceased to exist both in fact and in name. In Canada its veterans had blended into the general population and were indistinguishable from the rest of the men who tilled the fields and roamed the forests. In the same way, those who were in France also vanished from sight after they returned to their villages or fought the king's battles in other regiments and in other campaigns.

In a way the regiment's story comes to an anticlimactic end, particularly for those who would have had it come to a more glorious conclusion. As attrition took its toll, the regiment just diminished gradually so that all that remained were the few traces it had left on the annals of its age.

CHAPTER NINE

Conclusion

From the outset it has to be borne in mind that much of the impetus for sending the Carignan-Salières Regiment to Canada came from a desire to put Jean-Baptiste Colbert's mercantilist theories into practice, rather than from the pleas for help that had been coming for some years from leading figures in the colony. The hope was that mercantilism would facilitate the pursuance of Louis xiv's European ambitions by increasing the flow of wealth into his royal coffers. From that point of view the operation was a complete failure, for Canada at once became a great financial drain on the mother country and continued to be so, a hard fact that Colbert recognized in 1674 when he wound up the Compagnie des Indes occidentales. Its monopoly was sold to a private entrepreneur, who was more interested in the access it gave him to the slave and sugar trades than in the declining market for beaver skins.[1]

Discussion of that broader aspect, however, is not within the scope of this work, whose concern is solely to identify such effects as can be directly attributed to the deployment of the regiment in Canada. To that end it seems convenient to examine the regiment from two viewpoints: first, from the manner of its deployment, which reveals something of the regime that ordered it; and, second, from its presence in the colony, which affected life there in the short- and long-term.

From conception to completion, the operation of assembling the regiment at La Rochelle, shipping it across the Atlantic to Canada, and then for three years maintaining a line of supply across five thousand kilometres of ocean was a remarkable achievement. It was so remarkable, in fact, that it is very easy to forget that it took place between 1665 and 1668, long before the major seafaring states of Holland and England had even contemplated such ambitious enterprises. It called for a high degree of centralized control to coordinate the activities of the branches of government involved, as well as for an efficient bureaucracy to consolidate and carry out the orders and instructions emanating from them. It certainly taxed France's limited maritime resources to their utmost, and it also made great demands on the royal treasury, not only in meeting a considerable payroll but also in procuring large quantities of supplies, equipment, and munitions. The success of that side of the operation depended very much on the ability of one man, Colbert de Terron, the intendant of Rochefort, whose role in Canadian history has been largely overlooked.

Other than from that point of view, however, the Canadian venture cannot be considered an unqualified success. Shortcomings and deficiencies were revealed that impaired the regiment's ability to do the job it had been sent to do. It was improperly equipped for some of its duties, as well as for at least one of its campaigns. Furthermore, it was not trained to fight in the irregular type of warfare waged by its enemies, who were expert in the use of guerilla tactics. Although neither shortcoming can be blamed on negligence or mismanagement, they do reflect the general ignorance of conditions in Canada prevalent among those who advised the king. Even Colbert, who was probably as knowledgeable as anyone in that circle about conditions in the country, could base his judgment only on the intelligence he had gleaned from publications such as the *Jesuit Relations* and from letters written to him by the Jesuit father superior in Quebec, Paul Ragueneau. Michel Le Tellier, the minister of war, knew even less about Canada, and when it came to outfitting troops for service there, he could turn only to his knowledge of campaigning in Europe.[2]

That dearth of useful intelligence was certainly responsible, among other things, for the inability of those close to the king to convince him that cunning rather than dash, and caution rather than recklessness, were the qualities he should look for in those appointed to direct the war against the Iroquois. As a result, a man such as Courcelle became the governor of New France, and a part of the regiment was condemned to suffer the consequences of his incompetence in an ill-conceived campaign. He had little understanding of the demands of such an expedition, he compounded that ignorance by refusing to listen to advice from any he considered his social inferiors, and he crowned it by getting lost in the wilderness and losing two-thirds of his men to hypothermia and starvation. He could well have been an excellent officer on the plains of Europe, where his reckless ways could have brought him recognition and advancement, but in the Canadian wilderness, where not all the enemies were armed men, foolhardiness such as his was lethal.

The lingering resentment among senior regimental officers over the army reforms that had shorn them of much of their authority, which had been given to royal officials, such as Courcelle, also dogged the regiment in Canada. Its effects were apparent in the strained relations between the Marquis de Salières and his two immediate superiors, the governor and the general, which occasionally flared up into open squabbling.

Even so, alarming as some of those impediments to performance might seem, they are not sufficient to overshadow the sheer magnitude and audacity of the operation that took the Carignan-Salières Regiment to Canada. In short, it did not suffer from a breakdown of logistical support, but from a lack of accurate intelligence, which led to major decisions being made on the basis of inadequate or inaccurate information.

Turning to the effects the presence of the regiment, and later its veterans, had on life in Canada, it is necessary to say that they were not all beneficial. As well, incidents damaging to the unit's reputation are, as a general rule, better documented than those that could depict it favourably, which, consequently, leaves the impression that they were more numerous. So far as the evidence shows, it was only a minority of the soldiers who got into trouble, while the vast majority, although they may not all have led exemplary lives, at least led inconspicuous ones so that their deeds, and misdeeds, went unrecorded.

Much the same can be said for the entire regiment during its first year in Canada. In part because of its preoccupation with building forts, or with campaigning, and in between times with trying to settle into its new surroundings, it did not adversely affect the colony. It was a period during which the rapture of the first welcoming weeks had not completely worn off, and the unit's only negative impact on Canada was to be seen in minor irritations caused, for example, when food was commandeered or when the habitants were ordered to provide firewood for the soldiers' use.[3]

The ill-feelings that might have been generated were largely offset by an air of optimism that pervaded the colony. Its state of near siege was about to be lifted, and its domestic economy was being rapidly transformed as cash, used by the regiment to pay for all the goods and services obtained locally, replaced barter as the medium of exchange.[4]

In the subsequent two years of their Canadian tour of duty, as the troops became better acquainted with the colony, its people, and its opportunities, they gradually became more conspicuous. Some turned their attention to activities outside their military duties that were calculated to enrich them by legal and other means, mostly connected with the fur trade, which seemed to hold a strange fascination for them. It was also a period during which the regiment's image first became tarnished by criminal acts perpetrated by a few and by unscrupulous practices by some others in the fur trade.

Even so, it is not likely that many soldiers were complete scoundrels, and conversely, that many were complete saints. There were, of course, those who abjured Protestantism in 1665, or those who were brought back into the fold of the church they had abandoned, but they can hardly be said to have been motivated by their consciences, for they were given no choice in the matter and there is nothing to suggest that they led particularly pious lives afterwards. Neither did the religious fervour that possessed some of the men shortly after they had landed in Canada indicate much more than their heartfelt gratitude at having been spared a watery grave during the long and sometimes perilous voyage from France. Only two out of the twelve hundred soldiers in Canada showed signs of great devotion to the church – one officer, who left the army to enter the priesthood, and one enlisted man, who had faith enough to seek a miraculous cure for a crippling affliction. Although the rest of the troops might have attended to the observances of their religion with scrupulous care, it never dominated their lives to the point where they felt obligated to modify their behaviour.

In the years after 1668, the conventional wisdom has it that the approximately four hundred veterans who remained in Canada married, farmed the land, and became "the founders of Canadian families from which have come distinguished men, enlightened jurists, eminent barristers, renowned doctors, talented engineers, men of letters, devout priests, saintly bishops, etc."[5] The incidence of eminent personages among the descendants of veterans of the Carignan-Salières Regiment, however, has been neither greater nor smaller than it has been among any other segment of the population. It must also be considered that since so many of the former soldiers preferred the unfettered life of the *coureur de bois,* it would be reasonable to suspect that a good number entered into liaisons, both formal and informal, with Indian girls. Any children they fathered would have been absorbed into the tribe their mothers belonged to and, consequently, would have stood less chance than others of achieving eminence in white society.

It could not have been the vision of riches alone that attracted the former soldiers to the life of the *coureur de bois*. The attraction had to have been the way of life itself, regardless of its rewards and hardships, for, despite considerable evidence indicating that extreme poverty was not uncommon among former officers and enlisted men alike, they still persisted in following it (see appendix B).

Paradoxically that increasing poverty coincided, to a great extent, with the growing prosperity of Montreal as it emerged as the main base of the fur trade. It had always been in a more advantageous position than Trois-Rivières and Quebec were to benefit from the traffic, standing, as it did, at the western extremity of the colony and near the confluence of the Ottawa and the St Lawrence rivers, but until the destruction of the Mohawk villages and the ensuing peace, it had been exposed to Iroquois attacks.[6] The situation was different after the spring of 1667, the change hastened when some of the officers stationed there entered the fur trade in true opportunist fashion and thus helped the settlement shed the mantle of moral and commercial rectitude that had cloaked it during the Maisonneuve years. Thereafter it became a bustling business hub, a transformation that was not pleasing to some, but that set the pattern for the community's development to the present.[7]

It might also be argued that the regiment made a major contribution towards increasing the population of Canada, although not necessarily in the conventional sense that its veterans married and fathered legitimate children. Their main contribution towards peopling the colony was indirect in that their campaigns against the Mohawks gave it a few years of peace, a breathing space in which immigration, as well as marriages between immigrants to found new families, proceeded apace. From 1665 to 1668 the population almost doubled to well over six thousand, and it continued to grow thereafter, a result of both further immigration and natural increase. In the pre-Conquest period, however, it never exceeded sixty thousand, and in 1683 when war again broke out against the Iroquois, it was not even ten thousand.[8] Nevertheless, small as that figure was, the colony was far better able to defend itself than it had been eighteen years earlier when the Carignan-Salières Regiment arrived from France. Of all its contributions, the peace won for the colony has to have been the most important, for it gave the people enough time to consolidate their presence along the St Lawrence and to develop a measure of self-defence, in the form of militia companies, against their traditional enemies. It might be an exaggeration to say that the regiment ensured the survival of French culture in America, but it at least helped to do so. As if to attest to that, place-names that mark the location of seigneuries granted to some of its former officers in 1672 remain on the map.[9]

Whatever the legacy of the regiment, however, it did not introduce a superior bloodline in Canada, as has been suggested by some who have deliberately overstated its contribution to the country. Their motives for doing so are to be found in the particular brand of French-Canadian nationalism preached by the Abbé Lionel Groulx. Central to it is the belief that "France at a safe distance in time and place is needed to counteract the impact of the English-speaking world and to give density and energy to the culture mediated by French."[10] The Abbé himself was even more explicit when he wrote, "For our intellectual élite we ask Roman [Catholic] culture and French culture."[11]

His was an elitist, almost a racist, doctrine, which meant that it needed elitist paradigms to substantiate it. The story of the Carignan-Salières Regiment lent itself admirably to that use, especially since Marie de l'Incarnation had already given a lead in that direction. She had written that the unit was "composed of thirteen hundred élite men, all of whom went into combat as to triumph," and that "our French soldiers are so fervent they fear nothing, and there is nothing they do not do and undertake ... It seems to all these soldiers that they are going to besiege paradise, and they hope to capture and enter it, because it is for the good of the Faith and religion that they are going to do battle."[12]

For her it was a case of the army of the Lord's anointed coming to do the Lord's work in Canada, and it was the possibility of that kind of an interpretation that commended the story to the Abbé Groulx's disciples, two of whom lauded the regiment in similar vein when they wrote: "The men of the Carignan regiment were good soldiers; colonists who heeded their pastors and, under their care, increased, they and their descendants, truly brave and without deceit. They were good Canadians!"[13] Thus did the so-called "golden haze of glorious legend," which has clouded so much of the history of pre-Conquest Canada, descend on the story of the Carignan-Salières Regiment.[14]

Although the object of this work was to try to disperse enough of that haze to permit an accurate view of the only seventeenth-century French infantry regiment to serve in Canada, it should not be taken as an attempt to diminish the unit's reputation. It certainly was the "good regiment" of which Colbert wrote to Mgr de Laval in 1664, just as all the other French regiments of the day were, which together made up the most powerful army in Europe.

It follows that the men of the Carignan-Salières Regiment were ordinary foot soldiers, not the white knights they have been made out to be. For the most part, they were rough men, who in their off-duty hours caroused, womanized, gambled, grumbled, and dreamed of making their fortunes. Their story is thus given an overtone of universality, for it shows that infantrymen have changed remarkably little over the centuries. The sorts of things that the men of the regiment did, and the sorts of things that happened to them, have been duplicated over and over again in the long line of infantry units throughout recorded history. If this story has any underlying message, then that universality is it.

Equipment

The following tables itemize the clothing, provisions, and equipment the king sent to Canada to see the Carignan-Salières Regiment through its first year in the colony. Certain payments made on its behalf are also included. The tables were compiled from data contained in an accounting document signed by M. Chamot, the regiment's quartermaster, at La Rochelle on 15 June 1666, after he had been recalled from Canada to explain certain irregularities.[1] At times the arithmetic in the original document is incorrect; in these tables, it has been corrected. To facilitate comparisons with present-day units of measure and currency, the following conversion rates will be of some assistance. It must be borne in mind, however, that the rates are nothing more than approximations.[2]

UNITS OF LENGTH

1 *aune* = 1.12 metres
1 *pied* = 32.5 centimetres
1 *pouce* = 2.7 centimetres

UNITS OF VOLUME

The units of volume used in the document are usually kegs of different sizes. A *barril* held about 23 litres; a *barrique*, about 100 litres; a *tonneau*, about 160 litres. Salt is measured in terms of the *minot*, a unit of dry volume equal to approximately 40 litres.

UNITS OF WEIGHT

The basic unit of weight used in the document is the *livre*, which is about the same as the present imperial pound, or 454 grams. It can be subdivided into 16 *onces*, each roughly the equivalent of 1 imperial ounce, or 28 grams. Two thousand *livres* is a *tonneau*, and is about the same as a present-day short ton. It should not be confused with the unit of volume having the same name. If in doubt, the context in which the term is used generally gives a clue as to its meaning.

UNITS OF CURRENCY

All costs and prices in the document are given in terms of *livres (1.)*, *sols (s.)*, and *deniers (d.)*, which bear the following relationship to each other:

1 *livre* = 20 *sols*
1 *sol* = 12 *deniers*

Until 1717 there were two monetary systems in use, *argent de France* and *argent de Canada*. *Argent de Canada* had only 75 per cent of the value of *argent of France*, but since the document was drawn up at La Rochelle, it can be assumed that the amounts of money are given in terms of the latter. In both systems the *livre* was nothing more than a theoretical denomination used for accounting purposes. Coinage existed only in the values of:

Copper coins: 1 *denier*, 1 *liard* (3 *deniers*), 1 *sol*.
Silver coins: 1 *petit louis, petit écu*, or *écu blanc*, which was worth 3 *livres*, 12 *sols*; and 1 *gros écu à couronne*, which was worth 6 *livres*, 12 *sols*.
Gold coins: 1 *louis d'or*, which was worth 24 *livres*.

It is impossible to give a value for the *livre* in present-day currency, but the purchasing power of 1 *livre (argent de France)* would possibly approximate that of $12 (Canadian). Even that conversion rate should be used with extreme caution, however, for it is impossible to compare the value of an implement made by hand in 1665 with that of a similar item produced by modern, mass-production methods.

131 Appendix A

Table 1
Food Supplies

Quantity		Item	Rate	l.	s.	d.
501,866	*livres*	Coarse flour in 986 *barriques*	69*l.* per 1,000 *livres*	34,628.	15.	1
100		*Barriques* not included above	3*l.* each	300.	0.	0
150,120	*livres*	Lard in 784 *barrils*	15*l.* 16*s.* 3*d.* per 100 *livres*	23,737.	14.	6
115,370	*livres*	Milled flour in 226 *barriques*	68*l.* per 1,000 *livres*	7,845.	3.	2
4,102	*livres*	Olive oil	30*l.* 3*s.* per 100 *livres*	1,236.	15.	1
12	*minots*	Salt	30*l.* 10*s.* per *minot*	366.	0.	0
92	*barriques*	Brandy	46*l.* per *barrique*	4,508.	0.	0
2,000	*livres*	Butter	35*l.* per 100 *livres*	700.	0.	0
2	*tonneaux*	Prunes	40*l.* per *tonneau*	80.	0.	0
4	*barrils*	Raisins	25*l.* per *barril*	100.	0.	0
Total				73,502.	7.	10

Table 2
Clothing for Noncommissioned Men

Quantity	Item	Rate	l.	s.	d.
250	Outfits consisting of jerkins and breeches	18l. each	4,500.	0.	0
3,072 aunes	Fustian to make breeches and jerkins	3l. per aune	9,216.	0.	0
3,060 aunes	Coarse cloth to line clothing	25s. per aune	3,825.	0.	0
84 aunes	Serge to make stockings	54s. per aune	226.	16.	0
20 gross	Laces for shoes and breeches	40s. per gross	40.	0.	0
2,259	Shirts	35s. each	3,953.	5.	0
200	Better shirts for sergeants	37s. each	370.	0.	0
100	Smaller shirts	28s. 6d. each	142.	10.	0
473	Shrouds	50s. each	1,182.	10.	0
999 aunes	Cloth for linings	30s. per aune	1,498.	10.	0
250 aunes	Canvas for packing 80 bales of cloth (to be used for lining breeches)	12s. per aune	150.	0.	0
1,200	Trimmed black hats	26l. per dozen	2,600.	0.	0
600	Canvas bags	22s. 6d. each	675.	0.	0
50 livres	White thread	50s. per livre	125.	0.	0
2,400 pairs	Shoes, ready packed	56s. 6d. per pair	6,780.	0.	0
120 gross	Leather buttons for jerkins	35s. per gross	210.	0.	0
34 pieces	Ribbon for hatbands	4l. 10s. per piece	153.	0.	0
2,000	Needles	4l. per 1,000	8.	0.	0
Total			35,655.	11.	0

Table 3
Tools and Other Matériel for the Stores and for Issue to the Troops

Quantity		Item	Rate	l.	s.	d.
200		Flintlocks	13l. 15s. each	2,750.	0.	0
40,000		Musket flints	45s. per 1,000	90.	0.	0
100		Pistols	5l. each	500.	0.	0
200		Belts with pouches	40s. each	400.	0.	0
200		Bayonets with sheaths	25s. each	250.	0.	0
800		Powder horns	7s. each	280.	0.	0
1,000		Cleaning rods for muskets	2s. each	100.	0.	0
2,000	*livres*	Lead shot, hunting size	18l. 10s. per 100 *livres*	370.	0.	0
2		Anvils	144l. each	288.	0.	0
6		Surgeons' chests	271l. 15s. each	1,630.	10.	0
12		Shoemakers' lasts	8s. each	4.	16.	0
12		Shoemakers' knives	7s. each	4.	4.	0
100		Awls	1s. each	5.	0.	0
24		Awl handles	5s. each	6.	0.	0
6		Iron stitching awls	5s. each	1.	10.	0
6		Stitching awl handles	5s. each	1.	10.	0
4		Large shoemakers' hardwood heel burnishers	15s. each	3.	0.	0
4		Small shoemakers' hardwood heel burnishers	8s. each	1.	12.	0
2		Shoemakers' cutting out knives	15s. each	1.	10.	0
2		Knife handles	5s. each		10.	0
4		Iron pliers	30s. each	6.	0.	0
1	*livre*	Shoemakers' thread	5l. 10s. per *livre*	5.	10.	0
600		Assorted hobnails	12s. per 100	3.	12.	0
40	*livres*	Shoemakers' wax	40s. per *livre*	80.	0.	0
12		Assorted rods	1s. each		12.	0
100		Shoemakers' square needles	40s. per 100	2.	0.	0
100	*livres*	Hemp thread	20s. per *livre*	100.	0.	0
4		Choice grey cowhides	16l. each	64.	0.	0
40	strips	Choice strong leather	18l. per *strip*	720.	0.	0
100,000		Shoemakers' tacks	50s. per 1,000	250.	0.	0

134 Appendix A

Table 3 (continued)

Quantity	Item	Rate	l.	s.	d.
500	Mess tins	4l. 16s. per dozen	200.	0.	0
12	Sets containing 2 lancets and a razor	4l. 10s. each	54.	0.	0
12	Bleeding implements	12s. each	7.	4.	0
2	Large ornamented syringes	8l. each	16.	0.	0
28	Bleeding cups	10s. each	14.	0.	0
1	Copper pestle and mortar	15l. each	15.	0.	0
1	Small scale for the surgeon	6l. each	6.	0.	0
6,000	Lead ingots for the store	No price given			
2	Large bellows	60l. each	120.	0.	0
4 dozen	Medium-sized coarse files	30s. per dozen	6.	0.	0
30	Fine bastard files	12s. each	18.	0.	0
12	Medium files	10s. each	6.	0.	0
8	Large fine files	15s. each	6.	0.	0
4	Large coarse stones	32s. each	6.	8.	0
6	Medium stones	15s. each	4.	10.	0
2	Hand vises	30s. each	3.	0.	0
1	Large workshop vise	37l. each	37.	0.	0
1	Large two-billed anvil	7l. 10s. each	7.	10.	0
1	Bench anvil for metal burnishing	7l. 10s. each	7.	10.	0
2	Large striking hammers	3l. 10s. each	7.	0.	0
4	Medium hammers	40s. each	8.	0.	0
4	Carpenters' hammers	25s. each	5.	0.	0
2	Large chisels	12s. each	1.	4.	0
2	Augers	12s. each	1.	4.	0
2	Pliers for pulling nails	16s. each	1.	12.	0
1	Small screw plate with 5 screws	8l. each	8.	0.	0
2	Large screw plates with 4 screws	13l. each	26.	0.	0
2	Blast pipes for the forges	3l. 5s. each	6.	10.	0
2	Wrenches	30s. each	3.	0.	0
5	Hooks for the workshop	10s. each	2.	10.	0
2	Blacksmiths' tongs	5l. 10s. each	11.	0.	0
3	Rollers	5l. 10s. each	16.	10.	0

Table 3 (continued)

Quantity	Item	Rate	l.	s.	d.
2	Saw horses	9l. each	18.	0.	0
4 bundles	Cord	12s. per bundle	2.	8.	0
2	Dogfish skins	40s. each	4.	0.	0
20	Carpenters' bits	5s. each	5.	0.	0
4 livres	English glue	12s. per livre	2.	8.	0
2	Large rip saws	50s. each	5.	0.	0
2	Hand saws	20s. each	2.	0.	0
2	Tenon saws	15s. each	1.	10.	0
2	Medium saws	13s. 6d. each	1.	7.	0
2	Scroll saws	4l. each	8.	0.	0
8	(Entry not completely decipherable. Possibly it is "Assorted spokeshave blades, or draw-knife blades.")	15s. each	6.	0.	0
8	Assorted jointing plane blades	15s. each	6.	0.	0
4	Mortice chisels	15s. each	3.	0.	0
6	Adzes	45s. each	13.	10.	0
13	Plane blades	13s. each	8.	9.	0
10	Assorted large firmer chisels	16s. each	8.	0.	0
10	Medium chisels	8s. each	4.	0.	0
2	Plane blades	18s. each	1.	16.	0
2	Ripsaw blades	55s. each	5.	10.	0
2	Handsaw blades	25s. each	2.	10.	0
2	Scroll saw blades	20s. each	2.	0.	0
2	Saw handles	20s. each	2.	0.	0
2	Set squares	25s. each	2.	10.	0
2	Tenon saw handles	15s. each	1.	10.	0
2	Braces	25s. each	2.	10.	0
2	Grooving plane blades	3l. 10s. each	7.	0.	0
16	Chisel sleeves	5s. each	4.	0.	0
2	Jack plane blades	20s. each	2.	0.	0
4	Wheelbarrow axles	20s. each	4.	0.	0
2	Large copper dividers	37s. each	3.	14.	0
10,286 livres	Iron	10l. per 100 livres	1,028.	12.	0

Table 3 (continued)

Quantity	Item	Rate	l.	s.	d.
6 dozen	Assorted iron door fittings:				
	6 large	12l. each	72.	0.	0
	18 smaller ones	7l. each	126.	0.	0
	24 smaller still	5l. each	120.	0.	0
	24 for bedrooms	38s. each	45.	12.	0
6	Mortar mountings	3l. 10s. each	21.	0.	0
10,000	Large ships' nails	55s. per 100	275.	0.	0
10,000	Ships' nails	35s. per 100	175.	0.	0
10,000	Small ships' nails	25s. per 100	125.	0.	0
10,000	Slating nails	25s. per 100	125.	0.	0
1,000	Biscay axes	25s. 4d. each	1,266.	13.	4
50	Scythes	30s. each	75.	0.	0
100	Whetstones	3s. each	15.	0.	0
8 dozen	Drills	36s. per dozen	14.	8.	0
8 dozen	Strong door braces complete with hinges, weighing 557 livres altogether	6s. per livre	167.	2.	0
2 dozen	Assorted strap hinges	4l. 4s. per dozen	8.	8.	0
2 dozen	Strap hinges	3l. 12s. per dozen	7.	4.	0
4 dozen	Strap hinges	40s. per dozen	8.	0.	0
2 dozen	Door fastenings complete with latches	35s. each	42.	0.	0
400	Iron fittings	27s. each	540.	0.	0
10	Small axes	25s. each	12.	10.	0
24	Mattocks	40s. each	48.	0.	0
6	Moulds and templates	40s. each	12.	0.	0
20	Covers for dough	6l. 10s. each	130.	0.	0
3 barriques	Fish oil for the store	60l. per barrique	180.	0.	0
23 livres	Copper, contained in 4 cooking pots, 4 pastry bowls, and 2 large lamps	24s. per livre	27.	12.	0
400 livres	Candles	33l. per 100 livres	132.	0.	0
12	Large funnels	20s. each	12.	0.	0
8	Large copper scythes	25s. each	10.	0.	0
10 barrils	Tar for the store	No rate given			

Table 3 (continued)

Quantity	Item	Rate	l.	s.	d.
10,000 *livres*	Caulking pitch	60*l.* per 1,000 *livres*	600.	o.	o
2,000 *livres*	Oakum	10*l.* per 100 *livres*	200.	o.	o
440	Foresights for muskets	28*l.* per 100	123.	4.	o
200 *livres*	Spun yarn	24*l.* per 100 *livres*	48.	o.	o
50 *livres*	Linen thread	75*l.* per 100 *livres*	37.	10.	o
150 *aunes*	Canvas to make shallop sails	15*s.* per *aune*	112.	10.	o
798 *livres*	Iron, contained in 8 iron plates, 6 sledge hammers, 4 tripods, 8 wedges, 12 medium-sized hammer heads, 12 pairs of tongs, 4 rollers, 4 fire rakes	5*s.* per *livre*	199.	10.	o
150 *livres*	Alignment cord	40*l.* per 100 *livres*	60.	o.	o
12	Adzes	40*s.* each	24.	o.	o
100 *livres*	Tallow	30*l.* per 100 *livres*	30.	o.	o
2	Fishing nets	60*l.* each	120.	o.	o
12	Tinplate lanterns	30*s.* each	18.	o.	o
4	Grappling irons weighing 213 *livres* altogether	5*s.* per *livre*	53.	5.	o
4	Copper cauldrons weighing 40 *livres* each	5*s.* per *livre*	40.	o.	o
4	Copper handles for cauldrons weighing 13 *livres* altogether	6*s.* per *livre*	3.	18.	o
12	Pit saws having a total length of 55 *pieds*	20*s.* per *pied*	55.	o.	o
4	Heavy hawsers weighing 657 *livres* altogether	30*l.* per 100 *livres*	197.	2.	o
12	Large augers:				
	4 at 4 *pieds* long	35*s.* each	7.	o.	o
	2 at 5 *pieds* long	35*s.* each	3.	10.	o
	3 at 3 *pieds* long	30*s.* each	4.	10.	o
	1 at 3 *pieds* long	30*s.* each	1.	10.	o
	2 at 3 *pieds* long	30*s.* each	3.	o.	o
12	Masons' combined hammer and trowel	35*s.* each	21.	o.	o
4,000	Lead slabs	17*l.* per 100	680.	o.	o
40 *livres*	Candlewick	12*s.* per *livre*	24.	o.	o
4	Copper scales complete with weights	8*l.* each	32.	o.	o

Table 3 (continued)

Quantity		Item	Rate	l.	s.	d.
15		Oarlocks	7l. each	105.	0.	0
12		Large spatulas	12s. each	7.	4.	0
36		Small spatulas	5s. each	9.	0.	0
50	*livres*	Cotton thread	24s. per *livre*	60.	0.	0
2		Large measures made of tinplate	30s. each	3.	0.	0
2 bundles		Paper	100l. per bundle	200.	0.	0
6		Mattresses for the store	16l. each	96.	0.	0
12		Mattress covers for the store	6l. 10s. each	78.	0.	0
6		Palliasses, each with a bolster, for the store	8l. each	48.	0.	0
10	*ton-neaux*	Vinegar	52l. per *tonneau*	520.	0.	0
20	*ton-neaux*	Wine	64l. per *tonneau*	1,280.	0.	0
100 dozen		Pocket knives	1l. per dozen	100.	0.	0
100 dozen		Combs	10l. per gross	83.	6.	4
100		Thimbles	1s. each	5.	0.	0
46		Assorted scissors	20s. each	46.	0.	0
1,600	*livres*	Fine gunpowder	58l. per 100 *livres*	928.	0.	0
1,118	*aunes*	Serge for making stockings	29s. per *aune*	1,621.	2.	0
2,400		Cravats	13s. each	1,560.	0.	0
50	*livres*	Grey thread	40s. per *livre*	100.	0.	0
Total				23,060.	2.	8

Table 4
Items for the Officers of the Twenty-Four Companies

Quantity	Item	Rate	l.	s.	d.
	Paid to sundry merchants in La Rochelle for clothing, munitions, liquor, and other refreshments supplied in accordance with the verbal and written orders of officers. Those officers checked that the merchants conformed with the orders.		13,523.	0.	0

To the rest of the officers of the twenty-four companies, consisting of 15 captains, 10 lieutenants, 19 ensigns, and 5 officers on the headquarters staff there has been supplied as follows:

Quantity	Item	Rate	l.	s.	d.
33½ *tonneaux*	Wine for distribution as follows: 15 *tonneaux* to the captains; 9 *tonneaux* to the lieutenants at the rate of 2 *barriques* each; 4 *tonneaux* and 3 *barriques* to the ensigns; 2 *barriques* to the colonel; 2 *barriques* to the lieutenant-colonel; 3 *barriques* to the major; 1 *barrique* to the adjutant; 1 *barrique* to the sergeant-major	64*l.* per *tonneau*	2,144.	0.	0
76 *barriques*	Brandy for distribution, in *barriques,* as follows: 30 to the captains; 18 to the lieutenants; 19 to the ensigns; 1 to the colonel; 1 to the lieutenant-colonel; 3 to the major; 1 to the adjutant; 1 to the sergeant-major; 1 to the chaplain; 1 to the surgeon	46*l.* per *barrique*	3,496.	0.	0
4,020 *livres*	Tobacco for distribution, in *livres,* as follows: 2,400 to the captains; 720 to the lieutenants; 360 to the ensigns; 100 to the colonel; 100 to the lieutenant-colonel; 200 to the major; 100 to the adjutant; 40 to the sergeant-major	24*s.* 6*d.* per *livre*	4,924.	10.	0
96	Flintlocks supplied to the captains	13*l.* 10*s.* each	1,296.	0.	0

Table 4 (continued)

Quantity	Item	Rate	l.	s.	d.
2,410 *livres*	Fine gunpowder distributed, in *livres,* as follows: 1,500 to the captains; 540 to the lieutenants; 180 to the ensigns; 100 to the major; 50 to the adjutant; 30 to the sergeant-major; 10 to the surgeon	58*l.* per 100 *livres*	1,397.	16.	0
6,415 *livres*	Lead distributed, in *livres,* as follows: 3,200 to the captains; 1,800 to the lieutenants; 540 to the ensigns; 75 to the colonel; 400 to the major; 250 to the adjutant; 50 to the surgeon; 100 to the sergeant-major	18*l.* 10s. per 100 *livres,* bags and expenses included	1,186.	15.	6
32,000	Flints for flintlocks	45s. per 1,000	72.	0.	0

Other items supplied to the captains, lieutenants, and ensigns of the twenty-four companies:

154 *aunes*	Sedan cloth	10*l.* per *aune*	1,540.	0.	0
386 *aunes*	Brown drugget	50s. per *aune*	965.	0.	0
136 half pieces	Ribbon, half black and half russet	5*l.* 5s. per half piece	714.	0.	0
4 *livres*	Grey and brown silk	20*l.* 16s. per *livre*	83.	4.	0
4 *livres*	Grey and brown thread	48s. per *livre*	9.	12.	0
15 pieces	Grey and brown cloth, each piece containing from 10 to 12 *aunes*	12*l.* per piece	180.	0.	0
300 dozen	Grey and brown buttons	6s. per dozen	90.	0.	0
156 dozen	Grey and brown buttons	3s. per dozen	23.	8.	0
52	Skins to make pockets	10s. each	26.	0.	0
75 *aunes*	Grey and brown taffeta	5*l.* 10s. per *aune*	412.	10.	0
31 *aunes*	Silk lace	3*l.* per *aune*	93.	0.	0

Other items supplied to the five officers on the headquarters staff: the colonel, the lieutenant-colonel, the major, the adjutant, and the sergeant-major:

16,000	Flints for flintlocks	45s. per 1,000	36.	0.	0
86 *aunes*	Drugget	45s. per *aune*	193.	10.	0

Table 4 (continued)

Quantity	Item	Rate	l.	s.	d.
13 *aunes*	Linen	25s. per *aune*	16.	5.	0
2	Baldrics	7l. each	14.	0.	0
17	Flintlocks	13l. 10s. each	229.	10.	0
5 *onces*	Silk	25s. per *once*	6.	5.	0
5 *onces*	Thread	3s. per *once*		15.	0
15 *aunes*	Braid	3s. per *aune*	2.	5.	0
10	Skins to make pockets	10s. each	5.	0.	0
10 pieces	Black ribbon	10l. per piece	100.	0.	0
45 dozen	Buttons	5s. per dozen	11.	5.	0
41 dozen	Buttons	2s. 6d. per dozen	5.	2.	6
7½ *aunes*	Black taffeta	5l. 10s. per *aune*	41.	5.	0
5 *aunes*	Fine cotton cloth	58s. per *aune*	14.	10.	0
22 pairs	Shoes	3l. per pair	66.	0.	0
	Packing and shipping		5.	0.	0

Additional items supplied to officers in the twenty-four companies:

Quantity	Item	Rate	l.	s.	d.
504 pairs	Shoes distributed, in pairs, as follows: 192 to the captains; 108 to the lieutenants; 108 to the ensigns; 30 to the colonel; 9 to the lieutenant-colonel; 24 to the major; 15 to the adjutant; 6 to the sergeant-major; 6 to the chaplain; 6 to the surgeon	3l. per pair	1,512.	0.	0
82	Hats with bands distributed as follows: 36 to the captains; 18 to the lieutenants; 19 to the ensigns; 4 to the adjutant; 1 to the sergeant-major; 2 to the chaplain; 2 to the surgeon	6l. each	492.	0.	0
48 pairs	Chamois gloves for the captains	25s. per pair	60.	0.	0
49 pairs	Stockings for the captains	3l. 15s. per pair	183.	15.	0
3 pairs	Woollen stockings for the chaplain	3l. 15s. per pair	11.	5.	0
800 *livres*	Candles for the captains	33l. per 100 *livres*	264.	0.	0
86	Fine shirts for the captains	5l. 10s. each	473.	0.	0

Table 4 (continued)

Quantity	Item	Rate	l.	s.	d.
86	Thick shirts for the captains	3*l*. 10s. each	301.	0.	0
834 *aunes*	White cloth for the lieutenants, ensigns, and seven head-quarters officers	28s. per *aune*	1,167.	12.	0
834 *aunes*	Cloth for the lieutenants, ensigns, and seven head-quarters officers	22s. per *aune*	917.	8.	0
8	Shirts for an ensign	4 at 3*l*. 10s. each and 4 at 5*l*. each	34.	0.	0
15	Fashionable baldrics for the captains	8*l*. 10s. each	127.	10.	0
1	Baldric for the major	8*l*. 10s. each	8.	10.	0
1	Baldric for the adjutant	8*l*. 10s. each	8.	10.	0
18	Baldrics for the lieutenants	7*l*. 10s. each	135.	0.	0
19	Baldrics for the ensigns	7*l*. 10s. each	142.	10.	0
96	Dutch cheeses having a total weight of 960 *livres* for the captains	42*l*. per 100 *livres*	403.	4.	0
1,934 *livres*	Soap distributed, in *livres,* as follows: 800 to the captains; 720 to the lieutenants; 360 to the ensigns; 14 to the lieutenant-colonel; 40 to the sergeant-major	42*l*. per 100 *livres*	812.	5.	7
79 *livres*	White sewing thread distributed, in *livres,* as follows: 36 to the lieutenants; 36 to the ensigns; 1 to the major; 2 to the sergeant-major; 2 to the chaplain; 2 to the surgeon	50s. per *livre*	197.	10.	0
Total			40,174.	7.	7

Table 5
Items for Six Carpenters that His Majesty Maintains in Canada

Quantity	Item	Rate	l.	s.	d.
24	Shirts	3l. 10s. each	84.	0.	0
24	Cravats	18s. each	21.	12.	0
12 pairs	Drawers	30s. each	18.	0.	0
24	Handkerchiefs	10s. each	12.	0.	0
12 *aunes*	Cloth	25s. per *aune*	15.	0.	0
6	Complete outfits, including hoods and stockings	34l. each	204.	0.	0
12 pairs	Shoes	3l. per pair	36.	0.	0
6	Hats wtih bands	4l. 15s. each	28.	10.	0
6 *barriques*	Brandy	46l. per *barrique*	276.	0.	0
2 *barriques*	Wine	33l. per *barrique*	66.	0.	0
8 pairs	Shoes (supplied by M. Chamot)	3l. per pair	24.	0.	0
	Packing and shipping		9.	0.	0
	Balance of wages for the past year		462.	0.	0
Total			1,256.	2.	0

Table 6
Disbursements Made for Services Rendered

Nature of Service	l.	s.	d.
Salary for M. Chamot, superintendent of stores, at the rate of 50l. per month	600.	o.	o
Paid to the Sieur Le Gaigneur for the transportation of 806 *tonneaux* of stores from La Rochelle to Quebec	40,300.	o.	o
Paid to the Sieur Pettit for the transportation of stores	2,592.	o.	o
Paid to the Sieur de Lespinay for piloting the *Saint-Sébastien* down the St Lawrence in bad weather	800.	o.	o
Paid to M. de Barque for the transportation of a brewery to Belle-Isle	86.	o.	o
Total	44,378.	o.	o

TOTAL EXPENSES

Total for all expenses detailed in tables 1 to 6 is 218,026l. 11s. 1d.

It should be noted that the foregoing tables reveal that a great deal of clothing must have been supplied from Chamot's store to captains to replace worn and damaged items. Since it was a captain's responsibility to outfit his men, and he was provided with money to do so, there had to have been an arrangement whereby he was provided with the clothing in lieu of money to buy them.

Nominal Roll

The nominal roll presented here is obviously incomplete, for the twenty companies of the Carignan-Salières Regiment, together with the four that came from the Antilles with Tracy, totalled over twelve hundred men. Unfortunately no complete roll has come to light so far, and this one, which accounts for only a little more than a third of that number, is nothing more than a consolidation of the available information and, therefore, is far from comprehensive.

In addition to the men named in the roll, there are all the unnamed dead of whom the only record is the statistic of their death. References to them are to be found in several locations, all of which have to be treated with a considerable degree of caution, for it is not possible to check one against another. Marie de l'Incarnation, for example, wrote of 20 men dying aboard the *Saint-Sébastien* during its voyage to the St Lawrence, while, according to the *Annales de l'Hôtel-Dieu de Québec,* of the 130 men taken ashore from the ship, 35 died in the hospital. The two figures cannot be reconciled with each other, although they are probably referring, in part, to the same men.[1]

Similarly, François de Tapie de Monteil stated in his notebook that 400 men died during Courcelle's winter campaign, while the Jesuits wrote only of more than 60 dying.[2] Neither figure can be totally accurate, for they do not make the distinction between soldiers and the civilian volunteers who made up about 40 per cent of the force of 500 to 600 men. Furthermore, it is quite probable that the Jesuits' figure was kept deliberately vague so that it could more readily lend itself to misinterpretation.

It is difficult to determine losses with any accuracy also because there are no exact figures of the number of men who came to Canada in 1665 and of the number who returned to France in 1668.

The information contained in the roll was compiled from five main sources: the original list of soldiers remaining in Canada, the Abbé Cyprien

Tanguay's genealogical dictionary, *Dictionary of Canadian Biography*, François-Joseph Audet's presentation to the Royal Society of Canada in 1922, and the Leymarie Papers.[3] A. Leo Leymarie, a French journalist with a historical bent, carried out in the 1920s and 1930s a great deal of research into the personnel of the Carignan-Salières Regiment. The results of his labours are preserved in the National Archives of Canada. The copious dossier of anecdotal material he compiled has never been collated or published.

Table 1
Headquarters Staff

Rank	Name	Biographical Notes
Colonel	Henri Chastelard, Marquis de Salières	Returned to France in 1668 and remained in the army as colonel of the Soissons Regiment until he retired in 1676. He died in 1680 at the age of eighty-five. (See also in table 4.)
Lieutenant-colonel	Du Prat	Died at Fort Sainte-Thérèse in January 1666, presumably of natural causes. (See also in table 4.)
Major	Balthazard de La Flotte de La Fredière	A brute and a lecher who so incensed the residents of Montreal with his behaviour that they petitioned Tracy to send him back to France. (See also in table 4.)
Adjutant	François Féraud	Took over as Tracy's aide-de-camp late in 1666, after Alexandre de Chaumont left for France on official business. Féraud returned to France in 1668. (See also in table 4.)
Sergeant-major	François Pollet de La Combe-Pocatière	A half-pay captain who stayed in Canada and married at Quebec in 1669. His widow received the seigneurial concession of La Pocatière in October 1672, seven months after his death.
Chaplain	Jean-Baptiste Dubois d'Esgriseilles	According to the entry in the *Journal of the Jesuits* for 19 August 1665, presented a forged letter of introduction when he reached Quebec.
Surgeon	Vincent Basset Du Tartre	Presumably returned to France in 1667 or 1668.
Quartermaster	Chamot	Returned to France in October 1665, but came back to Canada the following June. He was killed in July 1666 in a Mohawk ambush near Fort Sainte-Anne.
Quartermaster	Nicolas Grisard Des Ormeaux	Was assistant quartermaster until he succeeded Chamot in July 1666. He presumably returned to France in 1668.
Assistant quartermaster	Labresche	Filled position left vacant by Des Ormeaux. He presumably returned to France in 1668.

Table 2
Officers whose Company Placement Is Not Known

Rank	Name	Biographical Notes
Lieutenant	d'Aiguemortes	Killed by the Mohawks on Courcelle's winter campaign in February 1666.
Lieutenant	de Chaulnes	Killed by the Iroquois, autumn 1666.
Lieutenant	Jean-Louis Douglas	Returned to France in 1668.
Lieutenant	Dugues	Returned to France in 1668.
Lieutenant	Du Luc	Drowned on Tracy's expedition to the Mohawk country in October 1666.
Lieutenant	Pierre Ferre de Lespinay	Returned to France in 1668.
Lieutenant	Flottant de l'Escure	Returned to France in 1668.
Lieutenant	François Gaude de Martinville	Returned to France in 1668.
Lieutenant	François de Masse de Vailly	A half-pay captain who returned to France in 1668.
Lieutenant	François de Monnery	Returned to France in 1668.
Lieutenant	Philippe de Montisson	Returned to France in 1668.
Lieutenant	de Rousère	Returned to France in 1668.
Ensign	Darienne	Stationed at Fort Sainte-Anne immediately before he returned to France in 1668.
Ensign	Dauboeuf	Returned to France in 1668.
Ensign	Truc	Returned to France in 1668.
Gentleman volunteer	de Beaubel	Returned to France in 1668.
Unknown	Modère Belac	Returned to France in 1668.
Unknown	de Chazy	Killed in a Mohawk ambush near Fort Sainte-Anne in July 1666.
Gentleman volunteer	Pierre Des Brandes	Died in hospital at Montreal in February 1666 at age twenty.
Unknown	Jean Dugal de Beaufresne (possibly Du Fresne)	Referred to as the "Major de Canada." He was on Tracy's expedition to the Mohawk country. Returned to France in 1668.

Table 2 (continued)

Rank	Name	Biographical Notes
Unknown	Pierre Dupas de Brache	Probably born in 1637. Remained in Canada and received permission to clear land on Ile Dupas. He and two other men were besieged in a hut there by Iroquois attackers. After 1668 he was active in the fur trade. In 1672 he received the land at the mouth of the Chicot River as a seigneurial concession. In 1677 he married at Quebec and died four days later.
Unknown	Gilbert Duperon	Returned to France in 1668.
Unknown	Jacques d'Harcuival	Returned to France in 1668.
Unknown	Henri La Frenaye Des Clays	Possibly the La Frenaye who had a trading post on the Bellevue seigneury.
Unknown	de La Haye	Returned to France in 1668.
Unknown	Morin	Killed in a Mohawk ambush near Fort Sainte-Anne in July 1666.
Unknown	Le Chevalier de Peguillon	Taken to the Hôtel-Dieu in Quebec off the *Saint-Sébastien* in September 1665 where he died a few days later.
Unknown	Charles-Gaspard Piot de Langloiserie	Probably a half-pay captain who remained in Canada. There is a record of a daughter in Quebec.
Gentleman volunteer	de Saint-Nicolas	Returned to France in 1668.
Gentleman volunteer	de Salampar	Returned to France in 1668.
Cadet	Gabriel de Berthé de Chailly et de La Joubardière	Born in 1647. In 1670 he set up a trading post opposite that of La Frenaye, in Bellevue seigneury. He became an ensign in the militia company formed by Perrot, the governor of Montreal. In 1672 he was charged with dealing in stolen furs. His holding in the Bellevue seigneury was sold in 1684.
Cadet	Louis de Berthé de Chailly et de La Joubardière	The brother of Gabriel. He probably returned to France in 1668.
Cadet	de Loubias	Brother of Arnoult de Broisle de Loubias, captain of the Loubias Company. He returned to France in 1668.

Table 3
Noncommissioned Personnel whose Company Placement Is Not Known
(Noms de guerre shown in parentheses)

Rank	Name	Biographical Notes
Sergeant	de Gouletrez	Returned to France in 1668.
Sergeant	Jean Lafond (La Fontaine)	Returned to France in 1668.
Soldier	René Benard (Bourjoli)	Born in 1630 and married at Trois-Rivières in 1666.
Soldier	Marc Butin	Drowned in Lake Champlain during Tracy's expedition, November 1666.
Soldier	(Champagne)	Charged, along with Langevin, with desertion and rape, 1667.
Soldier	Jean Coron	Born in 1644 and married at Montreal in 1670. He died in 1683.
Soldier	François de Cuque	Presumably settled in Canada.
Soldier	Ange Des Nogeaux	Drowned in Lake Champlain during Tracy's expedition, November 1666.
Soldier	Jean Esalquier de Merembeille	Died in hospital at Montreal in December 1665 at age twenty-six.
Soldier	Jacques Hurteau	Drowned in Lake Champlain during Tracy's expedition, November 1666.
Soldier	(Langevin)	Charged along with Champagne with desertion and rape, 1667.
Soldier	Jacques de Laune (La Vigne)	Related to Guillaume de Laune, a corporal in the La Fouille Company.
Soldier	Claude Maugrain	Convicted of indecent assault on a young girl and sentenced to receive twelve strokes of the birch.
Soldier	Jean Sagean	There is a record of his having married at Montreal.

Table 4
Company Rosters
(Noms de guerre shown in parentheses)

Rank	Name	Biographical Notes
BERTHIER COMPANY (DETACHED FROM THE ALLIER REGIMENT)		
Captain	Alexandre Berthier	Born in 1638. He was a Huguenot but abjured at Quebec in 1665. He went back to France in 1668, but returned to Canada in 1669. He married Marie Legardeur de Tilly in 1672. In the same year he received the seigneurial concession of Berthier-en-bas. In 1673 he bought the seigneury of the Sieur de Randin and, the following year, enlarged it and renamed it Berthier-en-haut. He was active in the military life of the colony until his death in 1708.
Lieutenant	Claude-Sébastien Le Bassier de Villieu de Dandeville	The son of a Savoy noble. He returned to France in 1667 and was replaced by Lavaltrie as the company lieutenant. He came back to Canada in 1670 as an ensign and served under Jacques de Chambly in Acadia. In 1672 he received the concession of the Villieu seigneury, which was sold on his death, in 1700, to Legardeur de Tilly and was, thereafter, known as the Tilly seigneury. Dandeville married at Nantes in 1668 and a daughter of the marriage was buried at Quebec in 1671, having died at the age of two.
Lieutenant	Séraphin Margane de Lavaltrie	Succeeded Dandeville in 1667, transferring from the Monteil Company of the Poitou Regiment to do so. He remained in Canada and married in 1668. He received a half-pay commission from the intendant and in 1672 received the seigneurial concession of Lavaltrie. He died there in 1699 at the age of sixty-six.
Ensign	Pierre Lautin de Cavitant	Returned to France in 1668.
Ensign	Prudent-Alexandre Taboureau de Veronne	Returned to France in 1668.
Soldier	(Belle-Isle)	Settled in Canada in 1668.
Soldier	Jacques Brin (La Pensée)	Settled in Canada in 1668.
Soldier	Louis Bureau (Sans Soucy)	Settled in Canada in 1668.

Table 4 (continued)

Rank	Name	Biographical Notes
Soldier	François Carcy (La Violette)	Married and settled in Canada in 1668.
Soldier	(Champagne)	Settled in Canada in 1668.
Soldier	François Couillard (La Fontaine)	Settled in Canada in 1668.
Soldier	Jean Gely (La Verdure)	Settled in Canada in 1668.
Soldier	Haudry	Settled in Canada in 1668.
Soldier	(Jolicoeur)	Settled in Canada in 1668.
Soldier	Michel Joron (Petit Bois)	Settled in Canada in 1668.
Soldier	(La Fleur)	Settled in Canada in 1668.
Soldier	(La Prairie)	Settled in Canada in 1668.
Soldier	(La Rozée)	Settled in Canada in 1668.
Soldier	(La Vaux)	Settled in Canada in 1668.
Soldier	(Le Catalan)	Settled in Canada in 1668.
Soldier	Le Jeune (La Violette)	Settled in Canada in 1668.
Soldier	Honoré Martel (La Montagne)	Settled in Canada in 1668.
Soldier	André Mignier (Lagasse)	Settled in Canada in 1668

CHAMBLY COMPANY

Captain	Jacques de Chambly	Built Fort Saint-Louis (later Fort Chambly) in 1665 and remained there as its commandant. During Tracy's expedition to the Mohawk country in 1666, he was put in command of the rear guard. Chambly returned to France in 1668, sold his commission, and joined the newly formed Troupes de la Marine. He returned to Canada in 1669 in command of a company of fifty men. In 1672, a year before he became the governor of Acadia, he received the concession of the seigneury of Chambly. In 1679 he was posted to Grenada, also as governor, and moved on to Martinique in the same role in 1680. He died there in 1687.
Lieutenant	Valentin Frapier de Beauregard	Replaced La Barthe as company lieutenant in 1667. He returned to France in 1668.

Table 4 (continued)

Rank	Name	Biographical Notes
Lieutenant	de La Barthe	Possibly the son of Lieutenant-Colonel Du Prat. He is thought to have left the army in 1667, for at that time he was replaced as company lieutenant.
Ensign	Jean-Vincent d'Abbadie de Saint-Castin	Remained in Canada after 1668 and served in Acadia where he became something of a legendary figure. He married an Abenaki chief's daughter. He died in 1707.
Ensign	Bernard Boucher de Roque	Returned to France in 1668 but, in all probability, came back to Canada in 1669 with Chambly. He received a seigneurial concession in 1672.
Sergeant	Pierre Mercan (La Pierre)	Born in 1626. Settled in Canada in 1668.
Soldier	Jean-Louis Baritault (La Marche)	Born in 1647. Settled in Canada in 1668.
Soldier	Louis Chiron (Chiron)	Born in 1647. Settled in Canada in 1668.
Soldier	(Grand-Fontaine)	Settled in Canada in 1668.
Soldier	(Jolicoeur)	Settled in Canada in 1668.
Soldier	La Roche de Perat	Settled in Canada in 1668.
Soldier	Christophe Laurent (Champagne)	Settled in Canada in 1668 and married at Quebec in 1669. He lived on the Sorel seigneury.
Soldier	Etienne Le Chevalier	Born in 1647. Settled in Canada in 1668.
Soldier	(Le Parisien)	Settled in Canada in 1668.
Soldier	Morin	Settled in Canada in 1668.
Soldier	Jean-Baptiste Poirier (La Jeunesse)	Born in 1647. Settled in Canada in 1668.
Soldier	René Poupart (La Fleur)	Born in 1650. Settled in Canada in 1668.
Soldier	Jean Radier (Du Buisson)	Born in 1647. Settled in Canada in 1668.

CONTRECOEUR COMPANY

Captain	Antoine Pécaudy de Contrecoeur	Born in 1596 and was granted letters of nobility in 1661. At the age of seventy-one he married a fifteen-year-old girl from Quebec, Barbe Denys. In 1672 he received the concession of the seigneury of Contrecoeur where he died in 1688.

Table 4 (continued)

Rank	Name	Biographical Notes
Lieutenant	André Jarret de Beauregard	Born in 1644. He was possibly a cousin of Jarret de Verchères. He remained in Canada, married in 1676, and died in 1690.
Ensign	François Jarret de Verchères	Born in 1641. He was a nephew of Pécaudy de Contrecoeur. He remained in Canada after 1668, married the following year, and took possession of what was to become the seigneury of Verchères. He received the concession in 1672 and died there in 1700.
Cadet	Pierre Julien	Probably returned to France in 1667 or 1668.
Corporal	Jean Moisan (Le Breton)	Died in hospital at Montreal in November 1665.
Soldier	Pierre Barbarin (Grand-Maison)	Settled in Canada in 1668 and married at Montreal in the same year.
Soldier	Guillaume Beautrefils (La Fleur)	Born in 1645. Settled in Canada in 1668.
Soldier	Etienne Benoist (La Jeunesse)	Settled in Canada in 1668.
Soldier	Bernard Bertin (Languedoc)	Settled in Canada in 1668.
Soldier	Gabriel Boutaux (La Ramé)	Settled in Canada in 1668.
Soldier	(Champagne)	Settled in Canada in 1668.
Soldier	Gaspard Dargan (Le Boesme)	Settled in Canada in 1668.
Soldier	Joseph Denis (Le Vallon)	Settled in Canada in 1668.
Soldier	Pierre Dues (La Chapelle)	Settled in Canada in 1668.
Soldier	Antoine Emery, Sieur de Coderre (Coderre)	Became Contrecoeur's steward on the seigneury. He married in Canada in 1674 and again in 1688.
Soldier	Pierre Favreau (Des Lauriers)	Settled in Canada in 1668.
Soldier	Bernard de Florensac (Le Gascon)	Died in hospital at Montreal in June 1666 at the age of thirty.
Soldier	Germain Gauthier (Saint-Germain)	Born in 1647. Settled in Canada in 1668.

Table 4 (continued)

Rank	Name	Biographical Notes
Soldier	Hubert Grangé (Dauphin)	Contrecoeur's valet, who died in hospital at Montreal in March 1667 at the age of twenty-five.
Soldier	Nicolas Guillaume (La Chaume)	Settled in Canada in 1668.
Soldier	Sicaire Guire (La Prairie)	Settled in Canada in 1668.
Soldier	Louis Lachaise (George d'Ambroise)	Settled in Canada in 1668.
Soldier	Maximin La Forge (La Forge)	Settled in Canada in 1668.
Soldier	(La Pensée)	Settled in Canada in 1668.
Soldier	(L'Esveillé)	Settled in Canada in 1668.
Soldier	Vivier Magdeleine (La Douceur)	Settled in Canada in 1668.
Soldier	François Pougnet (Beauregard)	Settled in Canada in 1668.
Soldier	Edme Salain (La Cave)	Settled in Canada in 1668.
Soldier	Jacques Supernant (Sans Soucy)	Settled in Canada in 1668.
Soldier	Pierre Tenaille (La Violette)	Died in hospital at Montreal in December 1665 at the age of twenty-five.

DES PORTES COMPANY (FORMERLY THE DU PRAT COMPANY)

Lieutenant-colonel	Du Prat	Died at Fort Sainte-Thérèse in January 1666.
Captain	Balthazar Des Portes	Born in 1638. He was a half-pay captain until he took command of the company after the death of Du Prat. He returned to France in 1668.
Lieutenant	Des Granges	See under La Varenne Company.
Lieutenant	Sieur de Rouverel	Transferred from the La Varenne Company in 1665 in an exchange involving Lieutenant Des Granges while still in France awaiting embarkation. He returned to France in 1668.
Cadet	Jean Gabarets	Died at Montreal in August 1668 at the age of thirty.

Table 4 (continued)

Rank	Name	Biographical Notes
Soldier	André Archin (Saint-André)	Settled in Canada in 1668.
Soldier	Pierre Amans (Amans)	Settled in Canada in 1668.
Soldier	Pierre Augrand (La Pierre)	Settled in Canada in 1668.
Soldier	d'Ausson	Settled in Canada in 1668.
Soldier	André Betourné (La Violette)	Settled in Canada in 1668.
Soldier	(Canadou)	Settled in Canada in 1668.
Soldier	(Champagne)	Settled in Canada in 1668.
Soldier	Renaud Chollet (La Liberté)	Settled in Canada in 1668.
Soldier	Antoine Combelle (Des Jardins)	Settled in Canada in 1668.
Soldier	Bernard Joachim (La Verdure)	Settled in Canada in 1668.
Soldier	(La Berthe)	Settled in Canada in 1668.
Soldier	(La Noce)	Settled in Canada in 1668.
Soldier	(Le Petit Des Lauriers)	Settled in Canada in 1668.
Soldier	Toussaint Lucas (Lagarde)	Settled in Canada in 1668.

DUGUÉ COMPANY (SOMETIMES CALLED THE BOISBRIAND COMPANY)

Captain	Michel-Sidrac Dugué de Boisbriand	In 1667 received permission from Talon to clear land on the Ile Sainte-Thérèse. In 1672 he received the concession of it as the seigneury of Boisbriand. He married in 1667 and in 1670 became the commandant of Montreal. Having more interest in the fur trade than in the life of a seigneur, he sold his fief in 1679. Six years later he received another seigneury, this one on the north shore of the St Lawrence and called Mille-Iles. He died in 1688 at the age of fifty.
Lieutenant	François de Sainte-Croix	Returned to France in 1668.
Ensign	Roch Thoery de L'Ormeau	Married at Quebec in 1667 and settled in Canada. He died in 1687.

Table 4 (continued)

Rank	Name	Biographical Notes
Cadet	Lavallé	Returned to France in 1668.
Sergeant	Laurent Cambin (La Rivière)	Settled in Canada in 1668.
Corporal	Pierre ... (La Pierre)	Drowned in July 1667 at the age of thirty-two.
Soldier	Guillaume Aubry (La Brière)	Drowned in Lake Champlain in November 1666 during Tracy's expedition to the Mohawk country.
Soldier	Antoine Bethelin (Saint-Jean Chastelleraud)	Settled in Canada in 1668.
Soldier	Jean Bricault (La Marche)	Settled in Canada in 1668.
Soldier	(La Faveur)	Settled in Canada in 1668.
Soldier	(L'Espérance)	Settled in Canada in 1668.
Soldier	Jacques Passard (Bretonnière)	Settled in Canada in 1668.
Soldier	Etienne Poitier (La Verdure)	Settled in Canada in 1668.
Soldier	(Rustique)	Died at Montreal in February 1666 at the age of thirty-two.
Soldier	(Sainte-Croix)	Settled in Canada in 1668.
Soldier	René Sauvageau de Maisonneuve (Maisonneuve)	Company surgeon, who settled in Canada in 1668. In that year he bought land at Pointe-aux-Trembles, married, and then went to live on the Lachenaie seigneury where he remained until his death in 1690.
Soldier	David Trouillard (La Pointe)	Died at Montreal in July 1667 at the age of forty-five.
Soldier	Pierre Trouillard (La Forest)	Brother of David Trouillard. He settled in Canada in 1668.

FROMENT COMPANY

Captain	Pierre Salvaye de Froment	Commanded what was perhaps the weakest company in the regiment. Before leaving Quebec for the Richelieu Valley in July 1665, he left 100 *louis d'or* with the Jesuits for safekeeping. He returned to France in 1667 or 1668 and died there in 1689.
Corporal	Pierre Poirrot (La Verdure)	Settled in Canada in 1668.

Table 4 (continued)

Rank	Name	Biographical Notes
Soldier	Sébastien Arnaud (La Douceur)	Settled in Canada in 1668.
Soldier	Louis Badaillac (La Plante)	Born in 1649 or 1650. He settled in Canada in 1668, married there, and lived on the Sorel seigneury.
Soldier	(Boutefeu)	Settled in Canada in 1668.
Soldier	Sépulture de Coue (La Fleur)	Killed at Trois-Rivières by the accidental firing of a cannon in August 1665.
Soldier	Louis Dauvernier (L'Orange)	Settled in Canada in 1668.
Soldier	(Desjardins)	Settled in Canada in 1668.
Soldier	Antoine Francoeur (Brule)	Settled in Canada in 1668 and lived on the Sorel seigneury.
Soldier	Jean Guillet (Saint-Marc)	Born in 1641. He settled in Canada in 1668 and lived on the Sorel siegneury.
Soldier	Jean Houry (Bellerose)	Probably settled in Canada in 1668.
Soldier	(Jolicoeur)	Settled in Canada in 1668.
Soldier	Pierre La Faye (Monturas)	Settled in Canada in 1668.
Soldier	Pierre Montarras (Monturas)	Settled in Canada in 1668.
Soldier	Léonard de Montreau (Francoeur)	Married at Montreal and settled in Canada in 1668.
Soldier	Bernard de Niger (Sansoucy)	Born in 1627. He settled in Canada in 1668 and lived on the Sorel seigneury.
Soldier	Pierre Queulin (Pierrot)	Settled in Canada in 1668.
Soldier	Etienne Rambault (Rambaux)	Born in 1637. He settled in Canada in 1668 and lived on the Sorel seigneury.

GRANDFONTAINE COMPANY

Captain	Hector d'Andigné de Grandfontaine	Returned to France in 1668 but came back to Canada the following year with the rank of major. He went to Acadia as governor in 1670, and served in that capacity until 1673 when he was replaced by Jacques de Chambly. At that time he went back to France and remained there.

Table 4 (continued)

Rank	Name	Biographical Notes
Lieutenant	François Provost	Born in 1638. When he came to Canada, he soon moved from the military to the civil sphere of duties. In 1666 he became garrison major in Quebec, a position confirmed in 1668. He married at Quebec in 1679 and shortly afterwards was appointed acting governor of the city in the absence of the incumbent. In 1699 he was made governor of Trois-Rivières, where he died in 1702.
Lieutenant	Pierre de Joybert de Soulanges et de Marson	Born in 1641 or 1642. He took over as company lieutenant in 1666, when Provost assumed the duties of garrison major in Quebec. He returned to France, most likely in 1667, but came back to Canada the following year when he took possession of Port-Royal, in Acadia, from the English. In 1671 Joybert went to Quebec after disagreements with Grandfontaine, the governor of Acadia. He married at Quebec the following year and soon after received the concession of an Acadian seigneury. By 1678 he had risen to the position of commandant of Acadia. He died very shortly afterwards.
Ensign	Pierre Bécart de Grandville	Born in 1645. He remained in Canada after 1668, marrying in that year at Quebec. In 1672 he received the seigneurial concession of Ilet de Portage. He returned to a military life in 1686 as a lieutenant in the Troupes de la Marine. He died at Quebec in 1708.
Soldier	André Babel (La Marche)	Settled in Canada in 1668.
Soldier	François Biville (Le Picart)	Settled in Canada in 1668.
Soldier	Louis Boulduc (Bosleduc)	Settled in Canada in 1668.
Soldier	Jean Bugeoni (L'Angevin)	Settled in Canada in 1668.
Soldier	Pierre Coquin (La Tonelle)	Settled in Canada in 1668.
Soldier	(Des Moulins)	Settled in Canada in 1668.
Soldier	René Dumas (Rencontre)	Settled in Canada in 1668.

Table 4 (continued)

Rank	Name	Biographical Notes
Soldier	Pierre Hudon (Beaulieu)	Settled in Canada in 1668.
Soldier	(Jolicoeur)	Settled in Canada in 1668.
Soldier	Julien La Bouche (La Touche)	Settled in Canada in 1668.
Soldier	Pierre La Croix (La Croix)	Settled in Canada in 1668.
Soldier	(La Flesche)	Settled in Canada in 1668.
Soldier	Aubin Lambert (Champagne)	Settled in Canada in 1668.
Soldier	Roger La Touche (La Touche)	Settled in Canada in 1668.
Soldier	(La Vigne)	Settled in Canada in 1668.
Soldier	(La Volonté)	Settled in Canada in 1668.
Soldier	(Le Parisien)	Settled in Canada in 1668.
Soldier	(Le Valon)	Settled in Canada in 1668.
Soldier	Jean Merienne (La Solaye)	Settled in Canada in 1668.
Soldier	Noel Pourveu (La Fortune)	Settled in Canada in 1668.
Soldier	Pierre-André Renoud (Locatte)	Settled in Canada in 1668.
Soldier	(Saint-Laurent)	Settled in Canada in 1668.

LA BRISANDIÈRE COMPANY (DETACHED FROM THE ORLÉANS REGIMENT)

Captain	... de La Brisandière	Returned to France in 1667 or 1668.
Ensign	Jean L'Aumonier de Traversy	Killed in an Iroquois ambush near Fort Sainte-Anne in July 1666.
Soldier	Pierre Balan (La Combe)	Settled in Canada in 1668.
Soldier	Fayat	Settled in Canada in 1668.
Soldier	Pierre Joncas (La Pierre)	Settled in Canada in 1668.
Soldier	Jean Parrier	Settled in Canada in 1668.
Soldier	Toupin	Settled in Canada in 1668.
Soldier	(Tranchemontagne)	Settled in Canada in 1668.

Table 4 (continued)

Rank	Name	Biographical Notes
LA COLONELLE COMPANY		
Captain	Jean-Baptiste Dubois de Cocreaumont et de Saint-Maurice	Besides being a company commander, he was the regimental gunnery officer and Talon's personal representative in the field. In the latter position it fell to him to take formal possession of the Mohawk lands in 1666 during Tracy's autumn expedition. He returned to France in 1667 or 1668.
Lieutenant	Sixte Cherrier de Mignarde	Returned to France in 1667 or 1668.
Lieutenant	François Féraud	Adjutant until he became Tracy's aide-de-camp, late in 1666, after Alexandre de Chaumont returned to France. He also returned there in 1668.
Ensign	Antoine La Frenaye de Brucy	Born in 1649 He purchased an ensign's commission on 26 August 1667. He remained in Canada in 1668 and entered the fur trade. In the course of his dealings he is known to have sold brandy to the Indians. He married in 1676 and died in 1684. For most of his life in Canada he lived on the seigneury of Ile Perrot, which he had received as a concession. He also owned a house on Saint-Paul Street in Montreal.
Ensign	Dominique Lefebvre Du Guesclin	Sold his commission to Brucy in August 1667 and then returned to France.
Sergeant	Jacques Guitant (Jolicoeur)	Married in Montreal on 14 June 1666. He settled in Canada in 1668 and entered the fur trade.
Soldier	Louis Denis (La Fontaine)	Born in 1649. Settled in Canada in 1668.
Soldier	Antoine Du Fresne	Born in 1636. He settled in Canada in 1668.
Soldier	(La Jauge)	Settled in Canada in 1668.
Soldier	(La Roze)	Settled in Canada in 1668.
Soldier	Guillaume Regnault	Born in 1644. He settled in Canada in 1668.
Soldier	Jean Rousssel (La Tulipe or Montauban)	Born in 1649. He settled in Canada in 1668.
Soldier	(Saint-Denis)	Settled in Canada in 1668.
Soldier	(Sans Soucy)	Settled in Canada in 1668.

Table 4 (continued)

Rank	Name	Biographical Notes

LA DURANTAYE COMPANY (DETACHED FROM THE CHAMBELLÉ REGIMENT)

Captain	Olivier Morel de La Durantaye	Born in 1640. He was at Fort Sainte-Anne in 1666 but returned to France in 1667 or 1668. Durantaye came back to Canada in 1669 and in 1672 received the concession of the seigneury of La Durantaye. He married in the colony and remained active in its military life until his death in 1716.
Lieutenant	de Saint-Aubert	Returned to France in 1667 or 1668.
Ensign	de L'Aubry	Returned to France in 1667 or 1668.
Soldier	Mathurin Besnard (La Jeunesse)	Settled in Canada in 1668.
Soldier	Mathurin Duchéron (Des Lauriers)	Settled in Canada in 1668.
Soldier	Jean-Pierre Forgues (Mont-Rouge)	Settled in Canada in 1668.
Soldier	(La Musique)	Settled in Canada in 1668.
Soldier	Michel Malet	Died in Montreal in February 1667 at the age of thirty.

LA FOUILLE COMPANY

| Captain | Jean-Maurice-Philippe de Vernon de La Fouille | Returned to France in 1668. |
| Lieutenant | Philippe Gaultier de Comporté | Born in 1641. He was the nephew of Captain de La Fouille. Involved in the assassination of a judge at La Mothe-Saint-Héray, while en route to La Rochelle in 1665, he was condemned to death in absentia. Soon after he became a lieutenant in his uncle's company. Remaining in Canada after 1668, he became Talon's commissioner of supplies in Quebec. In 1672 he married the daughter of one of the principal merchants in that city, and three years later was named churchwarden of a parish there. He became an official of the court in Quebec in 1677, and in 1680 received a royal pardon for his crime in France. He died in 1687 at the age of forty-six. |

Table 4 (continued)

Rank	Name	Biographical Notes
Ensign	Charles Dugey de Rozoy, Vicomte de Mannereuil	Received the concession of a seigneury near Lac Saint-Pierre, but since he never occupied it, he lost it and returned to France in 1682 where he became a captain in the Poitou Regiment. He came back to Canada ten years later, but only stayed until 1695 when he again returned to France.
Corporal	Guillaume de Laune	Probably returned to France in 1667 or 1668.
Soldier	(Beaulieu)	Settled in Canada in 1668.
Soldier	Jean Berard (La Riverdia)	Settled in Canada in 1668.
Soldier	François Bousbard (La Montagne)	Settled in Canada in 1668.
Soldier	(Boutebouilly)	Settled in Canada in 1668.
Soldier	Etienne Boyer (La Fontaine Milon)	Settled in Canada in 1668.
Soldier	Pierre Brunion (La Fontaine)	Settled in Canada in 1668.
Soldier	Jean-Baptiste Charron (La Ferrière)	Settled in Canada in 1668.
Soldier	Jean Cherbot (Des Moulins)	Settled in Canada in 1668.
Soldier	(Des Fontaines)	Settled in Canada in 1668.
Soldier	Antoine Dubois (Du Bois)	Settled in Canada in 1668.
Soldier	Guillaume Du Bord (La Fontaine)	Settled in Canada in 1668.
Soldier	(Esmardit)	Settled in Canada in 1668.
Soldier	Pierre Faye (Villefaignan)	Settled in Canada in 1668.
Soldier	Christophe Février (La Croix)	Settled in Canada in 1668.
Soldier	(Germaneau)	Settled in Canada in 1668.
Soldier	Paul Guyon (La Tremblade)	Settled in Canada in 1668.
Soldier	Jean Huitonneau (La Forest)	Settled in Canada in 1668.

Table 4 (continued)

Rank	Name	Biographical Notes
Soldier	Jean Jacquet de Gerlaise (Saint-Amand)	Settled in Canada in 1668.
Soldier	(La Barre)	Settled in Canada in 1668.
Soldier	(La Fortune)	Settled in Canda in 1668.
Soldier	(La Noiray)	Most probably the drummer involved in the disturbance at La Mothe-Saint-Héray in 1665 during the march to La Rochelle. He is also possibly Louis Deniort, who was sentenced to death in absentia by the court at Saint-Maixent. He settled in Canada in 1668.
Soldier	Jean Laspron (La Charité)	Settled in Canada in 1668.
Soldier	Noel Laurarée (L'Orange)	Settled in Canada in 1668.
Soldier	Jean Le Niay	Settled in Canada in 1668.
Soldier	(Le Petit Breton)	Settled in Canada in 1668.
Soldier	François Le Roux (Le Cardinal)	Settled in Canada in 1668.
Soldier	Jean Le Tellier (La Fortune)	Settled in Canada in 1668.
Soldier	(Maisonseule)	Settled in Canada in 1668.
Soldier	François Nepveu (La Croix)	Settled in Canada in 1668.
Soldier	Jacques Paviot (La Pensée)	Settled in Canada in 1668.
Soldier	Jean Peladeau (Saint-Jean)	Settled in Canada in 1668.
Soldier	(Saint-Amand)	Settled in Canada in 1668.
Soldier	(Saint-Germain)	Settled in Canada in 1668.
Soldier	Jacques Tetu (La Rivière)	Settled in Canada in 1668.
Soldier	(Villefroy)	Settled in Canada in 1668.

Table 4 (continued)

Rank	Name	Biographical Notes
LA FREDIÈRE COMPANY		
Major	Balthazard de La Flotte de La Fredière	A repulsive, avaricious, and debauched man, disliked by all except his uncle, the Marquis de Salières. He received a wound in the thigh during the skirmish near Schenectady in February 1666. Later in the same year he was sent by Tracy to build two strong points near Fort Saint-Louis. During 1666–67 he served as the military governor of Montreal and succeeded in angering the residents with his drunkeness, cruelty, womanizing, and unscrupulous practices of trading guns and liquor to the Indians. The outcome was that complaints were lodged with the general, the governor, and the intendant, who issued an order calling for the major's return to France. In September 1667 the Marquis de Salières protested strenuously about the order, but to no avail. La Fredière was sent back to France in the fall of 1667.
Lieutenant	Annibal Alexis de La Flotte de La Fredière	The brother of Balthazard. He returned to France in 1668.
Ensign	Jean-Nicolas de Brandis	Returned to France in 1668.
Soldier	André Barsa (Le Limousin)	Settled in Canada in 1668.
Soldier	Antoine Beaudoin (Saint-Antoine)	Settled in Canada in 1668.
Soldier	François Belair (Belair)	Settled in Canada in 1668. In 1670 he became a servant to Paul Dupuy, a former ensign in the Maximy Company, and Pierre Bécart de Grandville, who had held a similar rank in the Grandfontaine Company.
Soldier	Mathurin Bernier (La Marcelle)	Settled in Canada in 1668.
Soldier	François Boutron (Le Major)	Settled in Canada in 1668.

Table 4 (continued)

Rank	Name	Biographical Notes
Soldier	Jean-Vincent Chamaillard (La Fontaine)	Born in 1646. He settled in Canada in 1668.
Soldier	Jean Dalpé (Delpesches)	Born in 1648. He settled in Canada in 1668.
Soldier	Jean ... (Des Rosiers)	Found dead in the snow in January 1667. He was about thirty when he died.
Soldier	Louis Fortin (Le Grandeur)	Born in 1647. He settled in Canada in 1668.
Soldier	Jacques Genest (La Barre)	Settled in Canada in 1668.
Soldier	(La Bonté)	Settled in Canada in 1668.
Soldier	(La Chaume)	Settled in Canada in 1668.
Soldier	(La Jeunesse)	A Walloon who at age thirty was killed by the Iroquois in May 1666. He was buried at Montreal.
Soldier	(La Rose)	Settled in Canada in 1668.
Soldier	(La Verdure)	Settled in Canada in 1668.
Soldier	(La Vergne)	Settled in Canada in 1668.
Soldier	Guillaume ... (Le Petit Breton)	Died in hospital at Montreal in November 1665.
Soldier	Hilaire Limousin (Beaufort)	Born in 1633. He settled in Canada in 1668.
Soldier	Nicolas Moisan (La Palisse or Le Parisien)	Settled in Canada in 1668.
Soldier	René Orieux (La Fleur)	Settled in Canada in 1668.
Soldier	Jean Roussel (La Roussellière)	The company surgeon. He settled in Canada in 1668.
Soldier	Jean Roy (La Pensée)	Settled in Canada in 1668.
Soldier	Jacques Viau (L'Espérance)	Born in 1640 or 1644. He settled in Canada in 1668.
Soldier	Name unknown	Crushed to death by a tree he was felling while helping to build a strong point near Fort Saint-Louis in August 1666.

Table 4 (continued)

Rank	Name	Biographical Notes
LAMOTTE COMPANY		
Captain	Pierre Lamotte de Saint-Paul	The builder of Fort Sainte-Anne, which he completed on 26 July 1666. Lamotte remained in Canada after 1668 in command of the Montreal garrison. According to Nicolas Perrot, explorer, fur trader, and French commandant at Baie des Puants (Green Bay), the Lamotte Company was one of the last of the Carignan-Salières Regiment to be on active duty in Canada in 1669. The captain probably returned to France in 1670.
Lieutenant	Philippe Dufresnoy Carion	Born in 1631. He stayed on with the company in the Montreal garrison and then settled in Canada. He received a fief from the Sulpicians in 1671, and in the same year he carried out an armed attack on Thoery de L'Ormeau, a former ensign in the Dugué Company, who was a neighbour. He also married in that year. He died in 1684.
Ensign	Paul de Morel	Remained with the company in the Montreal garrison and also received a fief from the Sulpicians, contiguous with that of Dufresnoy Carion. Morel too was involved in the attack on Thoery de L'Ormeau.
Soldier	Michel Grouvillet de La Motte	Possibly related to the company commander. He died in hospital at Montreal in March 1667 at the age of eighteen.
Soldier	René Le Meunier (La Ramée)	Born in 1636. He settled in Canada in 1668.
Soldier	Etienne Pasquier	Born in 1621. He settled in Canada in 1668.
Soldier	Isaac Pasquier (La Vallée)	Born in 1636. He settled in Canada in 1668.
Soldier	Eustache Prévost (La Fleur)	Born in 1646. He settled in Canada in 1668.
Soldier	Jean René	Settled in Canada in 1668.
Soldier	Jean de Roy	Settled in Canada in 1668.

Table 4 (continued)

Rank	Name	Biographical Notes
LA NORAYE COMPANY		
Captain	Louis de Niort de La Noraye	Born in 1639. He married at Quebec in February 1672. He obtained a seigneurial concession in 1688 and died in 1708.
Ensign	Nicolas de Hautcourt de Beaumont	Sold his commission to Dubois de Saint-Maurice in 1667 and presumably returned to France thereafter.
Ensign	Felix Dubois de Saint-Maurice	Purchased his ensign's commission from Hautcourt de Beaumont in 1667. He probably returned to France in 1668.
Soldier	Jean Boesme (Bohémier)	Settled in Canada in 1668.
Soldier	(Champagne)	Settled in Canada in 1668.
Soldier	Jacques La Fontaine	Settled in Canada in 1668.
Soldier	Jacques La Querre (Rencontre)	Settled in Canada in 1668.
Soldier	Pierre Morin	Settled in Canada in 1668.
Soldier	Nicolas Prunier (Le Picard)	Settled in Canada in 1668.
Soldier	Nicolas Rousselol (La Prairie)	Settled in Canada in 1668.
Soldier	Michel Roy (Chastelleraud)	Settled in Canada in 1668.
Soldier	Alexandre Saint-Jean	Settled in Canada in 1668.
Soldier	François Trollain (Saint-Surin)	Settled in Canada in 1668.
LA TOUR COMPANY		
Captain	de La Tour	Already an aged man when he came to Canada. One of his first acts on arriving was to arrange for François Moussart, a drummer, to be placed with the Jesuits in Quebec so that he might continue his education. La Tour returned to France in 1668.
Ensign	Roland de La Font	Transferred to the Monteil Company of the Poitou Regiment in May 1666. He presumably returned to France in 1668.
Sergeant	Léonard Tresny	Settled in Canada in 1668.
Corporal	Pierre Payette (Saint-Amour)	Settled in Canada in 1668.

Table 4 (continued)

Rank	Name	Biographical Notes
Soldier	Blaise Belleau (La Rose)	Settled in Canada in 1668.
Soldier	Jean Besset (Brisetout)	Settled in Canada in 1668.
Soldier	(Champagne)	Settled in Canada in 1668.
Soldier	Aufray Coulon (Mabriau)	Settled in Canada in 1668.
Soldier	Antoine Duprée (Duprée Rochefort)	Settled in Canada in 1668.
Soldier	(La Fontaine)	Settled in Canada in 1668.
Soldier	René Le Breton (Le Breton)	Settled in Canada in 1668.
Soldier	(Le Picart)	Settled in Canada in 1668.
Soldier	(L'Irlande)	Settled in Canada in 1668.
Soldier	(Maison Blanche)	Settled in Canada in 1668.
Soldier	Jean Martinet (Font Blanche)	Settled in Canada in 1668.
Soldier	François Moussart	The company drummer placed in the charge of the Jesuits at Quebec by La Tour in order to complete his education.
Soldier	Michel Potier (L'Angevin)	Settled in Canada in 1668.

LA VARENNE COMPANY

Rank	Name	Biographical Notes
Captain	Roger de Bonneau de La Varenne	Returned to France in 1668.
Lieutenant	Des Granges	Originally with the Des Portes (then Du Prat) Company, but changed places with the Sieur de Rouverel following a disagreement between himself and La Varenne while the regiment was still in France. Des Granges returned to France in 1668.
Lieutenant	Sieur de Rouverel	See under Des Portes Company.
Gentleman volunteer	de Bassigny	Returned to France in 1668.
Soldier	Jacques Bannois (Bannois)	Settled in Canada in 1668.
Soldier	Jean Beaume (La Franchise)	Settled in Canada in 1668.

Table 4 (continued)

Rank	Name	Biographical Notes
Soldier	Charles Des Maignouz, Sieur de Laleu	Was with François Poisson when he died while hunting near Montreal in March 1667.
Soldier	Charles Duchesne (La Rivière)	Settled in Canada in 1668.
Soldier	Claude Du Parc	Killed by the Iroquois in June 1666 at the age of twenty.
Soldier	Jean Dusseault (Du Sceau)	Settled in Canada in 1668.
Soldier	Jean Fagueret (Petit Bois)	Settled in Canada in 1668.
Soldier	Mathieu Fayé (La Fayette)	Settled in Canada in 1668.
Soldier	Gabriel Fournier (La Verdure)	Settled in Canada in 1668.
Soldier	Claude Galope	The company surgeon. He was called in to verify the cause of death of François Poisson, who died on a hunting expedition near Montreal in March 1667.
Soldier	(La Montagne)	Settled in Canada in 1668.
Soldier	(Lavau)	Killed by the Iroquois in June 1666 at the age of twenty-five.
Soldier	(Le Chaudillon)	Settled in Canada in 1668.
Soldier	Antoine Le Gros (La Violette)	Settled in Canada in 1668.
Soldier	(L'Espérance)	Settled in Canada in 1668.
Soldier	Louis Mané (Sainte-Marie)	Settled in Canada in 1668.
Soldier	Jean Monflet (Champagne)	Settled in Canada in 1668.
Soldier	Jean Moreau (Jolicoeur)	Settled in Canada in 1668.
Soldier	Jacques de Moulin (De Moulin)	Settled in Canada in 1668.
Soldier	François Poisson	Froze to death while on a hunting trip near Montreal in March 1667. He was twenty-six years old at the time.

Table 4 (continued)

Rank	Name	Biographical Notes
Soldier	Guillaume Richard (Lafleur)	Settled in Canada in 1668 and became the first commandant of Fort Frontenac in 1673. He was killed in a skirmish with a band of Iroquois in 1690.
Soldier	(Salle Brune)	Settled in Canada in 1668.
Soldier	François Saluer de Monthieu	Drowned while bathing in June 1666 at the age of twenty-seven.

LOUBIAS COMPANY

Rank	Name	Biographical Notes
Captain	Arnoult de Broisle de Loubias	Arrested the Iroquois ambassadors at Trois-Rivières in July 1666. He returned to France with Tracy in 1667, but came back to Canada in 1669 with a company of fifty men. He took part in Courcelle's expedition to Cataracoui in 1671. In 1672 he received the concession of the seigneury of Lac Saint-Pierre, but he did not stay there long, returning to France again in 1674.
Lieutenant	René Gaultier de Varennes	Born in 1634. He married Pierre Boucher's daughter Marie in September 1667. In the same year he became the governor of Trois-Rivières, a post he held until his death in 1689. In 1672 he received the concession of the seigneury of Varennes and became active in the fur trade, along with his father-in-law.
Ensign	Pierre Mouet de Moras	Remained in Canada after 1668 and, in the same year, married at Trois-Rivières. In 1672 he received the concession of a seigneury, named Ile de Moras, on an island at the mouth of the Nicolet River. He settled on the island as a farmer and died there in 1693, leaving his family in extreme poverty.
Sergeant	Paul Cartier (La Roze)	Settled in Canada in 1668.
Sergeant	Jacques Labadie	Remained in Canada after 1668. In 1669 he was a member of the garrison at Trois-Rivières, and by 1671 he was in charge of it. In 1672 he received a fief on the outskirts of Trois-Rivières, which he rented to the Godefroy family on the condition that it be named Godefroy-Labadie. Two years later Labadie became the sergeant-major of the Trois-Rivières garrison, a post he retained until 1689. In 1676 he became a member of the Committee of Merchants at Trois-Rivières. He died there in 1707.

Table 4 (continued)

Rank	Name	Biographical Notes
Soldier	Jean Arcourt (La Jeunesse)	Settled in Canada in 1668.
Soldier	François Audouin (La Verdure)	Settled in Canada in 1668.
Soldier	Pierre Boulanger (Le Boulanger)	Settled in Canada in 1668.
Soldier	(Des Barreaux)	Settled in Canada in 1668.
Soldier	(Du Boulay)	Settled in Canada in 1668.
Soldier	(Du Marché)	Settled in Canada in 1668.
Soldier	Pierre Durand (Des Marchets)	Settled in Canada in 1668.
Soldier	Cobie Hébert (Montauban)	Settled in Canada in 1668.
Soldier	Jacques Julien (Le Dragon)	Settled in Canada in 1668 and lived on the Sorel seigneury.
Soldier	(La Fleur)	Settled in Canada in 1668.
Soldier	(La Marche)	Settled in Canada in 1668.
Soldier	(La Montagne)	Settled in Canada in 1668.
Soldier	(La Pensée)	Settled in Canada in 1668.
Soldier	(La Roye)	Settled in Canada in 1668.
Soldier	Le Petit (La Fontaine)	Settled in Canada in 1668.
Soldier	Jacques Le Prince	Settled in Canada in 1668.
Soldier	(Le Rigeur)	Settled in Canada in 1668.
Soldier	Pierre Lozeau (La Tour)	Settled in Canada in 1668. He lived on the Sorel seigneury until 1676 when he sold his holding and moved to Acadia.
Soldier	Pierre Lybault (La Rosée)	Settled in Canada in 1668.
Soldier	Elie Provost (La Violette)	Settled in Canada in 1668.
Soldier	Louis Robert (La Fontaine or La Pommeraye)	Settled in Canada in 1668.
Soldier	(Sansoucy)	Settled in Canada in 1668.

Table 4 (continued)

Rank	Name	Biographical Notes
Soldier	Charles Vanet (Le Parisien)	Born in 1649. He settled in Canada in 1668 and subsequently married. He lived on the Sorel seigneury and became the first church-warden in the parish there, a post he held until his death in 1723.
Soldier	Pierre Verrier (La Solaye)	Settled in Canada in 1668.

MAXIMY COMPANY

Captain	de Maximy	Returned to France in 1668.
Ensign	Paul Dupuy de Lisloye	Born in 1637. He remained in Canada in 1668 and, in the same year, married at Quebec. He became the fourth seigneur of the Ile aux Oies in 1671. After becoming lieutenant-particular for the provostship of Quebec, he took up arms again in 1687 to fight the Iroquois, and in 1690 against the English. He turned his seigneury over to the Hospitalières at Quebec before his death in 1713.
Cadet	Nicolas de Choisy	Returned to France in 1668.
Cadet	Florimond de La Chenais, Sieur du Puis	Returned to France in 1668.
Soldier	(Belle-Isle)	Settled in Canada in 1668.
Soldier	Jacques Bidet (de Russel)	Settled in Canada in 1668.
Soldier	Alexandre Boissard (Le Prince de Conty)	Settled in Canada in 1668.
Soldier	Nicolas-Vincent Boissoneau (Xaintonge)	Settled in Canada in 1668.
Soldier	Antoine Bordeleau (Dampierre)	Settled in Canada in 1668.
Soldier	Jacques Bussière (La Verdure)	Settled in Canada in 1668.
Soldier	Charles Dampierre (Saint-Martin)	Settled in Canada in 1668.
Soldier	Julien Dumont (La Fleur)	Settled in Canada in 1668.
Soldier	Jean-Baptiste Gourdon (La Chasse)	Settled in Canada in 1668.

Table 4 (continued)

Rank	Name	Biographical Notes
Soldier	Martin Guérand (Gratte Lard)	Settled in Canada in 1668.
Soldier	Gugnot (Le Tambour)	Settled in Canada in 1668.
Soldier	Paul Inaid (Le Provençal)	Settled in Canada in 1668.
Soldier	Julien ...	Settled in Canada in 1668.
Soldier	(La France)	Settled in Canada in 1668.
Soldier	(La Meslée)	Settled in Canada in 1668.
Soldier	(La Rhétorique)	Settled in Canada in 1668.
Soldier	Jean Lauget (Matta)	Settled in Canada in 1668.
Soldier	Antoine Leblan (Jolicoeur)	Settled in Canada in 1668.
Soldier	(Le Blanc)	Settled in Canada in 1668.
Soldier	René Le Merle (Le Merle)	Settled in Canada in 1668.
Soldier	Mathurin Ranbeau (Bourjoly)	Settled in Canada in 1668.
Soldier	Pierre Ronoset (Beaucourt)	Settled in Canada in 1668.
Soldier	Pierre Vignault	Settled in Canada in 1668.

MONTEIL COMPANY (DETACHED FROM THE POITOU REGIMENT)

Rank	Name	Biographical Notes
Captain	François de Tapie de Monteil et de Clérac	Kept a notebook for much of his army career, from 1661 to 1670, which contains background information on the day-to-day life of an officer in Canada. He returned to France on 5 November 1668, aboard the ship *Espérance*. He continued to serve in the army, following his return to Europe, until 1670.
Lieutenant	Louis de Canchy de Lerole	Took over the lieutenancy in May 1666, when Lavaltrie was transferred to the Berthier Company of the Allier Regiment. Until that time Lerole had been an ensign in the company. After being captured by the Mohawks near Fort Sainte-Anne in July 1666, he returned to Quebec with the Flemish Bastard at the end of the month. He returned to France in 1668. He was a relative of the Marquis de Tracy.

Table 4 (continued)

Rank	Name	Biographical Notes
Lieutenant	Séraphin Margane de Lavaltrie	See under Berthier Company.
Ensign	Roland de La Font	Became an ensign on 29 May 1666, after Canchy de Lerole had been promoted to lieutenant. He paid 454 *livres* for the commission, borrowing the money from Tapie de Monteil. He returned to France in 1668.
Sergeant	Michel Hébert (La Verdure)	Settled in Canada in 1668.
Soldier	(Aiment)	Returned to France in 1667 or 1668.
Soldier	Nicolas Audet (La Pointe)	Settled in Canada in 1668.
Soldier	François Bacquet (La Montagne)	Settled in Canada in 1668.
Soldier	Barreau	Settled in Canada in 1668.
Soldier	Laurent Belan (La Rivière)	Settled in Canada in 1668.
Soldier	Antoine Besiers	Settled in Canada in 1668.
Soldier	Bonneau	Settled in Canada in 1668.
Soldier	Léonard de Bord	Settled in Canada in 1668.
Soldier	Etienne Bourru (La Roze)	Died in October 1667.
Soldier	Etienne Charles (La Jeunesse)	Settled in Canada in 1668.
Soldier	Etienne Content (Berry)	Settled in Canada in 1668.
Soldier	François Dessureaux (La Plante)	Settled in Canada in 1668.
Soldier	Jacques Du Bois	Settled in Canada in 1668.
Soldier	Du Four	Settled in Canada in 1668.
Soldier	René Grimault	Settled in Canada in 1668.
Soldier	Pierre L'Abbé (La Croix)	Settled in Canada in 1668.
Soldier	(La Fortune)	Settled in Canada in 1668.
Soldier	Jacques de La Lande	Settled in Canada in 1668.
Soldier	(L'Amérique)	Returned to France in 1667 or 1668.
Soldier	(Le Parisien)	Settled in Canada in 1668.
Soldier	(L'Espérance)	Settled in Canada in 1668.

Table 4 (continued)

Rank	Name	Biographical Notes
Soldier	Leuradeau	Settled in Canada in 1668.
Soldier	Michel Rognan (La Roche)	Settled in Canada in 1668.
Soldier	Jean Saigneux (La Framboise)	Settled in Canada in 1668.
Soldier	Claude Salver or Salois	Settled in Canada in 1668.
Soldier	(Sans Soucy)	Settled in Canada in 1668.
Soldier	René Sorel (La Fleur)	Settled in Canada in 1668.
Soldier	Mathurin Villeneuve	Settled in Canada in 1668.
Soldier	Jean Vincent	Settled in Canada in 1668.

PETIT COMPANY

Rank	Name	Biographical Notes
Captain	Louis Petit	Born in 1629. Petit went on Courcelle's winter campaign. He remained in Canada after 1668 and entered the seminary at Quebec where he was ordained as a priest in 1670. He served as the parish priest on the Saint-Ours seigneury from 1675 to 1676 and then was named vicar general of Acadia. He served there until 1690 when he was taken prisoner by the English. After his release in 1691, he returned to Quebec where he died in 1709.
Soldier	René Bin (René Le Normand)	Settled in Canada in 1668.
Soldier	Michel Brouillet (La Violette)	Settled in Canada in 1668 and married at Fort Saint-Louis two years later. He remained on the Chambly seigneury until 1675 when he moved to Sorel.
Soldier	Jean Collet (Le Picard)	Married and settled in Canada in 1668. He remarried in 1688 and died in 1699.
Soldier	Jean Dontelet (de L'Isle)	Settled in Canada in 1668.
Soldier	Pierre Dupuis (La Montagne)	Settled in Canada in 1668.
Soldier	(Du Verger)	Settled in Canada in 1668.
Soldier	Jacques Huchereau (La Châtaigneraie)	Died in hospital at Montreal in April 1666 at the age of twenty.
Soldier	(La Forge)	Settled in Canada in 1668.

Table 4 (continued)

Rank	Name	Biographical Notes
Soldier	Gilles Luton (Bon Courage)	Settled in Canada in 1668.
Soldier	Jean de Paris (Champagne)	Settled in Canada in 1668.
Soldier	Paul Perrot (La Fleur)	Settled in Canada in 1668.
Soldier	(Poitevin)	Settled in Canada in 1668.

ROUGEMONT COMPANY

Captain	Etienne de Rougemont	Went on Courcelle's winter expedition to the Mohawk country and afterwards took command of Fort Sainte-Thérèse. He returned to France in 1668.
Sergeant	Hirais, or Hivars	Assassinated in February 1665 while still in France.
Soldier	Michel Fabulet	Died in hospital at Montreal in March 1667 at the age of twenty-two.
Soldier	Vincent Oly (La Rosée)	Settled in Canada in 1668.
Soldier	Bernard Ravenne	Died in hospital at Montreal in March 1666 at the age of nineteen.
Soldier	(Rencontre)	Settled in Canada in 1668.

SAINT-OURS COMPANY

Captain	Pierre de Saint-Ours d'Eschaillons	Born in 1640. He was the protégé of his illustrious relative Marshal d'Estrades. The captain remained in Canada after 1668, and in 1672 received the concession of the seigneury of Saint-Ours. Later the same year the concession was enlarged to mark the birth of his son. Another enhancement occurred in 1674 when Saint-Ours received two islands from Frontenac for his services to the colony. Notwithstanding his good fortune in that respect, by 1688 Saint-Ours was in an impoverished state, a condition that was relieved only in 1690 when he became the commandant of troops in Montreal. In 1704 he was honoured by being made a Chevalier of Saint-Louis. Saint-Ours remarried in 1708 and died in 1724 at the age of eighty-four.

Table 4 (continued)

Rank	Name	Biographical Notes
Lieutenant	Edmond de Suève	Born between 1617 and 1620. He remained in Canada after 1668. In 1672 he received, jointly with Thomas de Lanouguère, the concession of Sainte-Anne-de-la-Pérade. He apparently spent most of his time hunting, neglecting his land to the extent that in 1680 he was poverty stricken. After that things must have improved for him because by 1691 he was affluent enough to make a gift of land for the construction of a church. He died in 1707.
Ensign	Thomas de Lanouguère	Born in 1644. He remained in Canada after 1668. He married at Quebec in 1672, the same year that he received with Suève the concession of Sainte-Anne-de-la-Pérade. In 1674 he became the acting governor of Montreal. He died in 1678.
Sergeant	Jacques Babie de Ranville	Born in 1633. He settled in Canada in 1668. He bought land adjacent to Lake Champlain in that year and devoted himself to trade. He married in 1670 and died in 1688.
Sergeant	Etienne Charpentier (Saint-Laurent)	Born in 1631. He remained in Canada after 1668. He married in 1672 and received a concession of land from Saint-Ours, and bought more in 1675.
Soldier	Antoine Arnaud (La Rose)	Settled in Canada in 1668 and lived on the Saint-Ours seigneury. He sold his holding in 1675.
Soldier	Mathurin Baulsnier (La Perle)	Born in 1643. He settled in Canada in 1668 and received land on the Saint-Ours seigneury. He added to it in 1673, after his marriage. At that time his father-in-law moved in with him.
Soldier	Jean Bellet (La Gajaille)	Settled in Canada in 1668 and lived on the Saint-Ours seigneury.
Soldier	Mathieu Betanchon (La Lande)	Settled in Canada in 1668. He married and lived on the Saint-Ours seigneury.
Soldier	Nicolas Bonnin (Saint-Martin)	Settled in Canada in 1668 and lived on the Saint-Ours seigneury.
Soldier	Laurent Bony (La Vergne)	Born in 1643. He settled in Canada in 1668, married, and lived on the Saint-Ours seigneury until he died in 1708.
Soldier	Jean Bouvet, Sieur de La Chambre	Born in 1643. He served as the company surgeon. He settled in Canada in 1668 and lived on the Saint-Ours seigneury. He married in 1673 and died in 1694.

Table 4 (continued)

Rank	Name	Biographical Notes
Soldier	Jean Celurier (Des Lauriers)	Settled in Canada in 1668 and lived on the Saint-Ours seigneury.
Soldier	Jean Chastenay (La Guigne)	Settled in Canada in 1668 and lived on the Saint-Ours seigneury.
Soldier	François Chevrefils (La Lime)	Settled in Canada in 1668 and lived on the Saint-Ours seigneury. There, in 1673, he bought extra land and sold it a few days later at a profit. He married in the colony.
Soldier	Mathurin Colin (La Liberté)	Settled in Canada in 1668, married, and lived on the Saint-Ours seigneury. He later moved to Longueuil.
Soldier	Charles Desmarés	Settled in Canada in 1668 and lived on the Saint-Ours seigneury.
Soldier	Pierre Dextras (La Vigne)	Settled in Canada in 1668, married, and lived on the Saint-Ours seigneury.
Soldier	Jean Duval	Settled in Canada in 1668 and lived on the Saint-Ours seigneury. At an unspecified date he married. A builder by trade, he constructed a number of houses on the seigneury. He also built the church there, for which he was paid 200 *livres*.
Soldier	Jean Gajaille (Saint-Germain)	Settled in Canada in 1668 and lived on the Saint-Ours seigneury.
Soldier	Gilbert Guillaume (de Villard)	Settled in Canada in 1668 and lived on the Saint-Ours seigneury.
Soldier	Jean-François Herpin (Toureaugeau)	Settled in Canada in 1668. He married the following year and lived on the Saint-Ours seigneury.
Soldier	Mery Herpin (Poitevin)	Born in 1648. He settled in Canada in 1668 and lived on the Saint-Ours seigneury. He bought an addition to his holding there in 1677, but he spent most of his time in the fur trade. He married in 1689 and died in 1728.
Soldier	Louis Jean (La Fontaine)	Settled in Canada in 1668 and lived on the Saint-Ours seigneury. In 1673 he sold his original holding there and bought another one.
Soldier	(Jolicoeur)	Settled in Canada in 1668 and lived on the Saint-Ours seigneury.
Soldier	(La Chambre)	Settled in Canada in 1668 and lived on the Saint-Ours seigneury.

Table 4 (continued)

Rank	Name	Biographical Notes
Soldier	Pierre Lacougnier (La Croix)	Settled in Canada in 1668 and lived on the Saint-Ours seigneury.
Soldier	(La Fouche)	Settled in Canada in 1668 and lived on the Saint-Ours seigneury.
Soldier	François-César de La Gardelette	Born in 1648. He settled in Canada in 1668. He married and lived on the Saint-Ours seigneury until he died in 1732.
Soldier	(La Lande)	Settled in Canada in 1668 and lived on the Saint-Ours seigneury.
Soldier	(La Ramée)	Settled in Canada in 1668 and lived on the Saint-Ours seigneury.
Soldier	François La Rosée (La Rose)	Settled in Canada in 1668 and lived on the Saint-Ours seigneury.
Soldier	(Lavallée)	Settled in Canada in 1668. He became a wood-cutter on the Saint-Ours seigneury where he was killed by an Iroquois raiding party in 1692.
Soldier	(Le Bruné)	Settled in Canada in 1668 and lived on the Saint-Ours seigneury.
Soldier	Jean Lecomte	Settled in Canada in 1668 and lived on the Saint-Ours seigneury.
Soldier	André Marigny (L'Esveillé)	Born in 1643. He settled in Canada in 1668 and lived on the Saint-Ours seigneury. He died in 1703.
Soldier	Pierre Menard	Settled in Canada in 1668. He married and became both a notary and a shoemaker on the Saint-Ours seigneury.
Soldier	Pierre Meunier (La Pierre)	Born in 1648. He settled in Canada in 1668, married in 1675, and lived on the Saint-Ours seigneury.
Soldier	Jacques Pigeon (Petit Jean Des Mines)	Settled in Canada in 1668 and lived on the Saint-Ours seigneury.
Soldier	Jean-François Pinsonneau (La Fleur)	Born in 1646. He settled in Canada in 1668 and lived on the Saint-Ours seigneury.
Soldier	Lucas Poupart (La Fortune)	Born in 1651. He settled in Canada in 1668. He sold his holding on the Saint-Ours seigneury in 1673 and joined the Montreal garrison force.
Soldier	Jean Pradez (La Prade)	Miraculously cured of a paralyzed leg at the Church of Sainte-Anne-de-Beaupré in 1667.

Table 4 (continued)

Rank	Name	Biographical Notes
Soldier	Jean Renault (Montauban)	Settled in Canada in 1668 and lived on the Saint-Ours seigneury.
Soldier	(Saint-Antoine)	Settled in Canada in 1668 and lived on the Saint-Ours seigneury.
Soldier	André Sire	Settled in Canada in 1668 and lived on the Saint-Ours seigneury.
Soldier	(Xaintonge)	Settled in Canada in 1668 and lived on the Saint-Ours seigneury.

SALIÈRES COMPANY

Rank	Name	Biographical Notes
Colonel	Henri Chastelard, Marquis de Salières	Born about 1595. The marquis first joined the army in 1619. He became the colonel of the regiment when Colonel Blathazard retired. Following its amalgamation with the Carignan Regiment, he retained the position of active colonel. He returned to France in 1668 with what remained of his company and his regiment. The marquis retired from the army in 1676 and died in July 1680. He was buried at the Church of Saint-Sulpice in Paris.
Ensign	François Balthazard de Chastelard	Born in 1650. He was the son of the Marquis de Salières and returned to France with him in 1668 where he continued his military career.
Gentleman volunteer	Valentin de Hayes	Died at Saint-Gabriel's Farm, near Montreal, in July 1666.
Cadet	Lazide	Returned to France in 1668.
Sergeant	Jean Gats de Vivarette	Returned to France in 1668.
Sergeant	Pierre de Maffe (Le Frisé)	The senior sergeant. He returned to France in 1668.
Corporal	Pierre Masson	Returned to France in 1668.
Corporal	Claude Royer (La Mulle and La Treille)	The senior corporal. He returned to France in 1668.
Soldier	Jean Boucheret (La Tau)	Settled in Canada in 1668.
Soldier	Pierre Bouteau (La Ramée)	Settled in Canada in 1668.
Soldier	Jean Boutin (L'Esveille)	Name might have been Jean Poulin. He settled in Canada in 1668.

Table 4 (continued)

Rank	Name	Biographical Notes
Soldier	Nicolas Choquet (Champagne)	Born in 1643. He settled in Canada in 1668.
Soldier	Jean Courtois (Courtois)	Settled in Canada in 1668.
Soldier	Bernard Delpesche (Belair)	Born in 1641. He married at Montreal in 1667 and settled in Canada in 1668.
Soldier	François-Etienne Denison	Settled in Canada in 1668. In 1672 he was the temporary clerk of the court in Montreal.
Soldier	Du Buisson	Settled in Canada in 1668.
Soldier	Ricard Jean (Saint-Germain)	Died in hospital at Montreal in December 1665 at the age of twenty-six. He abjured Calvinism on his deathbed.
Soldier	François Le Clerc (La Violette)	Settled in Canada in 1668.
Soldier	François Lenoir (Rolland)	Born in 1642. He settled in Canada in 1668.
Soldier	Jean Lever (Dauphiné)	Died in January 1666.
Soldier	Pierre Perthius (La Lime)	Born in 1644. He settled in Canada in 1668.
Soldier	Jacques Pillerant (L'Isle d'Or)	Settled in Canada in 1668 and lived on the Repentigny seigneury unitl he returned to France in 1673. By 1681 he was back in Canada and living in Montreal.
Soldier	Jean Roy (Le Gascon or Petit Jean)	Born in 1641. He settled in Canada in 1668 and lived on the Saint-Ours seigneury.
Soldier	Bernard Vesin (Beausoleil)	Settled in Canada in 1668.

SAUREL COMPANY

| Captain | Pierre de Saurel | Born in 1628. He rebuilt Fort Richelieu and cleared a considerable amount of land around it. He remained in Canada after 1668 and married Catherine Legardeur de Tilly at Quebec in that year. In 1672 he received the area around Fort Richelieu as a seigneurial concession, which was named after him. Saurel must have entered the fur trade, for when he died in 1682, he was returning from the west. He was buried in Montreal. |

Table 4 (continued)

Rank	Name	Biographical Notes
Lieutenant	Antoine d'Amplemont de Hericourt	Returned to France in 1668.
Ensign	Hugues Randin	Remained in Canada after 1668 and in 1671 was put in charge of a mission to Acadia. The following year he received a seigneurial concession, which in 1673 he sold to Alexandre Berthier. Frontenac employed him as a cartographer and he drew up the plans for Fort Frontenac. In 1679 he was given another seigneury, this one in Acadia. Despite the ban on such activities, he entered the fur trade, and died while on an expedition into the interior about 1680. He was fifty-four years old when he died.
Sergeant	Jean Darbois (La Fleur)	Born in 1618 or 1621. He settled in Canada in 1668 and lived on the Sorel seigneury until 1676. At that time he gave up his holding to Antoine Chaudillon.
Soldier	Antoine Adhémar de Saint-Martin	Born in 1640. He married in 1667. In 1668, after deciding to remain in Canada, he became the bailiff and notary for four seigneuries. He married for a second time in 1684, having been a widower since 1683. He lived on the Sorel seigneury until his death in 1714.
Soldier	Julien Allard (La Barre)	Born in 1645. He settled in Canada in 1668 and lived on the Sorel seigneury.
Soldier	Antoine Bethune (La Taille)	Settled in Canada in 1668 and lived on the Sorel seigneury.
Soldier	Julien Boin (Du Fresne)	Born in 1641. He settled in Canada in 1668 and lived on the Sorel seigneury.
Soldier	Jean Bougrand (Champagne)	Born in 1641. He settled in Canada in 1668, married that same year, and lived on the Sorel seigneury.
Soldier	Antoine Chaudillon	Born in 1643. He settled in Canada in 1668 and married two years later. In 1676 he received some land on the Sorel seigneury from Jean Darbois on the condition that he take care of Darbois and his wife. The fact that he was the former company surgeon might have had something to do with the arrangement.

Table 4 (continued)

Rank	Name	Biographical Notes
Soldier	Etienne Clemenceau (La Chesnaye)	Settled in Canada in 1668 and lived on the Sorel seigneury.
Soldier	Claude Cognac (La Jeunesse)	Settled in Canada in 1668, married, and lived on the Sorel seigneury.
Soldier	Gilles Couturier (La Bonté)	Born in 1642. He settled in Canada in 1668 and married in 1674. A shoemaker by trade, he lived on the Sorel seigneury. In 1685 he bought a permit to enter the fur trade in partnership with two other men, one of whom was Jean-Baptiste Patissier.
Soldier	Desrochers	Arrested in 1667, along with Jean Sendil, also of the Saurel Company, for theft and counterfeiting. He was hanged for his crimes on 28 June 1667.
Soldier	Jean Dominique	Settled in Canada in 1668 and lived on the Sorel seigneury.
Soldier	Du Vemis	Settled in Canada in 1668 and lived on the Sorel seigneury.
Soldier	Pierre Enaud (Canada)	Settled in Canada in 1668 and lived on the Sorel seigneury
Soldier	Gabriel Gibaud (Poitevin)	Born in 1641. He married in 1667 and settled in Canada, living on the Sorel seigneury. He died in 1700 at Montreal.
Soldier	François Guire (La Rose)	Settled in Canada in 1668, married, and most likely lived on the Saint-Ours seigneury.
Soldier	François Le Breton (Le Breton)	Settled in Canada in 1668.
Soldier	Guillaume Le Breton (L'Andoise)	Born in 1636 or 1640. He settled in Canada in 1668 and lived on the Sorel seigneury.
Soldier	Pierre Letendre (La Liberté)	Born in 1636. He settled in Canada in 1668 and lived on the Sorel seigneury until his death in 1714.
Soldier	Jean Le Vannois (La Violette)	Born in 1627. He settled in Canada in 1668 and lived on the Sorel seigneury. In 1671 he was working as a casual labourer there.
Soldier	Mathias (La Violette)	Settled in Canada in 1668 and lived on the Saint-Ours seigneury.
Soldier	Martin Moreau (La Porte)	Settled in Canada in 1668 and lived on the Sorel seigneury until his death in 1704.

Table 4 (continued)

Rank	Name	Biographical Notes
Soldier	Nicolas Moye (Grancé)	Born in 1626. He settled in Canada in 1668 and lived on the Sorel seigneury until his death in 1713.
Soldier	Jean Olivier	Born in 1631. He settled in Canada in 1668. He married in 1673 and lived for a while on the Sorel seigneury. By 1687, however, he had moved and was living on the Berthier seigneury.
Soldier	Claude Pastourel (La Franchise)	Born in 1644. He settled in Canada in 1668.
Soldier	Jean-Baptiste Patissier (Saint-Amand)	Born in 1646. He settled in Canada in 1668 and lived on the Sorel seigneury until 1673 when he sold his holding of land there. He married in 1678 and in partnership with Gilles Couturier and another man bought a fur-trading permit for 2,000 *livres*.
Soldier	Jean Piette (Trempe La Crouste)	Born in 1641. He settled in Canada in 1668, married, and lived on the Sorel seigneury.
Soldier	Nicolas Pion (La Fontaine)	Settled in Canada in 1668 and lived on the Sorel seigneury.
Soldier	André Poutre (La Vigne)	Married at Quebec in 1667 and, afterwards, settled in Canada. After 1687 he abandoned his holding of land on the Sorel seigneury and moved to Montreal. He was probably a shoemaker.
Soldier	Jean Robin (La Pointe)	Born in 1643. He settled in Canada in 1668 and became a notary on the Sorel seigneury.
Soldier	(Saint-André)	Settled in Canada in 1668 and lived on the Sorel seigneury.
Soldier	Claude Saluart	The name might have been Claude Salois. He settled in Canada in 1668 and lived on the Sorel seigneury.
Soldier	Jean Sendil	Arrested in 1667, along with one Desrochers, for theft and counterfeiting. While Desrochers was hanged for his crimes, Sendil ended up having to spend a term of three years in the Jesuit House in Quebec.
Soldier	Pierre Vallet (La France)	Born in 1650. He settled in Canada in 1668 and lived on the Sorel seigneury.
Soldier	Pierre Volloing (L'Espérance)	Settled in Canada in 1668 and lived on the Sorel seigneury.

Notes

AC Archives des Colonies, Paris
AG Archives de la Guerre, Paris
AMG Archives du Ministère de Guerre, Paris
AN Archives nationales, Paris
ANQ Archives nationales du Québec, Sainte-Foy
BN Bibliothèque nationale, Paris
NAC National Archives of Canada, Ottawa

Except where otherwise stated in the notes, direct quotations in the text from French sources have been translated into English by the author.

PREFACE

1 Mason Wade, *The French-Canadian Outlook* (Toronto: McClelland and Stewart 1964), 3.
2 Benjamin Sulte, *Le Régiment de Carignan* (Montreal: G. Ducharme 1922), 6.
3 Régis Roy and Gérard Malchelosse, *Le Régiment de Carignan* (Montreal: G. Ducharme 1925), 12.
4 Ibid., 46–7.

CHAPTER ONE

1 J.-B. Colbert to Mgr de Laval, 18 March 1664, Archives du Séminaire de Québec, Lettres, carton N, no. 14. The name *Canada* as used in the preceding document, and throughout this work, refers only to those French possessions that would, today, be within the bound-

188 Notes to pages 3–6

aries of Quebec. It should not be confused with the term *New France,* which refers to the entirety of France's American colonies. This distinction is well explained by Gustave Lanctot, "Nouvelle-France ou Canada," *Revue d'histoire de l'Amérique française* 14, no. 2 (1960): 171–2.

2 P. Ragueneau to J.-B. Colbert, 28 November 1665, BN, Mélanges de Colbert, vol. 133 (transcript of the Mélanges de Colbert in NAC, MG7, IA6).

3 Bruce G. Trigger, *Natives and Newcomers: Canada's "Heroic Age" Reconsidered* (Kingston and Montreal: McGill-Queen's University Press 1985), 183–94.

4 Marcel Trudel, *La Population du Canada en 1663* (Montreal: Fides 1973), 11, 23, 26, 150–1.

5 *Edits, ordonnances royaux, déclarations et arrêts du Conseil d'état du roi concernant le Canada,* 2 vols. (Quebec: P.E. Desbarats 1803), 1: 20–1.

6 Lucien Campeau, *Les Cent-Associés et le peuplement de la Nouvelle France, 1633–1663* (Montreal: Editions Bellarmin 1974), 10–11, 152.

7 Trudel, *La Population du Canada,* 150.

8 Joyce Marshall, ed. and trans., *Word from New France: The Selected Letters of Marie de l'Incarnation* (Toronto: Oxford University Press 1967), 210, 256, 273–7, 296; Reuben Gold Thwaites, ed. and trans., *The Jesuit Relations and Allied Documents,* 73 vols. (Cleveland: Burrows Brothers Company 1896–1901), 46: 197–9.

9 Dubois Davaugour to the prince of Condé, 13 October 1661, Papiers de Condé, series P, vol. 25 (transcript in Camille de Rochemonteix, *Les Jésuites et la Nouvelle-France au XVII* siècle [Paris: Letouzy et Ané 1896], 526–7).

10 William J. Eccles, *France in America* (New York: Harper and Row 1972), 60; Inès Murat, *Colbert* (Paris: Fayard 1980), 204–7, 269–93.

11 *Edits, ordonnaces royaux,* 1: 19–21.

12 Ibid., 21–4.

13 Commission de M. de Tracy, 19 November 1663, Affaires étrangères (transcript in NAC, MG5, BI, vol. 6).

14 *Edits, ordonnaces royaux,* 1: 21–4.

15 J.-B. Colbert to the Marquis de Tracy, 15 November 1664, AC, CIIA, vol. 2, pt. 1 (transcript of AC, CIIA, in NAC, MGI, CIIA.)

16 The minister of war to Colbert de Terron, 23 January 1665, AMG, Archives acadiennes, vol. 191 (transcript of the Archives acadiennes in NAC, MG4, AI). The scope of the intendant of Rochefort's duties went far beyond the mere civil administration of the country to the immediate north of the Garonne estuary. Within his jurisdiction was the port of La Rochelle, the main point of departure for France's American possessions. A large part of his duties, therefore, was concerned

with the trans-Atlantic shipping traffic, and with ensuring the flow of people and goods to and from the colonies.

17 Murat, *Colbert,* 269.

18 In 1644 Thomas Francis of Savoy, prince of Carignano, raised a regiment of infantry to serve in an auxiliary capacity alongside the French army in Italy. He named it the Carignano Regiment, after his own principality. Fourteen years later, when the cost of its upkeep forced him to turn it over to the full control of France, its name was changed to the Carignan Regiment. After the Peace of Westphalia, the regiment continued campaigning in Italy where the conflict between France and Spain went on unabated. It remained there until 1653, when it was withdrawn to join the loyalist troops besieging Paris during the civil wars of the Fronde. Once they were over, the regiment returned to Italy, and it remained there until 1658 when the Peace of the Pyrenees ended the war with Spain. At that time some retrenchment of the French army became possible and, as a part of it, the regiment was amalgamated with another, the Salières Regiment.

The Salières Regiment had been raised, early in the Thirty Years' War, by Johann von Balthazard, after whom it was originally named. That name, however, changed when he retired in 1658 and turned his command over to his old comrade in arms, Henri Chastelard, Marquis de Salières. Thereafter, the new unit, styled the Carignan-Salières Regiment, served in garrisons along the northern and eastern frontiers of France.

In his monograph on the regiment, Benjamin Sulte, quoting from F.-X. Garneau's *Histoire du Canada depuis sa découverte jusqu'à nos jours,* states that when France responded to the call to help repel the Ottoman Turks from the Holy Roman Empire, the regiment formed part of the French contingent in the Imperial Army. Unfortunately, while it is certainly possible that some officers and men might have served against the Turks, so far no documentary evidence has come to light to show that they actually did. A search of French archival collections could conceivably turn up some such evidence, but, for the time being, it can be assumed only that the regiment remained on garrison duties until it was ordered to Canada in January 1665.

"Estat des trouppes d'Infanterie et de Cavalerie de l'armée d'Italie," 22 January 1659, vol. 154, Louis XIV to the prince of Carignano, 31 May 1659, vol. 156, the minister of war to M. de Choisy, 17 January 1665, vol. 191, AMG, Archives acadiennes; Note regarding Captain Antoine Pécaudy de Contrecoeur, 13 November 1663, AN, series Y, 204 (transcript of this item in NAC, MG30, D56, vol. 5, file 6); Gabriel Daniel, *Histoire de la milice françoise,* 2 vols. (Paris: J.-B. Coignard 1721), 2:

421–2; Louis Susane, *Histoire de l'ancienne infanterie française,* 8 vols. (Paris: J. Correard 1851), 5: 237–8; *Gazette de France,* 4 September 1664 (a précis of the relevant article, which deals with the participation of certain officers in the siege of Paris during the Fronde, is contained in NAC, MG30, D56, vol. 5, file 6).

19 "Estat du fond qui doit estre fait pour la subsistance des vingt-quatre Compagnies d'Infanterie qui servent en Canada pendant douze mois à commencer de celluy de janvier 1668," AC, D2C, vol. 47 (microfilm in NAC, MG1, D2C); the minister of war to Colbert de Terron, 23 January 1665, AMG, Archives acadiennes, vol. 191; Louis André, *Michel Le Tellier et l'organization de l'armée monarchique* (Paris: F. Alcan 1906), 167–88, 267; Daniel, *La Milice françoise,* 2: 67–72, 327–87.

The twenty companies were named Chambly, Contrecoeur, Dugué, Du Prat (later Des Portes), Froment, Grandfontaine, La Colonelle, La Fouille, La Fredière, Lamotte, La Noraye, La Tour, La Varenne, Loubias, Maximy, Petit, Rougement, Saint-Ours, Salières, and Saurel. With the exception of La Colonelle Company, all were named after their captains. The regiment actually had two companies that were assigned to colonels, the Salières Company, which was commanded by the Marquis de Salières, and the La Colonelle Company, which was nominally commanded by the reigning prince of Carignano, who remained the honorary colonel of the unit. This arrangement was unique to the Carignan-Salières Regiment.

In addition to the companies listed, the regiment was joined in Canada by four companies that came with Tracy from the Antilles. They were the Berthier Company of the Allier Regiment, the La Brisandière Company of the Orléans Regiment, the La Durantaye Company of the Chambellé Regiment, and the Monteil Company of the Poitou Regiment.

20 The minister of war to Commissaire du Chaunoy, 28 February 1665, AG, vol. 2 (transcript of the Archives de la Guerre in NAC, MG4, BI); André Corvisier, *Armées et sociétés en Europe de 1494 à 1789* (Paris: Presses universitaires de France 1976), 84; Daniel, *La Milice françoise,* 1: 285–8. A regiment was more of an administrative organization than the basic fighting unit, which was the company. The former was the body through which the king was able to exert his authority over the various company commanders via the colonel, who, with the assistance of his headquarters staff, ensured that the royal wishes, passed down to him by the minister of war, or by a superior officer acting on the king's behalf, were carried out.

21 J. Lough, "France under Louis XIV," *The New Cambridge Modern History,* 14 vols. (Cambridge: Cambridge University Press 1961), 5: 223–4.

22 "Estat du fond," AC, D2C, vol. 47; André, *Michel Le Tellier,* 169, 289;

Corvisier, *Armées et sociétés en Europe,* 78, 113–14, 174–8. The basic monthly rates of pay for officers were: captains, 75 *livres;* lieutenants, 30 *livres;* and ensigns, 22 *livres,* 10 *sols.* Each month the headquarters staff received an additional emolument to their basic pay. The colonel got an extra 50 *livres;* the lieutenant-colonel, 30 *livres;* and the major, 25 *livres.* Those headquarters officers who had no company attachment were paid as follows: adjutant, 50 *livres* a month; billeting officer/sergeant-major, 30 *livres;* chaplain, 15 *livres;* and regimental surgeon also got 15 *livres.* Enlisted men were paid at these monthly rates: sergeants, 15 *livres;* corporals, 10 *livres,* 10 *sols;* anspessades, 9 *livres;* and ordinary soldiers, 7 *livres,* 10 *sols.*

23 Note regarding Captain Antoine Pécaudy de Contrecoeur, 13 November 1663, AN, series Y, 204; the minister of war to M. de Choisy, 17 January 1665, AMG, Archives acadiennes, vol. 191.

24 The minister of war to M. de Salières, 9 February 1665, AMG, Archives acadiennes, vol. 191.

25 The minister of war to M. de la Gallissonière, 27 January 1665, AMG, Archives acadiennes, vol. 191.

26 Corvisier, *Armées et sociétés en Europe,* 93–4.

27 André, *Michel Le Tellier,* 339, 467.

28 Daniel, *La Milice françoise,* 2: 67–9.

29 The minister of war to M. de la Gallissonière, 27 January 1665, AMG, Archives acadiennes, vol. 191.

30 Ibid.

31 The minister of war to M. de Harlay, 3 February 1665, AMG, Archives acadiennes, vol. 191.

32 Corvisier, *Armée et sociétés en Europe,* 93.

33 Lough, "France under Louis XIV," 5: 232–3.

34 John B. Wolf, *Louis XIV* (New York: W.W. Norton 1968), 148–9. In support of his remarks on Louis XIV's army, Wolf quotes from the commission granted, in 1659, to Marshal de Turenne in which the king wrote, "We find ourselves obliged, for the conservation of our state as much as for its glory and our reputation, to maintain ... in peace as well as in war, a great number of troops, both infantry and cavalry, which will always be ready in good condition to act to keep our people in the obedience and respect that they owe us, to insure the peace and tranquility that we have won ... and to aid our allies."

35 The minister of war to M. de la Gallissonière, 27 January 1665, and the minister of war to M. de Salières, 9 February 1665, AMG, Archives acadiennes, vol. 191.

36 The minister of war to M. de Salières, 9 February 1665, AMG, Archives acadiennes, vol. 191.

37 Lettres de rémission de M. Gaultier de Comporté, June 1680, ANQ, TI–2/1, *Insinuations du Conseil souverain*, vol. 1; André, *Michel Le Tellier*, 267–70; Corvisier, *Armées et sociétés en Europe*, 82. André devotes chapter 5 to the system and manner of recruitment. The pages cited above summarize the chapter.

38 Lettres de rémission de M. Gaultier de Comporté, June 1680, ANQ, TI–2/1; Affaires criminelles, 1665, Archives départementales des Deux Sèvres, Siège royal de Saint-Maixent.

39 The minister of war to the Sieur de Launay, 30 March 1665, AMG, Archives acadiennes, vol. 192; the minister of war to Commissaire du Chaunoy, 28 February 1665, AG, vol. 2.

40 Colbert de Terron to J.-B. Colbert, 13 April 1665, BN, Mélanges de Colbert, vol. 128.

41 The minister of war to M. de Salières, 13 April 1665, AMG, Archives acadiennes, vol. 192. Cadets were usually young potential officers for whom no vacancy existed. However, they volunteered to serve without pay in a regiment to gain experience and recognition. The term "other capable persons," as used in the minister's letter, may be taken to refer to reserve officers, generally older men from disbanded regiments, who chose to serve in active units as supernumaries on a reduced rate of pay until such time as a vacancy might occur in the regular establishment. André deals with this subject at some length in *Michel Le Tellier,* 180–8.

42 Colbert de Terron to J.-B. Colbert, 16 November 1665, BN, Mélanges de Colbert, vol. 133. Although Colbert de Terron claimed in his letter that the colonel was just a bad-tempered man, later events suggest that his irascibility might, in part, have been due to an intense feeling of dread at the prospect of the forthcoming voyage, as well as to the testiness of old age, for, according to the *Jesuit Relations,* 49: 255, he was a man of "advanced age," who had "grown gray in military service."

43 The minister of war to Colbert de Terron, 9 February 1665, AG, vol. 2.

44 André, *Michel Le Tellier,* 268–9; Corvisier, *Armées et Sociétés en Europe,* 76–7; Daniel, *La Milice françoise,* 2: 86, 398.

45 "Total de toutte la dépense faite pour les troupes d'infanterie entretenues par le Roy en Canada …," 15 June 1666, AC, CIIA, vol. 2, pt. 2. The ribbon for making regimental cockades, as listed in the document, was black and russet in colour. The black indicated the regiment's connection with the ruling house of Savoy, and the russet that with the Marquis de Salières. Regimental cockades are discussed in R. la Roque de Roquebrune, "Uniformes et drapeaux des régiments au Canada sous Louis XIV et Louis XV," *Revue de l'université d'Ottawa* (September/October 1950): 327–42.

46 Colbert de Terron to J.-B. Colbert, 13 April 1665, BN, Mélanges de Colbert, vol. 128.

47 Jean Talon to J.-B. Colbert, 21 May 1665, AC, CIIA, vol. 2, pt. 1; the minister of war to Jean Talon, 29 May 1665, AMG, Archives acadiennes, vol. 193; Daniel, *La Milice françoise,* 2: 86, 398.

48 The minister of war to Jean Talon, 29 May 1665, AMG, Archives acadiennes, vol. 193.

49 "Total de toutte la dépense," AC, CIIA, vol. 2, pt. 2.

50 Colbert de Terron to J.-B. Colbert, 10 May 1665, BN, Mélanges de Colbert, vol. 129; Thwaites, *Jesuit Relations,* 49: 217, 223–5.

51 M. Delafosse, "La Rochelle et le Canada au XVIIe siècle," *Revue d'histoire de l'Amérique française* 4, no. 4 (1951): 469–511.

52 Minute, 28 February 1665, Archives départementales de la Charente-Maritime, La Rochelle, series E, Teuleron, 1665 (microfilm of the Archives départementales in NAC, MG6, A2). With a few exceptions it is impossible to say for certain in which ship each company travelled. There is documentary evidence that the Chambly, Froment, and La Tour companies sailed aboard the *Joyeux Siméon,* but not of the fourth company. The *Jesuit Relations* mention another ship, under the command of a man named Petit, that reached Quebec at about the same time as the *Joyeux Siméon.* In all likelihood it was the *Cat de Hollande,* also a chartered Dutch vessel, but there is no evidence of it having carried troops or supplies.

A letter from the Jesuit Paul Ragueneau to Jean-Baptiste Colbert puts the Marquis de Salières aboard the *Aigle d'Or,* and another one signed by several of the regiment's officers indicates that the La Fredière, Grandfontaine, and Lamotte companies were also on it. Although accounts assign the remainder of the companies to one of the other four ships, the *Paix,* the *Saint-Sébastien,* the *Justice,* and the *Jardin de Hollande,* they are, unfortunately, quite speculative and should not be given too much credence without further documentary evidence to support them.

Minute, 22 March 1665, Archives départementales de la Charente-Maritime, La Rochelle, series E, Teuleron, 1665; Colbert de Terron to J.-B. Colbert, 25 January 1665, vol. 127, 4 May 1665, vol. 129, 31 August 1665, vol. 131, P. Ragueneau to J.-B. Colbert, 28 November 1665, vol. 133, BN, Mélanges de Colbert; Thwaites, *Jesuit Relations,* 49: 161–3.

53 Colbert de Terron to J.-B. Colbert, 13 April 1665, vol. 128, P. Ragueneau to J.-B. Colbert, 28 November 1665, vol. 133, BN, Mélanges de Colbert.

54 Colbert de Terron to J.-B. Colbert, 21 September 1665, BN, Mélanges de Colbert, vol. 131; Delafosse, "La Rochelle et le Canada," 469–511.

55 Jean Talon to J.-B. Colbert, 4 May 1665, AC, CIIA, vol. 2, pt. 1.

56 Colbert de Terron to J.-B. Colbert, 27 April 1665, vol. 128, 4 May 1665, vol. 129, 18 May 1665, vol. 129, BN, Mélanges de Colbert.
57 Colbert de Terron to J.-B. Colbert, 27 April 1665, vol. 128, 4 May 1665, vol. 129, 10 May 1665, vol. 129, BN, Mélanges de Colbert.
58 Colbert de Terron to J.-B. Colbert, 18 May 1665, BN, Mélanges de Colbert, vol. 129; Minute, 22 November 1665, Archives départementales de la Charente-Maritime, La Rochelle, 1665, B.5666, no. 85; Germain Lesage, "L'arrivé du Régiment de Carignan," *Revue de l'université d'Ottawa,* no. 1 (1965): 11–34.
59 Marshall, *Word from New France,* 311–12.

CHAPTER TWO

1 P. Ragueneau to J.-B. Colbert, 28 November 1665, BN, Mélanges de Colbert, vol. 133 (transcript of the Mélanges de Colbert in NAC, MG7, IA6); Reuben Gold Thwaites, ed. and trans., *The Jesuit Relations and Allied Documents,* 73 vols. (Cleveland: Burrows Brothers Company 1896–1901), 49: 161, 50: 81.
2 Jeanne-Françoise Juchereau [de La Ferté] de Saint-Ignace and Marie-Andrée Duplessis de Sainte-Hélène, *Les Annales de l'Hôtel-Dieu de Québec, 1636–1716,* facsimile ed. (Quebec: Hôtel-Dieu de Québec 1939), 143.
3 P. Ragueneau to J.-B. Colbert, 28 November 1665, BN, Mélanges de Colbert, vol. 133; Thwaites, *Jesuit Relations,* 49: 223–5.
4 Juchereau and Duplessis, *Les Annales de l'Hôtel-Dieu,* 144–5; Joyce Marshall, ed. and trans., *Word from New France: The Selected Letters of Marie de l'Incarnation* (Toronto: Oxford University Press 1967), 308. Of Tracy's retinue, Mère Juchereau wrote: "This viceroy never goes anywhere without being preceded by twenty-four guards and four pages, followed by six lackeys and surrounded by a large number of richly dressed officers."
5 Thwaites, *Jesuit Relations,* 49: 225.
6 Juchereau and Duplessis, *Les Annales de l'Hôtel-Dieu,* 143.
7 Bruce G. Trigger, *Natives and Newcomers: Canada's "Heroic Age" Reconsidered* (Kingston and Montreal: McGill-Queen's University Press 1985), 263, 284.
8 Ibid., 273, 280.
9 Ibid., 275.
10 Ibid., 263–73, 275, 284. The Susquehannocks were an Iroquoian nation living along the north of Chesapeake Bay, in what is now part of Pennsylvania. After the middle of the seventeenth century, the supply of fur-bearing animals became so badly depleted in that area that they began to cast covetous eyes northwards, to the lucrative traffic

plying the extended routes from the more westerly members of the Iroquois Confederacy to Fort Orange. There followed a period of hostilities, sometimes called the Susquehannock War, although it was characterized more by skirmishes and ambushes than by open warfare. It persisted until the culminating battle, fought in 1675, in which the Senecas and the Cayugas combined to defeat the common foe.

11 P. Ragueneau to J.-B. Colbert, 28 November 1665, BN, Mélanges de Colbert, vol. 133; Thwaites, *Jesuit Relations,* 49: 265.

12 Some indication of the diverstiy of Paul Ragueneau's experience among Indian nations can be gathered from the numerous references to them in both the *Jesuit Relations* and Marie de l'Incarnation's letters.

13 Thwaites, *Jesuit Relations,* 49: 253.

14 Marshall, *Word from New France,* 307; Thwaites, *Jesuit Relations,* 49: 161, 237–9.

15 Marshall, *Word from New France,* 307.

16 Thwaites, *Jesuit Relations,* 49: 161–3.

17 P. Ragueneau to J.-B. Colbert, 17 September 1665, BN, Mélanges de Colbert, vol. 131; Thwaites, *Jesuit Relations,* 49: 237–9.

18 P. Ragueneau to J.-B. Colbert, 17 September 1665, vol. 131, P. Ragueneau to J.-B. Colbert, 28 November 1665, vol. 133, BN, Mélanges de Colbert; Thwaites, *Jesuit Relations,* 49: 163.

19 Registre paroissal de Trois-Rivières, 6 August 1665, Archives du Palais de Justice de Trois-Rivières.

20 Thwaites, *Jesuit Relations,* 49: 163, 253.

21 Colbert de Terron to J.-B. Colbert, 21 September 1665, vol. 131, P. Ragueneau to J.-B. Colbert, 28 November 1665, vol. 133, BN, Mélanges de Colbert; Thwaites, *Jesuit Relations,* 49: 163–5.

22 Various officers to J.-B. Colbert, 1 August 1665, vol. 131, Colbert de Terron to J.-B. Colbert, 16 November 1665, vol. 133, BN, Mélanges de Colbert.

23 The minister of war to M. de Salières, 19 April 1665, AMG, Archives acadiennes, vol. 192 (transcript of the Archives acadiennes in NAC, MG4, AI).

24 Louis André, *Michel Le Tellier et l'organization de l'armée monarchique* (Paris: F. Alcan 1906), 167–70.

25 "Mémoire de M. de Salières des choses qui se sont passées en Canada les plus considérables depuis qu'il est arrivé," BN, Fonds français, Fonds anciens, MS. 4569 (transcript in NAC, MG7, IA2).

26 *Edits, ordonnaces royaux, déclarations et arrêts du Conseil d'état du roi concernant le Canada,* 2 vols. (Quebec: P.E. Desbarats 1803), 1: 21–4.

27 André Vachon, "François de Laval," *Dictionary of Canadian Biography* 2: 358–72.

28 Louis XIV, *Oeuvres,* 6 vols. (Paris: Grimouard et Grouvelle 1806), 5: 375.

29 Marshall, *Word from New France*, 308, 311–12; Thwaites, *Jesuit Relations*, 49: 165.

30 Jean Talon to the king, 7 October 1665, AC, CIIA, vol. 2, pt. 1 (transcript of AC, CIIA, in NAC, MGI, CIIA); Thwaites, *Jesuit Relations*, 49: 169.

31 Thwaites, *Jesuit Relations*, 49: 165.

32 Ibid. Wherever they went, and whatever they were doing, Jesuits epitomized Ultramontanism. They owed total and unequivocal allegiance to the reigning pope, and whether they agreed with them or not, they obeyed his orders to the letter. Consequently, their loyalty, regardless of their nationality, was to the pope, and they condescended to submit to the governance of national rulers if, and only if, it did not conflict with his. The degree to which others were Ultramontanist in their leanings could be judged by the extent to which they conformed to the Jesuit pattern.

Gallicanism came into being as a result of the Concordat of 1515 whereby Francis I of France and Pope Leo X agreed to terms calculated to keep the country true to Catholicism in the face of the turmoil threatening to shake it apart. Essentially it gave the French monarch the right to nominate senior church officials, such as bishops and abbots. In return, the pope, after routinely approving the nominations, was recompensed by receiving the first year's stipends of the appointees. The Concordat gave the French king effective political control over the church in France so that, in some respects, it became a national, or Gallican, church and, thereafter, all those seeking preferment in it needed to look to the king rather than the pope.

33 J.-B. Colbert to the Marquis de Tracy, 15 November 1664, AC, CIIA, vol. 2, pt. 1.

34 Paul Hay, Marquis de Châtelat, *Traité de la politique de France* (Utrecht: Chez P. Elzevier 1670), 63. The passage in question is quoted in John B. Wolf, *Louis XIV* (New York: W.W. Norton 1968), 385.

35 Marshall, *Word from New France*, 312.

36 François Dollier de Casson, *A History of Montreal, 1640–1672*, trans. Ralph Flenly (London: Dent 1928), 301.

37 Thwaites, *Jesuit Relations*, 49: 171.

38 "Mémoire de M. de Salières." *Jesuit Relations* is in error here: Fort Richelieu was rebuilt by Saurel, and Fort Saint-Louis was constructed by Chambly. Marie de l'Incarnation made a similar error in a letter she wrote to her son on 18 October 1667 in which she mentioned "Fort Chambly (otherwise Sainte-Thérèse)." It would seem that both she and the author of the *Jesuit Relations* in 1665 had an imperfect idea of the locations and the names of Tracy's forts along the Richelieu River.

39 "Mémoire de M. de Salières." The custom upon which the colonel
    based his complaint dated back to 28 July 1661. Before that time a
    French infantry regiment was a somewhat decentralized body, not
    much more than a loose collection of near-autonomous companies,
    each of which was considered to be the property of its captain to
    whom the king paid a fee for its upkeep. The most senior captain
    was designated the lieutenant-colonel, who spoke for the regiment to
    an officer, the maître de camp. He, in turn, reported to the colonel-
    general of the infantry, who answered to the king for all the regi-
    ments of foot soldiers.

    Under the new system, implemented by the Royal Ordinances of
    26 and 28 July 1661, the office of colonel-general of infantry was abol-
    ished, and the former maîtres de camp became colonels over regi-
    ments. They did not necessarily have any seniority as company
    commanders in their units, and in most cases the lieutenant-colonel
    continued to be the most senior captain, although he no longer
    spoke for the regiment. The colonel did that, theoretically directly to
    the king but, in practice, through the minister of war or, in some
    instances, through field commanders appointed to take charge of
    major operations. Thereafter the lieutenant-colonel's role became
    mainly that of standing in for the colonel whenever he was absent
    from the regiment, a not infrequent occurrence if it was on garrison
    duties.

    The intention of the reform was to tighten the king's hold over
    his infantry regiments and so diminish the likelihood of their defec-
    tion, as had occurred during the Fronde in some units. To that end
    he simplified the pyramidical command structure by reducing the
    number of intermediate levels between himself and the lowest one,
    that occupied by the company commanders. See André, *Michel Le
    Tellier,* 167–70.

40 "Mémoire de M. de Salières."

41 The minister of war to M. de Salières, 19 April 1665, AMG, Archives
    acadiennes, vol. 192.

42 "Mémoire de M. de Salières."

43 The minister of war to the Marquis de Tracy, 25 December 1665, AMG,
    Archives acadiennes, vol. 196. In Wolf's *Louis XIV,* a similar case is
    cited on p. 220. It took place in 1672, during the early part of the
    Dutch War, when Turenne, who held a position similar to Tracy's,
    provoked equally energetic protests from three marshals of France
    who questioned his authority. They got the same short shrift from
    the king that Salières got from Tracy.

44 "Mémoire de M. de Salières"; P. Ragueneau to J.-B. Colbert, 28 Novem-
    ber 1665, BN, Mélanges de Colbert, vol. 133; Juchereau and Duplessis,

Les Annales de l'Hôtel-Dieu, 147; Marshall, *Word from New France,* 311; Thwaites, *Jesuit Relations,* 49: 167.

45 Registre de la Confrérie du Mont-Carmel, September 1665, Archives de Notre-Dame de Québec; Juchereau and Duplessis, *Les Annales de l'Hôtel-Dieu,* 147–8; Marshall, *Word from New France,* 312.

46 Juchereau and Duplessis, *Les Annales de l'Hôtel-Dieu,* 149.

47 Thwaites, *Jesuit Relations,* 49: 167.

48 "Mémoire de M. de Salières"; Marshall, *Word from New France,* 307; Thwaites, *Jesuit Relations,* 49: 253.

49 "Mémoire de M. de Salières"; Marshall, *Word from New France,* 307; Thwaites, *Jesuit Relations,* 49: 237, 253.

50 Thwaites, *Jesuit Relations,* 49: map facing p. 266.

51 "Mémoire de M. de Salières."

52 Ibid.

53 "Total de toutte la dépense faite pour les troupes d'infanterie entre-tenues par le Roy en Canada ...," 15 June 1666, AC, CIIA, vol. 2, pt. 2; Colbert de Terron to J.-B. Colbert, 18 May 1665, BN, Mélanges de Colbert, vol. 129.

54 André, *Michel le Tellier,* 467; André Corvisier, *Armées et sociétés en Europe de 1494 à 1789* (Paris: Presses universitaires de France 1976), 91–2.

55 "Mémoire de M. de Salières"; Thwaites, *Jesuit Relations,* 49: 255.

56 Ibid.

57 "Mémoire de M. de Salières."

58 Ibid.

59 Ibid. According to the *Jesuit Relations,* 49: 255, the fort was completed on the feast day of Sainte-Thérèse, 15 October. The Marquis de Salières's account indicates that the palisade was completed on that date, not the entire complex, which was finished some time between 15 and 26 October.

60 "Mémoire de M. de Salières."

61 Ibid.; Thwaites, *Jesuit Relations,* 49: 171–3. Fort Sainte-Anne, the fourth such structure that Tracy caused to be built in the Richelieu Valley area, was not begun until the spring of 1666. It was built under the direction of Captain Pierre Lamotte de Saint-Paul, on an island at the northern end of Lake Champlain that is still called Isle La Motte. The fort was completed in July of that year, possibly on the twenty-sixth, the feast day of Sainte-Anne. See Thwaites, *Jesuit Relations,* 50: 193.

62 Ibid., 49: map facing p. 266.

63 "Mémoire de M. de Salières"; Thwaites, *Jesuit Relations,* 50: 83.

64 "Mémoire de M. de Salières."

65 Ibid.; Thwaites, *Jesuit Relations,* 50: 83.

66 "Mémoire de M. de Salières."

67 Ibid.; Thwaites, *Jesuit Relations*, 49: 173.

68 "Mémoire de M. de Salières."

69 Ibid. It is not entirely clear why the colonel wrote to the Marquis de Louvois rather than to the minister himself. One explanation is that the general supervision of the Canadian venture had been delegated to the younger man by his father, a possibility that seems to be supported by the number of letters that came out of the ministry on matters related to it over his signature.

The colonel's action in going over Tracy's head by writing directly to Louvois tends to bear out the idea that he continued to regard Paris, not Quebec, as the seat of authority. That hypothesis is further borne out by his submission to the minister of what amounted to a diary covering the period from the day he landed in Canada to 14 September 1666, when he left for the Richelieu Valley to join Tracy's punitive expedition to the Mohawk country. In that document he succeeded in portraying Courcelle in a rather unfavourable manner without actually making any accusations or denunciations.

70 "Mémoire de M. de Salières"; Thwaites, *Jesuit Relations,* 49: 173.

CHAPTER THREE

1 "Pouvoir de Gouverneur, Lieutenant-Général en Canada, Acadie et l'Isle de Terre Neuve pour le Sr. de Courcelles," 23 March 1665, AN, BI (transcript of AN, BI, in NAC, MGI, BI).

2 Dossier Courcelle, BN, Pièces originales no. 28942, items 55.305 no. 71, 55.309 no. 9, and 55.310 no. 3 (transcript of the Pièces originales in NAC, MG7, 66A).

3 William J. Eccles, "Daniel de Rémy de Courcelle," *Dictionary of Canadian Biography* 1: 569–72.

4 J.-B. Colbert to M. de Courcelle, 15 May 1669, AN, BI; Reuben Gold Thwaites, ed. and trans., *The Jesuit Relations and Allied Documents,* 73 vols. (Cleveland: Burrows Brothers Company 1896–1901), 49: 173.

5 Régis Roy, writing in *Le Bulletin des recherches historiques,* suggests that those influential friends would have included the Comte d'Estrades, the ambassador to Holland and still nominally the viceroy in America; the Marquis de Feuquières, a former viceroy in America; and the Marquis de Tracy.

It is also possible that the queen mother, Anne of Austria, added her support for his candidacy. He had served as a captain in her regiment, presumably with some distinction, for that position led to his being chosen for the appointment at Thionville. What is more, it would not have been out of character for her, because she had also played a considerable part in securing Mgr de Laval's appointment as vicar apostolic in Quebec. Although her health was failing in 1665, it is unlikely that she would have allowed her condition to deter her from exerting her considerable influence over the king to ensure Courcelle's appointment.

The minister of war to M. de Courcelle, 18 March 1664, AMG, Archives acadiennes, vol. 184 (transcript of the Archives acadiennes in NAC, MG4, A1); Régis Roy, "Rémy de Courcelles," *Le Bulletin des recherches historiques* 20 (1914): 257–8; André Vachon, "François de Laval," *Dictionary of Canadian Biography* 2: 358–72; John B. Wolf, *Louis XIV* (New York: W.W. Norton 1968), 294–7.

6 Thwaites, *Jesuit Relations*, 50: 83, 133; Jeanne-Françoise Juchereau [de La Ferté] de Saint-Ignace and Marie-Andrée Duplessis de Sainte-Hélène, *Les Annales de l'Hôtel-Dieu de Québec, 1636–1716*, facsimile ed. (Quebec: Hôtel-Dieu de Québec 1939), 149.

7 "Mémoire de M. de Salières des choses qui se sont passées en Canada les plus considérables depuis qu'il est arrivé," BN, Fonds français, Fonds anciens, MS 4569 (transcript in NAC, MG7, 1A2).

8 Ibid.; Thwaites, *Jesuit Relations*, 50: 131, 181.

9 "Mémoire de M. de Salières"; Thwaites, *Jesuit Relations*, 49: 179, 50: 127–31.

10 "Mémoire de M. de Salières."

11 Ibid.; François Dollier de Casson, *A History of Montreal, 1640–1672*, trans. Ralph Flenly (London: Dent 1928), 299.

12 "Mémoire de M. de Salières"; Joyce Marshall, ed. and trans., *Word from New France: The Selected Letters of Marie de l'Incarnation* (Toronto: Oxford University Press 1967), 340.

13 Bruce G. Trigger, *Natives and Newcomers: Canada's "Heroic Age" Reconsidered* (Kingston and Montreal: McGill-Queen's University Press 1985), 229–51, 284.

14 "Mémoire de M. de Salières"; Thwaites, *Jesuit Relations*, 50: 127–31.

15 Trigger, *Natives and Newcomers*, 275.

16 Louis André, *Michel Le Tellier et l'organization de l'armée monarchique* (Paris: F. Alcan 1906), 361.

17 "Mémoire de M. de Salières"; Thwaites, *Jesuit Relations*, 50: 131–5, 181.

18 Thwaites, *Jesuit Relations*, 50: 131–5, 181–3.

19 Trigger, *Natives and Newcomers*, 262.

20 Dollier de Casson, *History of Montreal*, 303.

21 Ibid., 303–5.

22 Thwaites, *Jesuit Relations*, 50: 141, 201.

23 Marcel Trudel, *La Population du Canada en 1663* (Montreal: Fides 1973), 150.

24 "Mémoire de M. de Salières."

25 "Vers burlesques sur le voyage de Monsieur de Courcelles gouverneur et lieutenant général pour le Roy en la Nouvelle France en l'année

1666," ANQ (transcript in *Le Bulletin des recherches historiques* 33, no. 5 [1927]: 264–82).

26 Thwaites, *Jesuit Relations,* 50: 131–5, 181–5.

27 John Romeyn Brodhead, *Documents Relative to the Colonial History of the State of New York,* ed. Edmund Bailey O'Callaghan, 11 vols. (Albany: Weed, Parsons and Co. 1853–1861), 3: 118–19.

28 Thwaites, *Jesuit Relations,* 50: 183.

29 "Le Livre de raison de François de Tapie de Monteil, capitaine au régiment de Poitou (1661–1670)," Archives départementales de Lot et Garonne, Fonds de Raymond, MS. 137 (transcript in *Revue d'histoire de l'Amérique française* 14, no. 1 [1960]: 109–21).

30 "Mémoire de M. de Salières."

31 Ibid.

32 Ibid.; "Vers burlesques."

33 "Mémoire de M. de Salières."

34 Ibid.; "Vers burlesques."

35 "Vers burlesques"; Thwaites, *Jesuit Relations,* 50: 131.

36 "Mémoire de M. de Salières."

37 Ibid.; Thwaites, *Jesuit Relations,* 50: 131.

38 "Mémoire de M. de Salières."

39 Ibid.; Thwaites, *Jesuit Relations,* 50: 133–5.

40 Thwaites, *Jesuit Relations,* 50: 133, 181.

41 "Vers burlesques"; "Le Livre de raison de Tapie de Monteil"; Thwaites, *Jesuit Relations,* 50: 183.

42 "Vers burlesques"; Thwaites, *Jesuit Relations,* 50: 135.

43 Dollier de Casson, *History of Montreal,* 305.

44 "Vers burlesques." As far as can be ascertained, Courcelle's route should have taken him down Lake Champlain and Lake Saint-Sacrement, over the watershed into the upper Hudson Valley, across the river at its confluence with the Sacandaga, and up the latter's valley until it swung north. At that point it should have continued south-west, crossing the Adirondack foothills to reach the central Mohawk Valley.

45 "Vers burlesques"; "Mémoire de M. de Salières"; Thwaites, *Jesuit Relations,* 50: 181–3.

46 "Vers burlesques"; "Mémoire de M. de Salières."

47 "Mémoire de M. de Salières."

48 Ibid.; Dollier de Casson, *History of Montreal,* 303. The French officer who was killed was Lieutenant d'Aiguemortes. The officers who were wounded were Major Balthazard de La Flotte de La Fredière, Captain Petit, and Lieutenant Du Luc, all of whom received flesh wounds, and the volunteer who was hurt was a man called Vieux Pont from Trois-Rivières. See "Mémoire de M. de Salières."

49 "Vers burlesques"; Brodhead, *Colonial History of the State of New York*, 3: 118–19.

50 The king to the Marquis de Tracy, 24 March 1666, Ministère des Affaires étrangères, Correspondance politique, vol. 88 (transcript of Correspondance politique in NAC, MG5, A1).

51 Thwaites, *Jesuit Relations*, 50: 183.

52 "Vers burlesques"; Brodhead, *Colonial History of the State of New York*, 3: 118–19; Thwaites, *Jesuit Relations*, 50: 183.

53 "Vers burlesques"; "Mémoire de M. Salières"; Thwaites, *Jesuit Relations*, 50: 183.

54 "Mémoire de M. de Salières."

55 Ibid.

56 "Vers burlesques"; Thwaites, *Jesuit Relations*, 50: 183. The food cache had been placed by two Jesuits, Fathers Pierre Raffeix and Charles Boquet.

57 Thwaites, *Jesuit Relations*, 50: 183.

58 "Mémoire de M. de Salières."

59 Thwaites, *Jesuit Relations*, 50: 183–5. Assuming the figure of 400 dead to be reasonably accurate, it has to be remembered that it includes a number from the group of 200 Canadian volunteers. Statistically it can be expected that about 160 civilians died and 240 soldiers. Since the volunteers were probably better able to survive the ordeal than the soldiers were, it is likely that a smaller proportion of them died. It that were so, then it is entirely possible that more than 300 of the dead were soldiers.

60 J.-B. Colbert to the Marquis de Tracy, 15 November 1664, AC, CIIA, vol. 2, pt. 1 (transcript of AC, CIIA, in NAC, MG1, CIIA).

61 Thwaites, *Jesuit Relations*, 50: 185–7.

CHAPTER FOUR

1 Robert-Lionel Séguin, *Les Divertissements en Nouvelle-France* (Ottawa: National Museum of Canada 1968), 20–1.

2 Memorandum on Canada by M. de Tracy, 1667, AC, CIIA, vol. 2, pt. 2 (transcript of AC, CIIA, in NAC, MG1, CIIA); Joyce Marshall, ed. and trans., *Word from New France: The Selected Letters of Marie de l'Incarnation* (Toronto: Oxford University Press 1967), 330.

3 "Mémoire de M. de Salières des choses qui se sont passées en Canada les plus considérables depuis qu'il est arrivé," BN, Fonds français, Fonds anciens, MS. 4569 (transcript in NAC, MG7, IA2); Reuben Gold Thwaites, ed. and trans., *The Jesuit Relations and Allied Documents*, 73 vols. (Cleveland: Burrows Brothers Company 1896–1901), 50: 189.

4 François Dollier de Casson, *A History of Montreal, 1640–1672*, trans. Ralph Flenly (London: Dent 1928), 303.

5 Ibid., 301, 329.

6 "Le Livre de raison de François de Tapie de Monteil, capitaine au régiment de Poitou (1661–1670)," Archives départementales de Lot et Garonne, Fonds de Raymond, MS. 137 (transcript in *Revue d'histoire de l'Amérique française* 14, no. 1 [1960]: 109–21).

7 The minister of war to Colbert de Terron, 28 February 1666, AMG, Archives acadiennes, vol. 199 (transcript of the Archives acadiennes in NAC, MG4, AI).

8 Marshall, *Word from New France*, 314.

9 Dollier de Casson, *History of Montreal*, 301. The author could not have been writing from his own experience, for he did not arrive in Canada until September 1666.

10 Marcel Trudel, *La Population du Canada en 1663* (Montreal: Fides 1973), 150. The estimate of the average age of the men in the Carignan-Salières Regiment is based on a sample of ninety-four officers and men whose ages are known. Of them, twenty-one were officers whose average age in 1666 was approximately thirty. The seventy-three noncommissioned men had an average age of about twenty-five. The research upon which these figures are based was carried out by A. Leo Leymarie. His notes are preserved in NAC, MG30, D56, vol. 5, file 6, and their contents are summarized in appendix B.

11 Trudel, *La Population du Canada*, 150.

12 "Mémoire de M. de Salières"; Thwaites, *Jesuit Relations*, 50: 135–7.

13 "Mémoire de M. de Salières."

14 Ibid.

15 Ibid.

16 Thwaites, *Jesuit Relations*, 50: 189.

17 Marshall, *Word from New France*, 312.

18 *Traités de Paix conclus entre sa Majesté le Roy de France et les indiens du Canada* (Paris: Sébastien Mabre-Cramoisy 1667), 1–2.

19 "Mémoire de M. de Salières."

20 Ibid.; Thwaites, *Jesuit Relations*, 50: 191.

21 *Traités de Paix*, 3–5; Thwaites, *Jesuit Relations*, 50: 191.

22 "Mémoire de M. de Salières"; Thwaites, *Jesuit Relations*, 50: 191.

23 Jean Talon to the Marquis de Tracy, 1 September 1666, AC, CIIA, vol. 2, pt. 2; Thwaites, *Jesuit Relations*, 50: 139, 193. The *Dictionary of Canadian Biography*, 1: 555, states that a relative of Tracy's, most likely a nephew, was killed in the attack. Bruce Trigger, in *Natives and Newcomers: Canada's "Heroic Age" Reconsidered* (Kingston and Montreal: McGill-Queen's University Press 1985), 284, also says this. Both, how-

ever, are in error, for *Jesuit Relations,* 50: 193 and 197, makes it quite clear that the relative, Lieutenant de Lerole, was taken prisoner, and later brought back to Quebec by the Mohawks. Tracy himself, writing in his memorandum on Canada in 1667, indicates that the man was still alive by suggesting that he might be interested in settling in Canada. See Memorandum on Canada by M. de Tracy, 1667, AC, CIIA, vol. 2, pt. 2.

24 "Mémoire de M. de Salières"; Thwaites, *Jesuit Relations,* 50: 139, 193.
25 Trigger, *Natives and Newcomers,* 274.
26 M. de Tracy to Colonel Richard Nicolls, 30 April 1667, Great Britain, Colonial Office Records, COI, vol. 21 (transcript of vol. 21 in NAC, MGII, vol. 21); Thwaites, *Jesuit Relations,* 50: 193. Guillaume de Couture was well known to the Iroquois, and his selection by Tracy as his emissary was a very shrewd move. Of all the men in Canada, he was probably the only one whose voice carried any weight with the Mohawk chiefs. His association with them dated back to 1642 when he was captured near Fort Richelieu as he was returning to Huronia where he was employed as an indentured tradesman. Taken with other captives to the Mohawk villages, he suffered numerous tortures and humiliations before his courage in adversity commended him to his captors and he was adopted into a family that had recently lost a son. For the next three years he was, for all intents and purposes, a Mohawk. He wore Mohawk dress and learned to speak the Mohawk language fluently. So highly esteemed did he become, in fact, that he quickly rose to the rank of chief, and in 1645 he was one of the Mohawk delegates to peace negotiations in Quebec. He later went on to serve as Iroquois ambassador to the Huron and Neutral nations before finally returning to Canada in 1646. See Marshall, *Word from New France,* 110, 125, 138–43, 147–8, 152–4.
27 M. de Tracy to Colonel Richard Nicolls, 30 April 1667, Great Britain, Colonial Office Records, COI, vol. 21, and Colonel Richard Nicolls to M. de Tracy, 20 August 1666, COI, vol. 20 (transcript of vol. 20 in NAC, MGII, vol. 20); Thwaites, *Jesuit Relations,* 50: 197–9. The Flemish Bastard, as he was called, was born of a Dutch father and a Mohawk mother, most likely between 1620 and 1630. His Dutch name was Jan Smits, but it is not known what he was called by the Mohawks. His career as a chief spans a period of almost forty years, and during that time he was active in various aspects of Mohawk affairs. At some point in his life he is known to have accepted Christianity, most likely in the years immediately following Tracy's term as lieutenant-general. He probably died some time during the 1690s. See Thomas Grassmann, "Flemish Bastard," *Dictionary of Canadian Biography* 1: 307–8.

28 The king to M. de Tracy, 24 March 1666, Ministère des Affaires étrangères, Correspondance politique, vol. 88 (transcript of Correspondance politique in NAC, MG5, A1).

29 "Mémoire de M. de Salières"; Thwaites, *Jesuit Relations,* 50: 197.

30 "Mémoire de M. de Salières."

31 The king to M. de Tracy, 24 March 1666, Ministère des Affaires étrangères, Correspondance politique, vol. 88.

32 John Romeyn Brodhead, *Documents Relative to the Colonial History of the State of New York,* ed. Edmund Bailey O'Callaghan, 11 vols. (Albany: Weed, Parsons and Co. 1853–1861), 3: 120.

33 Ibid.; Thwaites, *Jesuit Relations,* 50: 193.

34 The king to M. de Tracy, 24 March 1666, Ministère des Affaires étrangères, Correspondance politique, vol. 88.

35 Brodhead, *Colonial History of the State of New York,* 3: 120–1.

36 Colonel Richard Nicolls to M. de Tracy, 20 August 1666, Great Britain, Colonial Office Records, CO1, vol. 20.

37 "Mémoire de M. de Salières."

38 Thwaites, *Jesuit Relations,* 50: 197.

39 "Mémoire de M. de Salières"; Thwaites, *Jesuit Relations,* 50: 139, 197, 199.

40 Minute, 6 May 1666, Archives départementales de la Charente-Maritime, La Rochelle, series .E, Teuleron, 1666 (microfilm in NAC, MG6, A2); "Mémoire de M. de Salières"; Thwaites, *Jesuit Relations,* 50: 193.

41 The king to M. de Tracy, 24 March 1666, Ministère des Affaires étrangères, Correspondance politique, vol. 88.

42 Ibid.

43 Jean Talon to M. de Tracy, 1 September 1666, AC, C11A, vol. 2, pt. 2.

44 Ibid.

45 Ibid.

46 Ibid.

47 Ibid.

48 Marshall, *Word from New France,* 319–20.

49 Ibid., 317–18, 321.

CHAPTER FIVE

1 Jeanne-Françoise Juchereau [de La Ferté] de Saint-Ignace and Marie-Andrée Duplessis de Sainte-Hélène, *Les Annales de l'Hôtel-Dieu de Québec, 1636–1716,* facsimile ed. (Quebec: Hôtel-Dieu de Québec 1939), 153.

2 "Mémoire de M. de Salières des choses qui se sont passées en Canada les plus considérables depuis qu'il est arrivé," BN, Fonds français, Fonds anciens, MS. 4569 (transcript in NAC, MG7, 1A2); Joyce Marshall, ed. and trans., *Word from New France: The Selected Letters of Marie*

de l'Incarnation (Toronto: Oxford University Press 1967), 321; Reuben Gold Thwaites, ed. and trans., *The Jesuit Relations and Allied Documents*, 73 vols. (Cleveland: Burrows Brothers Company 1896–1901), 49: 257, 50: 141.

The Jesuit estimate of from three to four hundred Mohawk warriors was probably very conservative. There can be no doubt that the various epidemics that had raged among the Indian population of northeastern America between the coming of the first Europeans and the middle of the seventeenth century took a great toll, and that from 50 to 70 per cent of an estimated seven to eleven thousand Mohawks died as a result of smallpox, influenza, measles, and other diseases brought by the newcomers. Taking mean values for each yields a post-epidemic population estimate of about thirty-five hundred, which by 1666 might have risen to somewhere between four and five thousand. Assuming the accuracy of the data, and a normal distribution within the population of sexes and ages, it seems possible, therefore, that when Tracy launched his campaign in the fall of 1666, the Mohawks could have fielded as many as a thousand warriors against him. See Bruce G. Trigger, *Natives and Newcomers: Canada's "Heroic Age" Reconsidered* (Montreal and Kingston: McGill-Queen's University Press 1985), 235–6.

3 Marshall, *Word from New France*, 320.

4 Thwaites, *Jesuit Relations*, 50: 141–3.

5 Marshall, *Word from New France*, 321–8.

6 Thwaites, *Jesuit Relations*, 50: 141–7, 201–5.

7 François Dollier de Casson, *A History of Montreal, 1640–1672*, trans. Ralph Flenly (London: Dent 1928), 305–7; Thwaites, *Jesuit Relations*, 50: 147.

8 Juchereau and Duplessis, *Les Annales de l'Hôtel-Dieu*, 150–4.

9 Thwaites, *Jesuit Relations*, 50: 141–3.

10 Marshall, *Word from New France*, 318; Thwaites, *Jesuit Relations*, 50: 141–3.

11 Tracy's health was a matter for concern throughout his term in Canada, not only for himself, but for others too, including the king. See the king to M. de Tracy, 24 March 1666, Ministère des Affaires étrangères, Correspondance politique, vol. 88 (transcript of Correspondance politique in NAC, MG5, AI).

12 Thwaites, *Jesuit Relations*, 50: 141, 201–3.

13 Ibid., 49: map facing p. 266.

14 Ibid., 50: 141.

15 Marshall, *Word from New France*, 321.

16 Ibid.

17 Ibid., 322, 326.

18 Horatio Hale, *The Iroquois Book of Rites* (Philadelphia: D.G. Brinton 1883), 184–6.
19 Marshall, *Word from New France,* 322; Thwaites, *Jesuit Relations,* 50: 141–3.
20 Marshall, *Word from New France,* 317, 321.
21 Ibid., 321–2.
22 Dollier de Casson, *History of Montreal,* 305–7.
23 Ibid., 307; Thwaites, *Jesuit Relations,* 50: 147, 201.
24 Dollier de Casson, *History of Montreal,* 307; Marshall, *Word from New France,* 322.
25 Marshall, *Word from New France,* 322–3; Thwaites, *Jesuit Relations,* 50: 143, 203.
26 Marshall, *Word from New France,* 323; Thwaites, *Jesuit Relations,* 50: 143, 203.
27 Marshall, *Word from New France,* 323, 324, 326; Thwaites, *Jesuit Relations,* 50: 145.
28 Marshall, *Word from New France,* 324; Thwaites, *Jesuit Relations,* 50: 145.
29 Marshall, *Word from New France,* 323; Thwaites, *Jesuit Relations,* 50: 145.
30 Jean Talon to the minister (probably Colbert), 13 November 1666, AC, CIIA, vol. 2, pt. 2 (transcript of AC, CIIA, in NAC, MGI, CIIA).
31 "Proces verbal de prise de possession des forts d'Agnier, 17 October 1666," AC, CIIA, vol. 2, pt. 2.
32 Jean Talon to M. de Tracy, 1 September 1666, AC, CIIA, vol. 2, pt. 2; the king to M. de Tracy, 24 March 1666, Ministère des Affaires étrangères, Correspondance politique, vol. 88.
33 Marshall, *Word from New France,* 323–4, 326; Thwaites, *Jesuit Relations,* 50: 145, 203.
34 Marshall, *Word from New France,* 324. Marie de l'Incarnation states that the child was a boy; yet the *Annales de l'Hôtel-Dieu de Québec* says that it was a girl, who was given into the custody of Jean Talon. He had her baptized under the name of Maria and then sent her to France, into the care of the Hospitalières de la Raquette in Paris, where she died two years afterwards. See Juchereau and Duplessis, *Les Annales de l'Hôtel-Dieu,* 153–4.
35 Marshall, *Word from New France,* 326.
36 Ibid., 325; Thwaites, *Jesuit Relations,* 50: 145–7.
37 Marshall, *Word from New France,* 326–7.
38 Thwaites, *Jesuit Relations,* 50: 145–7. One officer, Lieutenant Du Luc, and seven other men died in the mishap on Lake Champlain, at least four of whom are known to have been soldiers. They were Marc Butin, Jacques Hurteau, Ange Des Nogeaux, and Guillaume Aubry. See Registre de Montréal, entries dated 16 November 1666 (transcript in NAC, MG30, D56, vol. 5, file 6).
39 Thwaites, *Jesuit Relations,* 50: 203.

40 Juchereau and Duplessis, *Les Annales de l'Hôtel-Dieu,* 153–4; Marshall, *Word from New France,* 327.
41 Thwaites, *Jesuit Relations,* 50: 145.
42 Trigger, *Natives and Newcomers,* 340.
43 Colonel Richard Nicolls to M. de Tracy, 20 August 1666, Great Britain, Colonial Office Records, COI, vol. 20 (transcript in NAC, MGII, vol. 20).
44 Thwaites, *Jesuit Relations,* 50: 147.

CHAPTER SIX

1 Jean Talon to J.-B. Colbert, 13 November 1666, and Jean Talon to the minister, 13 November 1666, AC, CIIA, vol. 2, pt. 2 (transcript of AC, CIIA, in NAC, MGI, CIIA). What had not been possible to accomplish by force of arms, Talon proposed doing by diplomatic sleight of hand, suggesting that "if the king accommodated Holland by stipulating to England the necessity of restoring New Holland to the former, and prior to this found the means of negotiation with the Gentlemen of the Estates, I believe an agreement could be reached on reasonable terms" (Jean Talon to J.-B. Colbert, 13 November 1666, AC, CIIA, vol. 2, pt. 2).

Those so-called reasonable terms would have resulted in certain very obvious benefits to France, including gaining control of an all-season port of access to the commerce of northeastern America; making the Five Nations of the Iroquois Confederacy entirely dependent upon France for the products of European technology; enabling France to seize the Swedish colony at the mouth of the Delaware River; and containing the New England colonies within their existing borders, thereby effectively cutting them off from the fur trade.
2 Jean Talon to J.-B. Colbert, 13 November 1666, AC, CIIA, vol. 2, pt. 2.
3 Joyce Marshall, ed. and trans., *Word from New France: The Selected Letters of Marie de l'Incarnation* (Toronto: Oxford University Press 1967), 327.
4 Ibid., 327; Reuben Gold Thwaites, ed. and trans., *The Jesuit Relations and Allied Documents,* 73 vols. (Cleveland: Burrows Brothers Company 1896–1901), 50: 205.
5 Memorandum on Canada by M. de Tracy, 1667, AC, CIIA, vol. 2, pt. 2; François Dollier de Casson, *A History of Montreal, 1640–1672,* trans. Ralph Flenly (London: Dent 1928), 317; Marshall, *Word from New France,* 330; Thwaites, *Jesuit Relations,* 50: 245.
6 Dollier de Casson, *History of Montreal,* 311.
7 Ibid.
8 Ibid., 313.
9 Ibid., 315.

10 Ibid., 319–21.

11 Ibid., 317.

12 Ibid. Purslane, a flowering plant, is a member of the Portulaca family. Its leaves were eaten as a vegetable or used as seasoning.

13 Ibid., 319–21.

14 Ibid., 321–3.

15 Ibid., 323; Thwaites, *Jesuit Relations,* 50: 209.

16 *Traités de Paix conclus entre sa Majesté le Roy de France et les indiens du Canada* (Paris: Sébastien Mabre-Cramoisy 1667), 6–12; Thwaites, *Jesuit Relations,* 50: 209–11.

17 Thwaites, *Jesuit Relations,* 50: 211.

18 *Traités de Paix,* 6–12.

19 Ibid.; Thwaites, *Jesuit Relations,* 50: 239; Bruce G. Trigger, *Natives and Newcomers: Canada's "Heroic Age" Reconsidered* (Kingston and Montreal: McGill-Queen's University Press 1985), 291.

20 *Traités de Paix,* 6–12; Marshall, *Word from New France,* 328–9; Thwaites, *Jesuit Relations,* 51: 169.

21 Memorandum on Canada by M. de Tracy, 1667, AC, CIIA, vol. 2, pt. 2; Marshall, *Word from New France,* 330; Thwaites, *Jesuit Relations,* 50: 239, 245.

22 The minister of war to M. de Noraye, 15 December 1665, vol. 196, 28 February 1666, vol. 199, AMG, Archives acadiennes (transcript of Archives acadiennes in NAC, MG4, AI).

CHAPTER SEVEN

1 William J. Eccles, "The Social, Economic, and Political Significance of the Military Establishment in New France," *Candian Historical Review* 52, no. 1 (1971): 1–3; Robert-Lionel Séguin, *La Vie libertine en Nouvelle-France au dix-septième siècle,* 2 vols. (Montreal: Leméac 1972), 2: 378.

2 Joyce Marshall, ed. and trans., *Word from New France: The Selected Letters of Marie de l'Incarnation* (Toronto: Oxford University Press 1967), 335.

3 Jean Talon to the minister, 13 November 1666, AC, CIIA, vol. 2, pt. 2 (transcript of AC, CIIA, in NAC, MGI, CIIA); Marshall, *Word from New France,* 330.

4 Reuben Gold Thwaites, ed. and trans., *The Jesuit Relations and Allied Documents,* 73 vols. (Cleveland: Burrows Brothers Company 1896–1901), 49: 171; 50: 207, 211–13; 51: 173–5.

5 "Total de toutte la dépense faite pour les troupes d'infanterie entretenues par le Roy en Canada ..." 15 June 1666, AC, CIIA, vol. 2, pt. 2.

6 "Le Livre de raison de François de Tapie de Monteil, capitaine au régiment de Poitou (1661–1670)," Archives départementales de Lot et

Garonne, Fonds de Raymond, MS. 137 (transcript in *Revue d'histoire de l'Amérique française* 14, no. 1 [1960]: 109–21).

7 Louis André, *Michel Le Tellier et l'organization de l'armée monarchique* (Paris: F. Alcan 1906), 289.

8 *Jugements et délibérations du Conseil souverain de la Nouvelle-France,* 6 vols. (Quebec: A. Côté 1885–1891), 1: 402.

9 André, *Michel Le Tellier,* 429–30; André Corvisier, *Armées et sociétés en Europe de 1494 à 1789* (Paris: Presses universitaires de France 1976), 80–1.

10 "Le Livre de raison de Tapie de Monteil."

11 François Dollier de Casson, *A History of Montreal, 1640–1672,* trans. Ralph Flenly (London: Dent 1928), 328; "Arrest du Conseil souverain de Québec," 5 January 1667, *Collection de manuscrits contenant lettres, mémoires, et autres documents historiques relatifs à la Nouvelle-France,* 4 vols. (Quebec: A. Côté 1883), 1: 186–7.

12 *Jugements et délibérations du Conseil souverain,* 1: 420; *Ordonnances, commissions, etc. etc., des gouverneurs et intendants de la Nouvelle-France, 1639–1706,* 2 vols. (Beauceville: Eclaireur 1924), 1: 68.

13 *Jugements et délibérations du Conseil souverain,* 1: 420; Raymond Boyer, *Les Crimes et les châtiments du Canada français du XVIIe siècle* (Montreal: Cercle du Livre de France 1966), 97; Thwaites, *Jesuit Relations,* 50: 211.

14 Anonymous note, probably written by the Jesuit Claude Dablon, AN, Fonds canadien, x–1292. The contents of the preceding document are summarized in vol. 1, pp. 75–6 of Séguin's *La Vie libertine.*

15 Ibid.

16 *Jugements et délibérations du Conseil souverain,* 1: 389–90; Séguin, *La Vie libertine,* 1: 74–5.

17 Gustave Lanctot, "La Douceur de la vie en Nouvelle-France," *Magazine Maclean,* July 1964, 20.

18 Baron Louis-Armand de Lahontan, *New Voyages to North America,* ed. Reuben Gold Thwaites, 2 vols. (Chicago: A.C. McClurg and Company 1905), 2: 453–5. There have been a number of editions of Baron Lahontan's work, both in the original French and in other languages too. The English translation edited by Thwaites was first published in London in 1735.

19 Bruce G. Trigger, *Natives and Newcomers: Canada's "Heroic Age" Reconsidered* (Kingston and Montreal: McGill-Queen's University Press 1985), 195.

20 *Jugements et délibérations du Conseil souverain,* 1: 399; item headed "Maugrain, dit Picart ou Le Picart (Claude)," NAC, MG30, D56, vol. 5, file 6; Séguin, *La Vie libertine,* 1: 76.

21 Order to the Sieur de La Fredière, 27 August 1667, Collection Moreau

Saint-Méry, vol. 3, pt. 2 (transcript of the Collection Moreau Saint-Méry in NAC, MGI, F3).

22 "André Demers vs sieur de La fredière Cap^{ne} & Major au régiment de Carignan-Salière," 10 September 1667, Montreal, Archives judiciaires, Registre du baillage du district de Montréal; Etienne-Michel Faillon, *Histoire de la colonie française en Canada,* 3 vols. (Villemarie: Bibliothèque pariossiale 1865–66), 3: 384–8.

23 Serge Gagnon, "Etienne-Michel Faillon," *Dictionary of Canadian Biography* 9: 246–9.

24 "Mémoire de M. de Salières des choses qui se sont passées en Canada les plus considérables depuis qu'il est arrivé," BN, Fonds français, Fonds anciens, MS. 4569 (transcript in NAC, MG7, IA2); *Le Bulletin des recherches historiques* 11 (1905): 161–6; Faillon, *Histoire de la colonie française,* 3: 384–8.

25 "Total de toutte la dépense," AC, CIIA, vol. 2, pt. 2.

26 *Collection de manuscrits,* 1: 186–7; Faillon, *Histoire de la colonie française,* 3: 384–8.

27 "André Demers vs sieur de La fredière," Archives judiciaires, Registre du baillage du district de Montréal; Faillon, *Histoire de la colonie française,* 3: 384–8.

28 Faillon, *Histoire de la colonie française,* 3: 384–8.

29 Ibid.

30 Ibid.; *Le Bulletin des recherches historiques* 11 (1905): 86–8; Thwaites, *Jesuit Relations,* 50: 209.

31 Order to the Sieur de La Fredière, 27 August 1667, Collection Moreau Saint-Méry, vol. 3, pt. 2.

32 The Marquis de Salières to Jean Talon, 1 September 1667, Collection Moreau Saint-Méry, vol. 3, pt. 2.

33 The last obvious link between the regiment and the ruling house of Savoy was broken soon after it returned to France in 1668, when the name Carignan was dropped in favour of Soissons. The change was, perhaps, more symbolic than significant, for the Comte de Soissons, after whom the regiment became named, was none other than the Prince Eugène Maurice of Carignano, whose claim to the French title went back to 1625 when his mother, Marie de Bourbon-Soissons, married Thomas Francis of Savoy.

34 Footnote by the Marquis de Tracy to the order to the Sieur de La Fredière, 27 August 1667, Collection Moreau Saint-Méry, vol. 3, pt. 2.

35 Jean Talon to the Marquis de Louvois, 19 November 1667, AMG, Archives acadiennes, vol. 463 (microfilm in NAC, MG4, AI).

36 Ibid.

37 Jean Talon to J.-B. Colbert, 27 October 1667, AC, CIIA, vol. 2, pt. 2.

38 Memorandum on Canada by M. de Tracy, 1667, AC, CIIA, vol. 2, pt. 2;

F. Grenier, "Antoine Pécaudy de Contrecoeur," *Dictionary of Canadian Biography* 1: 535–6.

39 Ibid.

40 Albert Tessier, "René Gaultier de Varennes," *Dictionary of Canadian Biography* 1: 326–7; Raymond Douville, "Pierre Boucher," *Dictionary of Canadian Biography* 2: 82–7.

41 W. Stanford Reid, "Michel-Sidrac Dugué de Boisbriand," *Dictionary of Canadian Biography* 1: 295.

42 E. Cheminade, "Emigrants au Canada venant du Nivernais," *Nova Francia* 1, no. 2 (1925): 75–6.

43 Marshall, *Word from New France*, 330; Cyprien Tanguay, *Dictionnaire généalogique des familles canadiennes*, 7 vols. (Montreal: E. Senécal 1871–90), 1: 2, 177, 266, 498.

44 Items headed "Adhémar, Antoine," and "Poutre, dit La Vigne (André)," NAC, MG30, D56, vol. 5, file 6.

45 Pierre-André Leclerc, "Le Mariage sous le régime français," *Revue d'histoire de l'Amérique française* 13, no. 2 (1959): 230–46; Robert-Lionel Séguin, *Les Divertissements en Nouvelle-France* (Ottawa: National Museum of Canada 1968), 22–4; Thwaites, *Jesuit Relations,* 50: 207.

46 Jean Talon to the Marquis de Louvois, 19 November 1667, AMG, Archives acadiennes, vol. 463; Jean Talon to J.-B. Colbert, 27 October 1667, AC, CIIA, vol. 2, pt. 2.

47 "Le Livre de raison de Tapie de Monteil."

48 Transcript of an account of a miracle written in 1668 by a missionary named Morel, Archives du Séminaire de Saint-Sulpice, Paris, Cahiers de notes de M. l'Abbé Faillon, cahier Y, entry no. 650 (transcript in NAC, MG30, D56, vol. 5, file 6).

49 Ibid.; Thwaites, *Jesuit Relations,* 50: 211.

CHAPTER EIGHT

1 Royal Memorandum to the Sieur Talon, 27 March 1665, AN, series B (transcript of AN, series B, in NAC, MGI, BI).

2 Memorandum on Canada by M. de Tracy, 1667, AC, CIIA, vol. 2, pt. 2 (transcript of AC, CIIA, in NAC, MGI, CIIA).

3 Ibid.; Joyce Marshall, ed. and trans., *Word from New France: The Selected Letters of Marie de l'Incarnation* (Toronto: Oxford University Press 1967), 330.

4 Memorandum on Canada by M. de Tracy, 1667, AC, CIIA, vol. 2, pt. 2.

5 Ibid.

6 Jean Talon to J.-B. Colbert, 29 October 1667, AC, CIIA, vol. 2, pt. 2.

7 Memorandum on Canada by M. de Tracy, 1667, AC, CIIA, vol. 2, pt. 2.

8 Reuben Gold Thwaites, ed. and trans., *The Jesuit Relations and Allied Documents,* 73 vols. (Cleveland: Burrows Brothers Company 1896–1901), 50: 215.

9 Roll of soldiers from the Carignan-Salières Regiment who settled in Canada, AC, D2C, vol. 47 (transcript in NAC, MG1, D2C); order dated 23 March 1669, Archives de la Marine, Orders and Dispatches, vol. 9 (microfilm of Orders and Dispatches in NAC, MG2, B2); items headed "Chambly," "Froment," "La Tour," "Lerole," and "Petit," NAC, MG30, D56, vol. 5, file 6; Cyprien Tanguay, *Répertoire général du Clergé canadien par ordre chronologique* (Quebec: C. Darveau 1868), 52.

10 André Corvisier, *Armées et sociétés en Europe de 1494 à 1789* (Paris: Presses universitaires de France 1976), 82.

11 Order dated 23 March 1669, Archives de la Marine, Orders and Dispatches, vol. 9.

12 "Le Livre de raison de François de Tapie de Monteil, capitaine au régiment de Poitou (1661–1670)," Archives départementales de Lot et Garonne, Fonds Raymond, MS. 137 (transcript in *Revue d'histoire de l'Amérique française* 14, no. 1 [1960]: 109–21).

13 The minister of war to M. de Salières, 5 December 1669, AMG, Archives acadiennes, vol. 221 (transcript of Archives acadiennes in NAC, MG4, A1); Gabriel Daniel, *Histoire de la milice françoise,* 2 vols. (Paris: J.-B. Coignard 1721), 2: 422.

14 "Le Livre de raison de Tapie de Monteil."

15 J.-B. Colbert to M. de Courcelle, 15 May 1669, AN, series B.

16 J.-B. Colbert to Jean Talon, 20 February 1668, AC, CIIA, vol. 3; Thwaites, *Jesuit Relations,* 51: 171.

17 Marshall, *Word from New France,* 315.

18 Ibid., 331.

19 Jean Talon to J.-B. Colbert, 10 November 1670, AC, CIIA, vol. 3.

20 Ibid.

21 Emma Helen Blair, ed. and trans., *The Indian Tribes of the Upper Mississippi and the Region of the Great Lakes; as Described by Nicolas Perrot, French Commandant in the Northwest,* 2 vols. (Cleveland: Arthur H. Clarke Company 1911), 1: 204.

22 R. Cole Harris and John Warkentin, *Canada before Confederation* (New York: Oxford University Press 1977), 49.

23 Jean Talon to J.-B. Colbert, 10 November 1670, AC, CIIA, vol. 3.

24 Marshall, *Word from New France,* 345, 353.

25 J.-B. Colbert to Jean Talon, 20 February 1668, AC, CIIA, vol. 3; Marshall, *Word from New France,* 353.

26 Blair, *Indian Tribes,* 204–7; Marshall, *Word from New France,* 353.

27 Ibid.

28 Ibid.

29 Ibid.
30 Ibid.
31 Ibid.
32 Bruce G. Trigger, *Natives and Newcomers: Canada's "Heroic Age" Reconsidered* (Kingston and Montreal: McGill-Queen's University Press 1985), 285; Marshall, *Word from New France*, 355.
33 Item headed "Philippe de Carrion du Fresnay," NAC, MG30, D56, vol. 5, file 6; Blair, *Indian Tribes*, 204–7.
34 Marshall, *Word from New France*, 355–8. In the incident referred to, three Frenchmen, in order to steal a valuable shipment of furs, killed six members of the Mahican nation. Their chiefs, thinking the Iroquois were to blame, declared war on them. Before anything came of it, however, there was a falling out among the thieves, and their crime was revealed. When the truth became known to the Mahicans and the Iroquois, they turned on the French and attacked a house, killing three of its occupants. The fate of the three Frenchmen who had killed the Mahicans is not known, although it seems likely that they fled and thus escaped any punishment for their crime.
35 J.-B. Colbert to M. de Courcelle, 15 May 1668, AN, BI.
36 Ibid.
37 Inès Murat, *Colbert* (Paris: Fayard 1980), 267.
38 Orders dated 23 March 1669 and 29 March 1669, Archives de la Marine, Orders and Dispatches, vol. 9.
39 Undertaking from Captains Berthier, Chambly, Durantaye, Grandfontaine, and Loubias to raise companies of soldiers, fifty men strong, for which they would be paid one thousand *écus*, Archives de la Marine (transcript in NAC, MG30, D56, vol. 5, file 6).
40 Marshall, *Word from New France*, 354.
41 The king to M. de Courcelle, 3 April 1669, AC, CIIA, vol. 3.
42 Various documented anecdotal items under the names of the officers concerned in NAC, MG30, D56, vol. 5, file 6. The contents of these items are summarized in appendix B. Similar information is to be found in Pierre-George Roy, *Inventaire des concessions en fief et seigneurie, fois et hommages, et aveux et dénombrements*, 6 vols. (Beauceville: Eclaireur 1927–29).
43 Marcel Trudel, *The Seigneurial System* (Ottawa: Canadian Historical Association 1971), 7.
44 Dossier of the 47th Infantry Regiment, AG, Archives historiques; Daniel, *La Milice françoise*, 2: 421–2; Louis Susane, *Histoire de l'ancienne infanterie française*, 8 vols. (Paris: J. Correard 1851), 5: 236–40.
45 "Le Livre de raison de Tapie de Monteil"; Dossier on Alexandre de Prouville, Marquis de Tracy, BN, Pièces originales, no. 2391, dossier no. 53.598, document no. 1 (transcript in NAC, MG7, vol. 66A, no. 28875).

46 The minister of war to M. de Salières, 10 December 1668, AMG, Archives acadiennes, vol. 221.

47 Transcript of L. Aubiman, ed., *Mémoires du Père René Rapin,* 5 vols. (Paris: 1865), 3: 183–4, in NAC. MG30, D56, vol. 5, file 6; Thwaites, *Jesuit Relations,* 51: 171–3.

48 Dossier of the 47th Infantry Regiment, AG, Archives historiques; Daniel, *La Milice françoise,* 2: 421–2.

49 Transcript of Aubiman, *Mémoires du Père René Rapin,* 3: 183–4.

CHAPTER NINE

1 William J. Eccles, "A Belated Review of Harold Adams Innis' *The Fur Trade in Canada,*" *The Canadian Historical Review* 60, no. 4 (1979): 422.

2 Although Father Ragueneau wrote regularly to Colbert, the contents of his reports had more to do with comings and goings than with the sort of intelligence useful to someone planning a military operation. So even though he had access to both the letters and the *Relations,* Colbert would still have been relatively ignorant about the conditions the Carignan-Salières Regiment would encounter when it attacked the Iroquois.

3 Joyce Marshall, ed. and trans., *Word from New France: The Selected Letters of Marie de l'Incarnation* (Toronto: Oxford University Press 1967), 315; Reuben Gold Thwaites, ed. and trans., *The Jesuit Relations and Allied Documents,* 73 vols. (Cleveland: Burrows Brothers Company 1896–1901), 49: 165.

4 Marshall, *Word from New France,* 314.

5 Régis Roy and Gérard Malchelosse, *Le Régiment de Carignan* (Montreal: G. Ducharme 1925), 47.

6 Bruce G. Trigger, *Natives and Newcomers: Canada's "Heroic Age" Reconsidered* (Kingston and Montreal: McGill-Queen's University Press 1985), 332–3.

7 François Dollier de Casson, *A History of Montreal, 1640–1672,* trans. Ralph Flenly (London: Dent 1928), 329.

8 *Censuses of Canada, 1665–1871,* 5 vols. (Ottawa: Queen's Printer 1876), vol. 4.

9 The list of place-names includes Berthierville, Boisbriand, Chambly, Contrecoeur, La Durantaye, La Pocatière, Saint-Ours, Sorel, Varennes, and Verchères.

10 *Montreal Gazette,* 14 July 1988.

11 Lionel Groulx, "Consignes de demain," *Soirées de l'Action française* (Montreal: Editions de l'Action française 1926), 10.

12 Marshall, *Word from New France,* 317–18, 321.

13 Roy and Malchelosse, *Le Régiment de Carignan*, 47.
14 Mason Wade, *The French-Canadian Outlook* (Toronto: McClelland and Stewart 1964), 3.

APPENDIX A

1 "Total de toutte la dépense faite pour les troupes d'infanterie entretenues par le Roy en Canada ...," 15 June 1666, AC, CIIA, vol. 2, pt. 2 (transcript in NAC, MGI, CIIA).
2 Marcel Trudel, *Initiation à la Nouvelle-France: histoire et institutions* (Montreal: Holt, Rinehart and Winston 1968), 197–9, 235–9.

APPENDIX B

1 Joyce Marshall, ed. and trans., *Word from New France: The Selected Letters of Marie de l'Incarnation* (Toronto: Oxford University Press 1967), 311; Jeanne-Françoise Juchereau [de La Ferté] de Saint-Ignace and Marie-Andrée Duplessis de Sainte-Hélène, *Les Annales de l'Hôtel-Dieu de Québec, 1636–1716*, facsimile ed. (Quebec: Hôtel-Dieu de Québec 1939), 147–9.
2 "Le Livre de raison de François de Tapie de Monteil, capitaine au régiment de Poitou (1661–1670)," Archives départementales de Lot et Garonne, Fonds de Raymond, MS. 137 (transcript in *Revue d'histoire de l'Amérique française* 14, no. 1 [1960]: 109–21); Reuben Gold Thwaites, ed. and trans., *The Jesuit Relations and Allied Documents*, 73 vols. (Cleveland: Burrows Brothers Company 1896–1901), 50: 183.
3 Roll of soldiers from the Carignan-Salières Regiment who settled in Canada, AC, D2C, vol. 47 (transcript in NAC, MGI, D2C); Cyprien Tanguay, *Dictionnaire généalogique des familles canadiennes*, 7 vols. (Quebec: E. Senécal 1890), vols. 1 and 2; *Dictionary of Canadian Biography*; François-Joseph Audet, "Le Régiment de Carignan," *Mémoires de la Société royale du Canada* 16 (1922): 129–41; A. Leo Leymarie Papers, NAC, MG30 D56, vol. 5, file 6. Where conflicts exist between the five sources with respect to dates and the spelling of names, the weight of authority is allotted to *Dictionary of Canadian Biography*.

Two other sources could be consulted for biographical information about the men listed in this appendix: *Dictionnaire national des canadiens français, 1608–1760*, 3 vols. (Montreal: Institut généalogique Drouin 1950); René Jetté, *Dictionnaire généalogique des familles du Québec: des origines à 1730* (Montreal: Les Presses de l'université de Montréal 1983).

Index

Adhémar de Saint-Martin,
Antoine, 105, 183
Adirondacks, 75, 76, 78
Aigle d'Or, 16, 22–3, 31
Albanel, Father Charles,
21, 52, 73, 78
Albany, 50, 61, 80
Algonkin Indians: in the
campaigns, 39, 47, 69,
78; firearms used by,
42; and fur trade, 3;
and Mohawks, 62, 78
Andigné de Grand-
fontaine, Captain
Hector d', 117, 158
*Annales de l'Hôtel-Dieu
de Québec*, 73, 145
Army reforms, 15, 92, 124
Arnoult de Broisle de
Loubias, Captain, 61,
117, 171
Autumn campaign:
accounts of, 73–4;
Courcelle on, 74, 79,
80, 81; logistics of, 72,
74, 76–8; mishaps
during, 78;
misrepresentation of,
71, 83; Mohawk
encounters during, 78,
79; and religion, 78,
106; results of, 71–2,
83–5; return from, 82–3;
route of, 75–6; route

map, 77; turning point
in, 80–1; and weather,
77, 82. *See also*
Prouville de Tracy,
Alexandre de

Beaugendre (Desrochers),
Paul, 95–6, 184
Berthier, Captain
Alexandre, 24, 74, 117,
151
Beschefer, Father Thierry,
60–1
Blue Coats, 49. *See also*
Volunteers
Bonneau-Chabot, Sieur
de, 11
Bonneau de La Varenne,
Captain Roger, 52, 58,
169
Boucher, Marie, 104, 109
Boucher, Pierre, 4, 104
Brèse, 15–16, 18
Brothels, 97
Burel, Jeanne, 105

Campaigns against
Mohawks. *See* Autumn
campaign; Winter cam-
paign
Canada: definition, 187n1
Canchy de Lerole,
Lieutenant Louis de, 61,
109, 110, 174

Carignan-Salières
Regiment: arming of,
15, 85; campaigns of,
37–53, 55, 63, 73–84;
conduct of, 8–12, 26,
92, 93, 113–15, 125;
demography of, 57;
embarkation of, 3, 13,
16–17; foreign status of,
101; and fur trade, 22;
Groulx on, 127; history
of, 7, 120, 121; impact
of, on Canada, 18, 56,
110, 124, 126, 127; and
marriage, 113; and mili-
tia, 118; misconceptions
regarding, 71; mission
of, to Canada, 6–7,
122–4; and Nicolls, 66;
and religion, 24, 106,
125; repatriation of, 91,
108; reputation of,
127–8; revised role of,
82; strength of, 110;
summary justice in,
9–10, 92, 101, 114; and
volunteers, 42, 43. *See
also* Companies
Catholic Church, 24. *See
also* Jesuits; Laval,
Bishop François de
Cayuga Iroquois: and
French, 3; and
Mohawks, 41; and

peace, 39, 66, 90; and Susquehannocks, 20. *See also* Susquehannock War

Chambly, Captain Jacques de: biographical note, 152; and campaigns, 47, 74; at Fort Saint-Louis, 21, 108; repatriation of, 110; at Trois-Rivières, 22; and Troupes de la Marine, 117

Chambly seigneury, 54; map, 120. *See also* Fort Saint-Louis

Chamot, 61, 147

Champagne (soldier), 96, 97, 150

Charles II, 65

Chartier de Lotbinière, René-Louis, 43, 44, 48

Chastelard, François Balthazard de, 121, 181

Chastelard de Salières, Henri de: and army reforms, 92, 124; and autumn campaign, 74; biographical note, 147, 181; as the colonel, 9, 10–11, 23, 27, 33, 35; and command structure, 23, 35; and Courcelle, 34–5, 44; death of, 121; disembarkation of, 23; as a fort builder, 28–34; as a garrison commander, 35, 39–40, 58–60; journal of, 43; repatriation of, 110, 119–20, 121; and settlement, 109; and Soissons Regiment, 121; and Tracy, 27–8, 101; traits and character of, 13–14, 23, 32, 46, 101, 121; and winter campaign, 42–7, 52

Chastellain, Father Pierre, 53

Château Trompette, 120–1

Chaumonot, Father Pierre-Joseph-Marie, 21

Chaumont, Alexandre de, 73

Cherrier de Mignarde, Lieutenant Sixte, 33, 161

Choisy, Nicolas de, 94, 173

Chomedey de Maisonneuve, Paul de, 4, 56

Coindreau, Ester, 98

Colbert, Jean-Baptiste: and Canada, 110, 117, 119; and Jesuits, 25; mercantilism of, 5, 122; minister of marine, 116; miscalculations by, 115, 122, 123; and reinforcements, 116, 117; and seigneurial expansion, 119; and Talon, 103

Colbert de Terron, Jean: experience of, 7; and flintlocks, 85; importance of, 6, 123; and inspection, 14, 15; and Salières, 13–14; and shipping, 15–16

Command structure, 23. *See also* Prouville de Tracy, Alexandre de; Rémy de Courcelle, Daniel de

Commerce in Canada, 56

Compagnie de la Nouvelle-France, 4, 5

Compagnie des Cent-Associés. *See* Compagnie de la Nouvelle-France

Compagnie des Indes occidentales, 6, 122

Companies: Berthier, 151–2; Chambly, 152–3; Contrecoeur, 34, 155–6; Des Portes (Du Prat), 34, 155–6; Dugué (Boisbriand), 156–7; Froment, 14, 22, 157–8; Grandfontaine, 34, 158–60; La Brisandière, 160; La Colonelle, 33, 34, 81, 161; La Durantaye, 87, 162; La Fouille, 11,

162–4; La Fredière, 34, 165–6; Lamotte, 34, 87, 167; La Noraye, 168; La Tour, 168–9; La Varenne, 169–71; Loubias, 171–3; Maximy, 94, 173–4; Monteil, 61, 120, 174–6; Petit, 176–7; Rougemont, 12, 34, 177; Saint-Ours, 177–81; Salières, 34, 121, 181–2; Saurel, 27, 95, 182–5

Connecticut. *See* Massachusetts and Connecticut

Conseil Souverain: credibility of, 102; establishment of, 5; judicial functions of, 92–4, 96–9; and Laval, 24; military bias of, 92, 94

Contrecoeur seigneury: map, 120

Coue, Sépulture de, 22, 158

Courcelle. *See* Rémy de Courcelle

Couture (Cousture), Guillaume de, 61–2, 86

Dablon, Father Claude, 24–5, 96

Daniel, Abbé Gabriel, 110

Delpesche, Bernard, 105, 182

Demers, André, 99–100

Denys, Barbe, 103–4

Denys, Simon, 104

Desertion, 50, 96

Des Portes, Captain Balthazar, 33, 46, 47, 155

Discipline, responsibility for, in Canada, 100–1

Disembarkation, 17, 18, 23, 28, 106

Disorders: in Canada, 26; in France, 8, 9, 11, 12

Dollier de Casson, François: on autumn campaign, 73, 78; at Fort Sainte-Anne, 87–9; on guerilla tactics, 55; on trading practices,

77; on troops' conduct, 26, 56–7

Drunkenness, 48, 93
Dubois Davaugour, Pierre, 4, 25
Dubois de Cocreaumont et de Saint-Maurice, Captain Jean-Baptiste, 81–2, 161
Dubois d'Esgriseilles, Father Jean-Baptiste, 78, 147
Dugué de Boisbriand, Captain Michel-Sidrac, 104, 156
Du Prat, Lieutenant-Colonel, 34, 46, 47, 147, 155
Durand, Suzanne, 105

Edict of Nantes, 24
Embarkation, 16–17
English colonies, 65. See also Massachusetts and Connecticut; New York
Enlisted men: business opportunities for, 95, 113–15; conduct of, 25–7; occupations of former, 115; reasons of, for joining army, 112; terms of engagement of, 7, 110. See also Officers; Recruitment
Executions, 86, 96, 114
Expansionism, 60

Faillon, Abbé Etienne-Michel, 99
Ferre de Lespinay, Lieutenant Pierre, 109, 148
Filles du roi, 105, 113
Flemish Bastard: and peace talks, 62, 66, 69, 86; goes to Quebec, 62, 89; and Saurel, 62; and Tracy, 72
Flintlocks, 15, 85
Forestier, 89
Fort Richelieu: agriculture

and settlement at, 86, 91, 108; continuing importance of, 119; Courcelle and Salières at, 35; crime at, 95
Forts, 29, 54, 72, 85, 91. See also names of individual forts
Fort Sainte-Anne: abandonment of, 91; access to, 34, 63; Algonkins at, 33; attack at, 61–2; and autumn campaign, 72–4, 76; conditions at, 78, 87, 88; scurvy at, 87–9, 106
Fort Sainte-Thérèse: abandonment of, 91; access to, 34, 63; Algonkins at, 33; construction of, 30–4; Courcelle at, 34, 47–8; incident near, 60; reconnaissance from, 33, 34; and winter campaign, 39, 53
Fort Saint-Jean, 91
Fort Saint-Louis: agriculture and settlement at, 86, 91, 108; construction of, 21, 29–30; continuing importance of, 119; Courcelle and Salières at, 35; defences strengthened at, 63; Dollier de Casson at, 87; and winter campaign, 39, 42, 45
Fort Ticonderoga, 76
47th Infantry Regiment, 121
French justice, Indian view of, 114
Fur trade: attraction of, 125–6; and Canadian economy, 3; and crime, 113–15; and Indians, 3, 19–20; and Jesuits, 91; and officers, 55, 95, 112; and peace treaty, 90; and soldiers, 111, 112, 125

Gaigneur, Pierre, 16

Garakontié, 39–40
Gaultier de Varennes, Lieutenant René, 104, 109, 171
Gencenay, Pierre de (Jean Sendil), 95–6, 185
Gibaud, Gabriel, 105, 184
Governor of New France. See Rémy de Courcelle, Daniel de
Governor of New York. See Nicolls, Colonel Richard
Groulx, Abbé Lionel, 127
Guerilla warfare, 50, 123
Guyart, Marie, dite Marie de l'Incarnation: appeals to France, 4; on filles du roi, 113; on the Flemish Bastard, 69, 72; on Garakontié, 39; on Iroquois raids, 59; on settlement, 111; on troops, 17, 25–6, 56, 73, 93, 117, 127

Hivars, Sergeant, 12, 177
Hôtel-Dieu de Québec, 28, 94
Hudson River, 75, 76
Huguenots, 24, 106, 125
Huron Indians, 3, 4

Ile aux Oies, 119
Ile Perrot, 119
Iles Percées (Boucherville), 104
Indian women, 98
Inspection: by Colbert de Terron, 15; procedures in, 15, 31; purpose of, 14–15; results of, 15, 16; by Tracy, 23–4
Intendant of New France. See Talon, Jean
Intendant of Rochefort. See Colbert de Terron
Iroquois Confederacy: and epidemics, 40; hostages from, 91; and Mahicans, 116;

Mohawks in, 19; nature of, 20; and peace, 66, 108; raids by, 3, 55, 59. *See also* Cayuga Iroquois; Mohawk Iroquois; Oneida Iroquois; Onondaga Iroquois; Seneca Iroquois

Jardin de Hollande, 17, 31
Jesuits: and autumn campaign, 73, 83; and fur trade, 91; and Iroquois, 60; and Laval, 24, 25; and peace treaty, 90; and winter campaign, 43, 44, 45
Jodoin, Claude, 100
Jourdain, Marguerite, 105
Joyeux Siméon, 16, 17, 18
Jurisdictional rivalry, civilian and military, 92
Justice, 17, 28

La Flotte de La Fredière, Major Balthazard de: biographical note, 147, 165; builds fortifications, 63; legal dilemma over, 100–2; military governorship of, 99; traits and character of, 98–100
Lake Champlain, 74, 76, 83
Lake Saint-Sacrement, 74, 76, 83
La Mothe-Saint-Héray, 11, 12
Lamotte de Saint-Paul, Captain Pierre, 87–9, 94, 167
Langevin, 96, 97, 150
La Noiray, 11, 164
La Porte, Marianne de, 98
La Tour, Captain de, 21, 109, 110, 168
Laval, Bishop François de: appeals to France, 4; and Colbert, 3, 127; and Conseil Souverain, 24; intolerance of, 24; and Jesuits, 24, 25; and

Salières, 59; and Tracy, 19, 25
Leboeuf, Marguerite, 97
Legardeur de Repentigny, Jean-Baptiste, 21
Le Moyne, Charles, 39, 46
Lepage, Marie-Rogère, 104–5
Le Prestre de Vauban, Sébastien, 29
Le Tellier, Michel: army reforms of, 15, 92; and Canada, 6, 117, 123; and Carignan-Salières Regiment, 12, 13, 115; and Salières, 27, 121; and Tracy, 28
Logistics, 7, 30. *See also* Inspection; Matériel; Shipping; Ships
Lorraine Guards, 121
Lorraine Regiment, 121
Louis XIV: advisers to, 123; American ambitions of, 81, 82; and army, 10; and Canada, 5, 40, 115, 116, 117, 119; and Carignan-Salières Regiment, 9–11, 108, 110; and the church, 24, 25; European orientation of, 4, 122; and Tracy, 63, 64, 67
Louvois, François-Michel Le Tellier, Marquis de, 35, 102, 106, 117

Mahican Indians, 115–16
Mance, Jeanne, 58
Marchenoir, 8–9
Marie de l'Incarnation. *See* Guyart
Marriage: between soldiers and colonists, 103–6; efforts to increase rate of, 112–13; Talon on, 102–3, 112
Martinet, Lieutenant-Colonel Jean, 15
Massachusetts and Connecticut: and Canada, 63; and Nicolls, 63–6

Matériel: ignorance about, 31–2; inadequacy of, 30, 31, 43
Maugrain, Claude (Le Picart), 98, 150
Mercier, Father Louis, 73
Militia, 42, 116–18. *See also* Volunteers
Minister of marine, 116, 117. *See also* Colbert, Jean-Baptiste
Mohawk Iroquois: and autumn campaign, 71, 78–83; and the Confederacy, 20, 41; factions within, 61; and the French, 3, 41, 43, 60, 66, 67–9, 71, 86, 89; and New York, 61, 63, 64, 67; and peace, 41, 90; strength of, 72, 81, 108; tactics of, in warfare, 50; and winter campaign, 41–2, 50
Mohawk Valley, 76, 78, 91
Mohawk villages, 74, 76, 77, 78, 79–82
Montagnais Indians, 3
Montreal: and fur trade, 126; and La Fredière, 100; troops at, 35, 72, 85, 93; vulnerability of, 55
Morel de La Durantaye, Captain Olivier, 117, 162
Moussart, François, 22, 169
Moyen, Marie, 104

New France, 3, 108; definition, 187–8n1
New York: and autumn campaign, 67, 71, 82; and Tracy, 84. *See also* Nicolls, Colonel Richard
Nicolls, Colonel Richard: and Canada, 63–6; and the Mohawks, 61, 63, 65–6; and the New England colonies, 63–6; and Tracy, 84

Officers: AWOL, 8, 10–11,

13, 38; business practices of, 55–6, 93–4; conditions of service, 8; fraudulent practices among, 14–15; and fur trade, 95, 113–15; marriages and romances of, 102–3, 106; return of, 117; seigneurial grants to, 118–19, 126; and settlement, 109, 115; social background of, 8. *See also* Fur trade; Troops

Oléron, 13

Oneida Iroquois: and the French, 3, 41, 61; and the Mohawks, 20, 41, 82; and peace, 39, 60, 90

Onondaga Iroquois: and the French, 3, 41; and the Mohawks, 41; and peace, 39, 60–1, 90; and the Susquehannocks, 20. *See also* Susquehannock War

Ottawa Indians, 20, 22, 116

Paille, Sieur de, 12

Paix, 16, 22–3, 31

Paon de Hollande, 67

Peace talks, procedure at, 40

Peace treaty, 90–1, 126

Pécaudy de Contrecoeur, Captain Antoine, 103–4, 109, 153

Pepin, Antoine, 94

Perché Regiment, 121

Peronaille, 8–9

Petit, Captain Louis, 109, 110, 176

Pointe-Claire, 114

Poutre, André, 105, 185

Pradez, Jean, 106, 107, 180

Prostitutes, 96–7

Prouville de Tracy, Alexandre de: appointment of, 5–6; authority of, 23, 27, 28, 102; and autumn campaign, 43,

62–70, 71–84, 85–6; at Château Trompette, 120–1; and church, 19, 25; and Conseil Souverain, 92, 94–5; and Contrecoeur, 103; and Courcelle, 37, 52; death of, 121; and diplomacy, 39, 41, 60–2, 65; disembarkation of, 18; embarkation of, 7, 15–16; and fortification, 20–1, 27–8, 40, 63, 87, 91; imposition by, 25; inspection by, 23–4; and La Fredière, 100, 102; military escort of, 18, 19; miscalculation by, 115; and plan for defence of New France, 108–9; repatriation of, 109; and Saurel's expedition, 61; traits and character of, 19, 25, 61, 74; and winter campaign, 39, 41, 42

Quebec: and autumn campaign, 72; and fur trade, 126; peace talks at, 40–1, 59, 60–1, 66, 69, 90; relative safety of, 55; troops at, 19, 93; and winter campaign, 42

Raffeix, Father Pierre, 47, 73, 78

Ragueneau, Father Paul, 20, 73, 123

Rape, 96

Ré, 13

Recruitment, 7–8, 11, 24

"Relation of the March of the Governor of Canada into New York," 43–5

Religion, 24, 28. *See also* Carignan-Salières Regiment: and religion; Catholic Church

Rémy de Courcelle, Daniel de: appointment

of, 38; arrival of, 29; and autumn campaign, 67, 74, 79, 80, 82, 83; and command structure, 23; and Conseil Souverain, 92, 94–5; embarkation of, 17; at Fort Sainte-Thérèse, 34, 47–8; and Jesuits, 52–3; and La Fredière, 100, 102; and lines of communication, 34–5; and militia, 116–18; policies of, 109, 119; and Salières, 35, 44; traits and character of, 37–8, 48, 61, 74, 123; and winter campaign, 34, 37–53, 63, 65, 76

Repatriates, 110

Richelieu River, 21

Richelieu Valley: defence of, 57, 99, 119; and Mohawks, 20; settlement in, 115, 118, 119

Royal government, 5–6

Sacandaga Lake, 75

Sacandaga River, 75, 76

Sacandaga Swamp, 75, 83

Saffray de Mézy, Augustin de, 25

Sageot, Geneviève, 105

Sainte-Anne-de-Beaupré, 106

Saint-Jean-d'Angély, 12

Saint-Maixent, 11

Saint-Ours seigneury: map, 120

Saint-Sébastien, 16–17, 28, 29

Saint-Sulpice, Church of, 121

Salières. *See* Chastelard de Salières

Salvaye de Froment, Captain Pierre, 22, 109, 110, 157

Saurel, Captain Pierre de: biographical note, 182; expedition of, 43, 61,

64; and the Flemish
Bastard, 62–3, 66; at
Fort Richelieu, 27, 101,
108
Schenectady: negotiations
at, 50–1; skirmish at,
44, 49–50, 53, 63, 99
Scurvy: causes of, 16; at
Fort Sainte-Anne, 87–9;
at Quebec, 28–9; and
religious fervour, 28, 106
Seigneurial system, 118–19;
map, 120
Seneca Iroquois: and the
French, 3, 58, 60; and
the Mohawks, 41; and
peace, 39, 58, 59–60,
90; and the Susque-
hannocks, 20. See also
Susquehannock War
Settlements: appeals of,
for help, 3, 4, 122;
demography of, 4, 57,
126; and peace treaties,
118, 126; and the troops,
57, 92, 124. See also
Montreal; Quebec;
Trois-Rivières
Shipping: needs in, 16;
problems over, 16–17,
123; use of Dutch, 16
Ships: *Aigle d'Or,* 16,
22–3, 31; *Brèse,* 15–16,
18; *Jardin de Hollande,*
17, 31; *Joyeux Siméon,*
16, 17, 18; *Justice,* 16–17,
28; *Paix,* 16, 22–3, 31;
Paon de Hollande, 67;
Saint-Sébastien, 16–17,
28, 29; *Terron,* 15–16
Snowshoes, 44–7. *See
also* Winter campaign
Social changes in
Canada, 56–8
Soissons Regiment, 121

Soldier settlers: activities
of, 125; assimilation of,
119; deterrents to, 111;
inducements to, 111, 112;
and marriage, 112, 113;
military usefulness of,
115; and nationalism,
127; number of, 110
Sorel seigneury, 54; map,
120. *See also* Fort
Richelieu
Susquehannock War, 20,
40, 60, 90

Talon, Jean: arrival of, 29;
and autumn campaign,
67–9; Canadian policy
of, 119; and Colbert, 85;
and Conseil Souverain,
92; and Courcelle, 52;
embarkation of, 17; and
flintlocks, 85; and in-
spection, 15; as a legal
officer, 93, 94, 96, 100,
102; Louis XIV instructs,
108; mistakes of, 102,
115; repatriation of, 116;
requests reinforcements,
116; and Salières, 43;
and soldier settlers,
102–3, 106, 112–13, 115;
and Tracy's defence
plan, 109
Tapie de Monteil et de
Clérac, Captain Fran-
çois de: biographical
note, 174; business acti-
vities of, 94, 95; at Château Trompette, 120;
repatriation of, 110; and
romance, 106; on winter
campaign 43, 45, 48, 110
Terron, 15–16
Thoery de L'Ormeau,
Ensign Roch, 104–5, 156

Thomas, Anne, 100
Tracy. *See* Prouville de
Tracy
Trois-Rivières: drunken-
ness at, 93; and fur
trade, 22, 126; troops
at, 22, 42, 93, 104;
vulnerability of, 55
Troops: and civilians, 54,
93; wariness of, 59, 86,
89. *See also*
Carignan-Salières Regi-
ment; Enlisted men;
Officers
Troupes de la Marine,
116–17, 120

Varennes seigneury: map,
120
Verchères seigneury:
map, 120
Vernon de La Fouille,
Captain Jean-Maurice-
Philippe de, 11, 162
Volunteers, 42–3, 49, 57,
109

War in Europe, 62, 66
Winter campaign: accounts
of, 43–5; accoutring of,
44, 46–7; aftermath of,
53, 54; and Algonkin
Indians, 47, 51; and
Anglo-Mohawk rela-
tions, 61–2; casualties
during, 45, 52, 110;
components of, 42; and
European tradition, 41;
plans for, 38–9; return
from, 52; and weather,
46, 51. *See also* Rémy
de Courcelle, Daniel
de; Schenectady

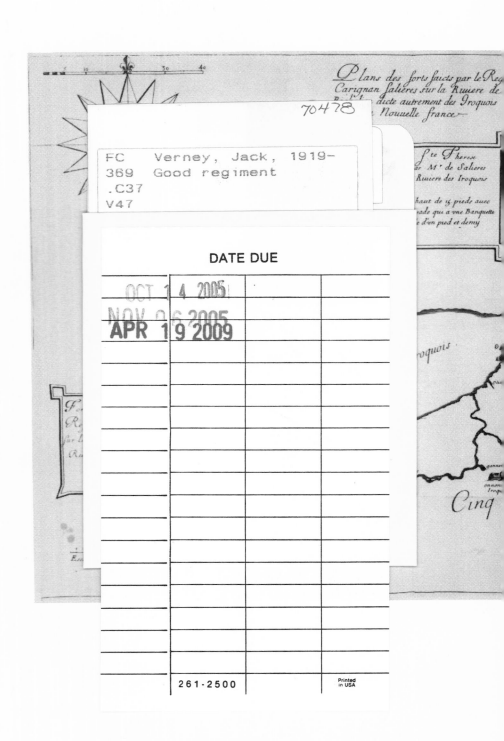